BRITAIN'S FUTURE

by

DAVID P. CALLEO

author of

EUROPE'S FUTURE

COLERIDGE AND THE IDEA OF THE MODERN STATE

To
WALLACE NOTESTEIN

BRITAIN'S FUTURE

by

DAVID P. CALLEO

HODDER AND STOUGHTON

Copyright © 1968 by David P. Calleo

First printed 1968

SBN 340 02936 6

Printed in Great Britain for Hodder and Stoughton Limited,
St. Paul's House, Warwick Lane, London, E.C.4,
by Willmer Brothers Limited, Birkenhead

Preface

Britain's future international role forms a vast and indefinable topic. My task has not been to decide what role Britain will or ought to choose, but rather to spell out the serious arguments for what now appear to be the main alternatives. Naturally, these arguments involve economic, political, military and cultural considerations, and hence cut across several different academic disciplines and techniques of analysis. Considering all these kinds of problems together makes rather strenuous demands on the author's lucidity and the reader's attention. But the exercise will serve some purpose if it suggests the relatedness of decisions in these different fields and does something to break down the unrealistic isolation in which they are so often considered. If there is a unifying technique throughout, it comes from the author's predisposition to look at these matters as an historian of ideas, searching for the underlying assumptions, values, ideals and goals behind each of the major proposals.

Studying contemporary ideas and events has numerous disadvantages, but some compensations. Perhaps the most important is the opportunity to speak at length with the men whose views and actions are important to the issues being decided. In this regard I have been singularly fortunate in spending a year as Research Fellow at Nuffield College, Oxford. It is hard to imagine a more satisfactory vantage point than that unique institution. I should like to thank the Warden, Fellows and students of the College generally, and in particular to acknowledge the special help of Uwe Kitzinger, Sir Donald MacDougall, John E. Nash, Peter Oppenheimer, Sir Robert Shone, Robert Skidelsky, and Philip Williams. I should also like to thank the Master and Fellows of University College for their generous and lively hospitality during my stay at Oxford.

5

A number of political, academic and business figures have been kind enough to talk to me at length about the problems raised in this book. I should particularly like to thank George Brown, Alastair Buchan, Alan Bullock, Richard Crossman, Lord Gladwyn, Sir Roy Harrod, Edward Heath, Professor Nicholas Kaldor, John Keane, Sir Frank Lee, Reginald Maudling, Christopher Mayhew, Sir Oswald Mosley, John Paul, Lord Sherfield, Andrew Shonfield, George Thomson, Air Marshal Sir Geoffrey Tuttle, and Peter Walker.

I am no less grateful for talks with civil servants in the British, French and German governments, and the Common Market Commission. In addition, a series of conferences and lectures have been extraordinarily helpful at critical moments. The meetings and library at Chatham House were of great value throughout the year. A few days at Wilton Park confirmed once again my long-standing admiration for that excellent institution. The book was greatly assisted by a conference on Atlantic relations at Ditchley Park and by a conference on Britain in Europe sponsored by the Federal Trust.

The whole project was initially made possible by a Fellowship from the Guggenheim Foundation and generous help for expenses from the Social Science Research Council and Nuffield College. I also thank my former colleagues at Yale for yet another year off to study European politics.

Throughout the writing of this book I have been singularly blessed with a series of admirable research assistants, each of whom has contributed special knowledge and insight. I take this opportunity to acknowledge the contributions of Caroline Bowes Lyon, John Brunner, Frances Cairncross, Cynthia Frey and Jeremy Hardie. The manuscript itself has involved massive labours, and I am grateful for the long hours and good advice of the two undergraduates who helped me over the summer, Phillip Hodson and Richard Livingston.

This book was completed by the date given below, though minor revisions were made up to January, 1968, and also at the proof-correcting stage.

August 31, 1967
Killingworth, Connecticut.

Contents

Contents

I.
Britain
in Search of
a Role

Two discouraging decades have made many among the British strongly dissatisfied with their country's present situation and prospects. Perhaps it is going too far to call contemporary Britain "the sick man of Europe". It has, however, become commonplace to speak of Britain, shorn of an Empire, as searching unhappily for a new role—indeed, almost a new identity.[1] For a great people, with so splendid a past, the search is bound to be perplexing and painful. The outcome, of course, is of more than casual interest to Britain's neighbours. For Britain's decisions cannot help but be profoundly significant for the future of the whole western world.

Britain's Future discusses some of the problems facing Britain in finding a new role. The book forms a natural continuation of my *Europe's Future: the Grand Alternatives,* written a few years ago, about the conflicting Gaullist and Federalist ideals for the rebuilding of Europe. I thought then that a Gaullist Europe of States was the only practical way to proceed towards a working European union. It also seemed to me, however, that unless and until Britain joined Europe, the ancient divisions among the continentals would keep a Europe of States from developing into a stable grouping. By Britain's joining Europe I meant not only that the Six would have to accept Britain as a partner, but that Britain would have to commit herself fundamentally to their enterprise—to the building of a great power in Europe.[2] This new book, written with perhaps more sympathy for Britain's hesitations, discusses what such a European commitment might mean for Britain and then examines some serious arguments for the main alternatives—a

Britain built around American or Commonwealth ties, or a Britain thrown back on her own island.

In so momentous and incalculable an enterprise as the fundamental reorientation of a great power, the practical decisions are unlikely to present themselves as sharply defined alternatives. There is certainly a danger in making immensely complicated decisions seem too simple and clear-cut. But there is a greater danger from obscuring the great choices under a heap of particular and limited calculations. The destiny of Great Britain and Europe ought to depend on some considerations beyond the price of butter and eggs or the tactical posturings of a handful of politicians.

Butter and eggs, of course, have their place. The economic needs of the country must be looked after. But though economics must be served, it need not, indeed it cannot, dominate these great decisions. For it should not be forgotten that, for all her troubles, Britain is an immensely rich country and her land, wealth, and ingenuity will not suddenly disappear because the British follow one course rather than another. Nearly all the major solutions for her future seem feasible economically. It is not Britain's prosperity that is at stake, but her happiness and, one might say, her national greatness. The real issue, in short, is England's likely place and contribution to the world if she invests her future in the Commonwealth, or Europe, or America—or withdraws into herself.

In the long run, nothing can keep Britain out of Europe if she genuinely wants to be there. The real question is whether the British are fundamentally sympathetic to the aspirations of those who want to build a great power in Europe. In the end, the issue may be decided by the heart rather than the head. Great decisions generally are. But the head can counsel the heart about consequences and means. Faith and reason fused can be an irresistible force. And it is not altogether impossible, in certain rare and splendid moments of history, that statesmen actually know what they are doing and that great things are accomplished by men with open eyes.

It is important to begin by putting Britain's search for a role in some sort of perspective. Quite naturally, few English politicians have been eager to take on the painful task of reorientation. All postwar governments, Labour and Conservative alike, have done their best to avoid abandoning the old world role. Churchill summarized the postwar policy in his celebrated doctrine of the "three circles".[3] Britain was to remain simultaneously a great European power, the centre of a world commonwealth, and the special ally of the United States. To many, so traditionalist a programme has appeared increasingly beyond Britain's means; thus, in June 1961, a large number in Britain welcomed Macmillan's announcement that the Government would enter negotiations with the Common Market. It seemed to presage a decisive step out of the three circles into a more limited but promising role. On the other hand, to the Leader of the Opposition, Hugh Gaitskell, Macmillan's new policy suggested "the end of a thousand years of history".[4]

It is clear enough what Gaitskell meant. Macmillan's new policy did certainly point to a change in Britain's position from the days of Chatham and Palmerston. From a long historical look, however, what seems most surprising about that traditional position is not that Britain is losing it, but that she ever came to hold it in the first place. How was it possible for a country which had, in 1700, only one-third the population of France, to be, roughly half a century later, the pre-eminent power in the world outside Europe?[5] It is still more surprising that Britain held her extraordinary position for nearly two centuries.

No doubt, the singular talents, virtues and vices of the British contributed greatly to their success, but their genius could not have carried them so far had not history presented them with an extraordinary opportunity. The tumultuous upheavals of the seventeenth century had ultimately resulted in a Europe so finely divided that no one within it could dominate the others. Britain's more powerful rivals, caught by geography, continued to exhaust themselves in the attempt. Britain, always the balancer, helped the weak against the strong, and thus ensured that no one could resolve Europe's divisions by conquest. Britain's was a most comfortable policy, neatly combining interest and altruism. For while the continentals were caught up in their own dissensions, Britain invested her energies in manufacturing, trade and empire. The rapid advance of Western technology gradually made it possible for the Europeans to dominate the rest of the globe. It was not the continent, but England that gathered the principal rewards.

The pattern was well established in the eighteenth century and, at the beginning of the nineteenth, the defeat of Napoleon, organized by England, triumphantly confirmed Europe's divisions and

11

Britain's world pre-eminence. Moreover, the revolutionary political and economic forces of the modern world seemed to conspire in Britain's favour. Through talent and luck, she avoided a revolution and developed into a stable modern state, while the continental governments remained enfeebled for the whole century by liberal, socialist and nationalist fevers. Until the rise of Germany, no one could attempt to lead Europe. True, on the fringes of the Western world, America and Russia were rival world powers with vastly greater potential. But both America and Russia were preoccupied by their "manifest" continental destinies and distracted by the political indigestion and administrative incoherence attendant upon their size and diversity. With the three great Western centres of potential power thus sterilized, and the rest of the world caught in technological backwardness and apathy, Britain came to occupy an international position strikingly out of proportion with her relatively slender home base.

The whole experience, of course, had the most profound effects on the country's economic and cultural development. The British naturally became "outward looking", more aware than anyone else of the world's far corners. The repeal of the Corn Laws in 1846 formally abandoned any mercantilist attempt at being a self-sufficient island economy. Britain was to concentrate on industry, commerce, finance, and government. By 1900 her population had jumped amazingly to equal that of France. Her people and increasingly her factories were nourished from abroad.[6] In short, Britain had become a great head with the whole world as her body.

Not surprisingly, free trade became a cardinal tenet of British policy. When the protectionism of newly-developing competitors undermined free trade and began to threaten the vital flow of British commerce, Britain countered with the idea of a vast imperial preference system, a natural reaction for a body-politic whose vital nerves and arteries encircled the globe.[7] These theories were the understandable rationalizations of a head eager to remain in close contact with its body.

Britain's imperial position, splendid as it was, remained fundamentally precarious. The Empire depended upon a very special combination of factors not likely to endure indefinitely. Europe had to remain in a division so finely balanced that no one power could gain hegemony. Once either Russia or America evolved into a world power, backed by the resources of a continental economy, Britain's days of world supremacy were clearly numbered. Moreover, if the backward countries ever shook off their political and technological apathy, Britain was unlikely to hold the Empire.

In the twentieth century each of these developments has occurred—sometimes helped by British capital, administration and education. It is not so much that Britain has failed as that events have finally put an end to a highly unnatural situation. As Europe has exhausted itself with its endless civil war, the two great colossi on the fringes have filled out their potential as "superpowers". Britain predictably cannot keep up. Meanwhile, the rest of the world has at last emerged from its long sleep, and Britain, exhausted by war, lacks the force and the blandishments to hold on either to Empire or Commonwealth. Finally, Europe shows an unprecedented urge towards voluntary union. Britain's traditional aloofness now threatens to isolate her from the great events on her doorstep.

History then has presented Britain with a dramatic reversal of fortune. Accustomed to looking outward, where does she turn now? To alien Europe, to overpowering America, to a heterogeneous Commonwealth—or inward to her own crowded island? It is a most trying time, one that might easily derange a less sensible people. If Britain is to achieve a new position worthy of her past glories and present talents, it will require leadership unusually endowed with creative political imagination. Unfortunately, imagination is an unfashionable faculty in the rather niggling analytical atmosphere of present English culture. But, at this critical moment in their history, the British may again find in themselves those imaginative and practical talents that were able to create the first stable constitutional state in Europe and join it successfully to a vast empire.

Any grand policy for Britain's future will, of course, have to come to terms with the limitations and opportunities of the imperial heritage. The precarious grandeur of the past is gone, but the Empire's head is still very large and it still needs a body. Britain is still too big for her island. That is the problem which any new role must take into account.

II.
The
Economic
Base

1. *Trade and Growth*

Nothing seems to suggest Britain's fundamental over-extension more clearly than her domestic economy. And indeed nothing has made the British more aware of the precariousness of their present role than their recurring economic difficulties. Not that these difficulties are new. Indeed many of the problems which constitute the substance of this chapter have been with the British economy since the nineteen twenties and, indeed, find their origins in the economic patterns and attitudes of the last century. But the wartime loss of so much of Britain's foreign investment, the inheritance left from Britain's early technological and imperial advantages, has removed that margin which formerly permitted greater complacency.[1]

It would be a mistake, nevertheless, to assume that Britain's future role is necessarily to be determined purely by economics. Simple economic determinism is an antiquated doctrine, whether invoked by Marxists or enthusiasts of the Common Market. In the activities of governments, political considerations often overpower economic goals, not least of all in the Marxist countries themselves. Nevertheless, the fundamental economic needs of a nation must somehow be satisfied if national life is to flourish in other spheres, indeed if it is to continue at all. Britain must cope with her economic problems, but her comparatively great wealth ensures that there are several possible ways to do so.

Before going on to study the broad political aspects of Britain's search for a role, it would be well to pause to consider the

14

country's essential economic situation. How does Britain compare in her economic base and performance with similar neighbouring states and trading partners? What are the current explanations for Britain's relatively poor performance?

To begin with the land and the people, Britain's size, 244,000 square kilometres makes her geographically the smallest of the larger Western European powers. France, with 551,200 sq. km., is more than twice as large, while West Germany, with 248,500 sq. km., is closest in size and, in fact, only slightly larger.

It is population rather than size that establishes Britain as a major European country. With 54,595,000 inhabitants, Britain is second in Western Europe in total population, and third in density (224 persons/sq. km.). Again, she is very close to the slightly more populous West Germany (59,041,000 and 238 persons/sq. km.). Italy, the third most populous, follows closely behind in total (51,546,000), but drops substantially in density (171 persons/sq. km.). France follows (48,940,000) with a much lower density (89 persons/sq. km.). Britain's birth rate (18.4 per 1000 of population) puts her slightly ahead of West Germany (17.7) and France (18.1) though slightly behind Italy (18.8) and the USA (19.4).

Table A
AREA, POPULATION, DENSITY AND BIRTH-RATES 1965

	Area '000 sq. km.	Population '000	Density per sq. km.	Birth-Rate per 1000 population
France	551.2	48,940	89	18.1
Germany	248.5	59,041	238	17.7
Italy	301.2	51,546	171	18.8
Japan	369.7	97,960	265	18.6
Spain	504.7	31,604	63	21.3
Netherlands	33.5	12,292	367	19.9
United Kingdom	244.0	54,595	224	18.4
United States	9363.4	194,572	21	19.4

Source: EEC Basic Statistics 1966, pp. 15, 18.

Table B (page 16) shows Britain with less agricultural land (12,409,000 hectares) than France (33,926,000 hectares), Spain (22,232,000 hectares) or Italy (19,582,000 hectares). Again, Britain most clearly resembles West Germany, which has only slightly more

15

B

agricultural land (14,090,000 hectares). Britain, however, devotes far less of her population to agriculture (3%) than either West Germany (11%), France (18%), Italy (25%), or even the US (6%).

Table B
AGRICULTURAL LAND AND LABOUR FORCE

	Agricultural area '000 hectares 1964	Percentage of civilian labour force in agriculture 1965
France	33,926	18
Germany	14,090	11
Italy	19,582	25
Japan	6,990	25
Spain	22,232	34
Netherlands	2,281	n.a.
United Kingdom	12,409	3
United States	441,366	6

Source: EEC Basic Statistics 1966, pp. 24, 45.

Britain's large population and small agricultural production mean, not surprisingly, that Britain needs to import a large quantity of food. In 1965 $4·8 billions worth of food, drink, and tobacco was imported—30% of Britain's total imports and half of the island's total food consumption. Against food imports, however, must be counted Britain's $911 million of agricultural exports. Thus the net food bill from abroad in 1965 was $3,879 million. Moreover, she faces a heavy net import bill for raw materials—$2,555 million in 1965 (see Table C, page 17).

This figure points to a fundamental fact of Britain's economic life. To break even, the island needs to earn a surplus of nearly $4,000 million each year from non-agricultural trade and services to pay for her food alone. For better or for worse, this is the legacy of Britain's having transformed herself, thanks to the doctrines of free trade and an early technological lead, into the industrial and commercial head of a world empire.

It is interesting to compare Britain's problems in feeding herself with those of other European countries. France imports a considerable amount of food but exports nearly as much. Her net food bill in 1965 was only $173 million. Italy's was only $761 million. The United States had a net surplus of $505 million. Once again, it is Western Germany, shorn of her agricultural hinterland, that most closely resembles Britain. Germany both imported and exported less than Britain, but her net bill was nearer the same magnitude, $3,216 million, than that of anyone else in Europe. She, too, has to import great quantities of raw materials—$2,439 million in 1965. The Federal Republic, like the United Kingdom, must export or die. France, in contrast to both, is nearly self-supporting in food, and imports far less raw material—$957 million in 1965. That obviously constitutes a significant distinction in the fundamental economic situations of the three great Western European powers.

Table C
AGRICULTURAL AND RAW MATERIAL IMPORTS

$ million 1965	Food, beverages and tobacco		Crude materials oils and fats		Total imports
	Imports	Exports	Imports	Exports	
France	1,772	1,599	1,702	745	10,336
Germany	3,651	435	3,017	578	17,472
Italy	1,611	850	1,638	251	7,347
United Kingdom	4,790	911	3,110	555	16,138
United States	4,011	4,516	3,152	3,326	21,282

Source: EEC Basic Statistics 1966, pp. 120, 122. Imports c.i.f. (except for USA) Exports f.o.b.

It is not surprising that Britain and West Germany are Europe's greatest trading nations. In 1965, British imports, with 9·3% of the world's total, dropped behind West Germany's (10·1%) to make Britain the world's third largest importer. The United States led with 12·3% and France came fourth with 6%. In exports, the relative standings were much the same, although Germany had surpassed Britain as early as 1959. In 1965 the United States led exports with 14·5% of the world's total; Germany came second with 9·6%; Britain came third with 7·4%; and France fourth with 5·4%.

The trade figures in Table D (page 18) yield some interesting observations. To begin with, they show, both absolutely and proportionately, how much more Western Europe collectively participates in world trade than does the United States[2]. They also show that France and West Germany are increasing their share of world trade in both imports and exports much more rapidly than either

Britain or the US. Germany's rate has been over twice that of Britain. Turning from the proportion of world trade to the balance of imports and exports, the figures show that the US has a large trade surplus and that France generally has at most a moderate deficit[3]—not a surprising record for two advanced industrial nations that are more or less self-sufficient agriculturally.[4] More surprising is that Germany, in spite of her heavy agricultural deficit, shows a steady and comfortable surplus.[5]

Table D
SHARES IN WORLD TRADE AND TRADE GROWTH 1965

| | Imports | | Exports | | Imports % |
	% of world	% change since 1958	% of world	% change since 1958	of GNP
France	6.0	84	5.4	96	11.1
Germany	10.1	137	9.6	103	15.6
Italy	4.2	128	3.9	179	12.9
United Kingdom	9.3	54	7.4	48	16.3
United States	12.3	61	14.5	52	3.1

Source: EEC Basic Statistics 1966, pp. 101–105. Imports c.i.f. (except for USA) Exports f.o.b.

Table E
BALANCE OF TRADE 1958–65

$ Millions	1958	1959	1960	1961	1962	1963	1964	1965
France	(488)	520	584	542	(158)	(643)	(1077)	(288)
Germany	1446	1327	1312	1746	984	1597	1602	420
Italy	(639)	(456)	(1077)	(1040)	(1402)	(2534)	(1294)	(159)
United Kingdom	(1212)	(1463)	(2365)	(1560)	(1519)	(1642)	(3096)	(2428)
United States	4543	2035	5344	6001	5046	5908	7387	5721

Source: EEC Basic Statistics 1966 p. 107. Imports c.i.f. (except for USA) Exports f.o.b.

Britain alone produces a persistent and significant trade deficit, averaging $1,650 million per annum from 1958 to 1961 and $2,171 million from 1962 to 1965. In 1965, far from her worst year, Britain's visible exports covered only 95% of her imports. Invisibles paid for a further 3%, leaving a deficit on current transactions of about 2%.[6] Furthermore, over the last few years, the trade gap has been growing; imports have tended to grow more rapidly than exports, while invisibles have shown no compensating improvement. British exports, in fact, have grown less rapidly than those of any other major trading nation.[7] Perhaps even worse, the composition of her imports has shifted steadily from food to competitive manufactures. Between 1955 and 1965, manufactures grew from 23·4 to 39·1 of total imports. Finished manufactures jumped from 5·6% to 15·3%. Food, on the other hand, declined from 37% of imports to 29·7%.[8] British industry, it would seem, is increasingly losing its share of the market, not only abroad, but also at home. British manufactured goods increasingly fail to compete. Why? The usual explanations point not so much to particular features affecting exports directly but to the general state of the postwar economy.

The slow growth of British trade only parallels the slow growth of the economy in general. Britain's economy, like her trading position, ranks as second in Europe and third in the world. In 1965 Britain's GNP was estimated at $98·9 billion, which

Table F1

GNP GROWTH RATES

$ in '000 m.	Average annual rate of growth 1955-1965	Rate of growth per head 1955-1965
France	5.0	3.7
Germany	5.6	4.3
Italy	5.6	4.8
United Kingdom	3.1	2.4
United States	3.4	1.8

Source: EEC Basic Statistics 1966, pp. 35, 39.

Table F2

ACTUAL GNP AND PROJECTIONS
(Based on 1965 figures in US $'000 millions)

	Actual		Projected		Average Annual % Change
	1960	1965	1972	1977	1965–1977
Germany	83.4	112.2	140.5	160.7	3.6
France	69.3	94.0	126.9	150.4	5.0
Italy	40.8	56.8	74.3	86.7	4.4
EEC (Total)	222.2	299.5	389.0	452.9	4.3
United Kingdom	82.2	98.9	120.4	135.7	3.1
EFTA (Total)	130.2	162.2	203.0	231.8	3.6
EFTA (Continental)	48.0	63.3	82.6	96.1	4.3
USA	541.0	681.0	904.8	1065.1	4.7

Source: Maxwell Stamp Associates, *The Free Trade Area Option*, The Atlantic Trade Study, London, 1967, p. 79.

19

contrasts with \$112·2 billion for West Germany, \$94·0 billion for France, and \$681·0 billion for the US. But the British growth rate, between 1955 and 1965, was only 3·1% per annum and 2·4% per capita in contrast to 5·6% and 4·3% for West Germany, 5·0% and 3·7% for France, and 3·4% and 1·8% for the United States. In short, Britain's rate of growth has been substantially less than that of Germany and France, though on a per capita basis it is higher than that of the US.[9] Projections into the future show Britain dropping further and further behind, not only Germany and Japan,[10] but France. What are the basic features of the way the British organize their economy? Do they offer any clues to the country's relatively sluggish performance?

Britain has the second largest European labour force, with a larger proportion of the population working (47%) than in West Germany (46%), France (40%), or the United States (39%).

Table G

	Labour Force '000	Labour force as % of population	Labour force as % of population aged between 15-64
	1965	1965	1960
France	19688	40	74.0
Germany	26846	46	71.5
Italy	19732	39	67.4
United Kingdom	25676	47	72.0
United States	75635	39	67.8

Source: EEC Basic Statistics 1966, p. 23; Maddison, p. 31.

Table H
DISTRIBUTION OF LABOUR FORCE 1965

	% of labour force			
	Agriculture	Industry	Services	Unemployed
France	18	39	42	1
Germany	11	49	39	1
Italy	25	39	32	4
United Kingdom	3	47	49	1
United States	6	31	58	5

Source: EEC Basic Statistics 1966, p. 25

Furthermore, as has already been pointed out, Britain devotes a far smaller proportion of her labour force to agriculture (3%) than even West Germany (11%) or the US (6%). The saving from agriculture, however, goes not to industry, but to services. In the percentage of the labour force devoted to industry, Britain with 47% is just behind West Germany (49%) and well ahead of France (39%) and the US (31%). But in the proportion of total labour in services Britain's 49% is substantially greater than her fast-growing European rivals, the Federal Republic (39%) and France (42%), though less than the relatively slow-growing United States (58%).

A comparative study of the way in which Britain's national income is distributed also reveals a number of differences between Britain and her three major rivals.

Britain leads her main European rivals in the proportion of national income devoted to the compensation of employees. Britain's 73·1% is in striking contrast to West Germany's 66·0% and France's 64·9% though close to America's 70·0%.

Britain leads all but the US (18·1%) in the proportion of national income consumed by government—16·7% for Britain in contrast to 15·5% for West Germany and 13·3% for France.

Table I
DISTRIBUTION OF NATIONAL INCOME 1965

	Compensation of employees	Income from property and enterpreneurship	Government income from property	Less: Interest on public debt
	%	%	%	%
France	64.9	36.0	0.7	1.6
Germany	66.0	32.4	2.4	0.8
Italy	59.9	39.8	2.6	2.3
United Kingdom	73.1	28.6	3.0	4.7
United States	70.0	31.6	n.a.	1.6

Source: EEC Basic Statistics 1966, p. 37.

Britain also pays a far greater proportion than her rivals of her national income as interest on the public debt—4·7% in contrast with 0·8% for West Germany, 1·6% for France, and 1·6% for the US.

Britain does just barely seem to lead all four in the proportion of national income spent on private consumption (64·0%). The proportion is slightly higher than the US (62.6%) and France (63·8%) but much higher than West Germany (56·9%).

A probable cause of Britain's slow rate of growth emerges clearly in the way Britain, like the US but unlike the continentals, devotes a relatively low percentage of her Gross National Product to asset formation. In 1965, for example, Britain devoted 17·7% of the GNP to domestic asset formation—better than the US at 17·1%, but behind France (21·7%) and Germany (26·6%).

Table J
EXPENDITURE ON GROSS NATIONAL PRODUCT 1965

	Private Consumption	Public Consumption	Gross domestic fixed asset formation	Change in stocks, and net exports
France	63.8	13.3	21.7	1.2
Germany	56.9	15.5	26.6	1.0
Italy	62.3	14.7	18.9	4.1
United Kingdom	64.0	16.7	17.7	1.6
United States	62.6	18.1	17.1	2.2

Source: EEC Basic Statistics 1966, p. 38

Various features of the British economy reflect this failure to invest and perhaps offer a partial explanation for it as well. It is often said that British manufacturing is relatively inefficient and therefore unprofitable. Figures for 1959, for instance, show that the ratio of gross profits to gross value added in manufacturing was 31% in Britain, only 20·4% in the US, but 40·3% in Germany.[11] There are, of course, several possible causes of a comparatively low rate of profit—for example, relatively high wages, bad management, poor distribution, inferior or unattractive products, etc. Among these causes, however, might be obsolescent equipment, itself a result of a low rate of investment. If wages and prices should be roughly comparable in Britain to what they are on the continent, then less efficient equipment would squeeze profits.

Reliable figures on relative costs are extremely elusive. That Britain's plant is less efficient than the continent's is, however, suggested by another set of figures for 1959 showing that the ratio of profits to the net value of fixed capital and inventories, while 17·9% for Britain and 15·7% for the US, was 27·4% for Germany.[12] Low rates of profit are said to provide a clue to the declining competitiveness of British exports. The profit rate is too small to be worth the investment in an export sales and service network. Low profit rates might also explain the lack of investment generally.

Obviously these arguments are circular and contain a great many loose ends. Measurements of comparative costs and efficiency are fragmentary. It nevertheless seems clear that, whatever the reasons, the rate of investment in England is lower than in France or Germany, and there is a strong commonsense presumption that this results in declining British productivity, profits and competitiveness. Up to 1960, at any rate, labour productivity in England did not seem markedly lower than in France or Germany, although in all three it was less than half that of the US.[13] The postwar trend, however, has been relatively unfavourable to Britain, no doubt because of the lower rate of capital investment. From 1955 to 1960, for example, the average annual growth of output per man hour was 2·3% for Britain and 2·0% for the US, but 3·6% for France and 5·9% for Germany.[14] By 1965, British wage costs per unit of output appeared substantially higher than in Germany or France.[15]

Table K

1965 TRENDS IN PRODUCTIVITY AND WAGE COSTS IN MANUFACTURING INDUSTRY

(Value in US $. Index 1960 = 100)

	Average Hourly Wage Costs		Output/Man Hour		Wage Costs/Unit Output	
	Value	Index	Value	Index	Value	Index
USA	3.20	119	4.44	120	.72	99
Canada	2.15	109	3.64	115	.59	105
France	1.29	147	1.74	125	.74	118
W. Germany	1.52	163	2.36	129	.65	126
UK	1.20	132	1.38	115	.87	115
Japan	.45	173	.72	147	.62	118

Sources: Swedish Employers Confederation, Bureau of Statistics: "Direct and Total Wage Costs for Workers". US Bureau of Labour Statistics: *Bulletin*, 1518, June, 1966.
National Institute Economic Review, Statistical Tables, May, 1967.

There is always obviously a risk in selecting figures from several countries. They may easily represent statistical variations, temporary aberrations or short-term cyclical trends. Nevertheless, the general outline of postwar Britain's economic situation seems clear enough. The British economy is unbalanced in the sense that to feed the island's population and factories requires importing a great deal of food and raw material.[16] In this sense Britain is like

postwar Western Germany and unlike agriculturally self-support-
ing France and the United States. Britain's trade is enormous—
just behind Germany's in total volume of exports and imports.
But Britain's balance of trade has been seriously and increasingly
unfavourable, while Germany's has generally yielded a substantially favourable balance. Furthermore, the volume of Britain's
trade—both exports and imports—has been growing at a rate,
which, while comparable to the US, has been far behind Germany
and France.

Britain's economy resembles the American rather than the
German in many other features—the high proportion of the GNP
that goes to employees, the high rate of private and public consumption,[17] the low rate of investment, and the slow growth of
the GNP. These are all features that may be acceptable for a
nation with an agricultural surplus and a favourable trade balance.
Trade is a far smaller factor in the American economy: US
imports are only 3% of GNP, whereas they are 16% for Britain.
If the rate of growth is slow in the United States, Americans find
consolation in a national income per capita twice that of either
Britain, France or Germany. Are these similarities with the United
States appropriate for Britain or do they suggest a country living
beyond her means? So impertinent a question would, of course,
never arise if Britain, like France and Germany, enjoyed a
balanced trade and a comparably high rate of growth.

The basic question therefore remains: why has the British
economy grown so slowly while the rest of Europe has been boom-
ing?

The explanations are numerous. Some are cultural and socio-
logical. Criticisms of the moral and cultural atmosphere of postwar British society have been abundant in recent years.[18] The
British frequently accuse themselves, often with a touch of self-
satisfaction, of having become lazy, self-indulgent and incompetent.
Half the population, it is said, is caught up in snobbish nostalgia—
in the gentlemanly cult of diffident incompetence. Meanwhile, the
other "modern" half of Britain has thrown over all traditions of
self-discipline and restraint for a "pop" world of enthusiastic but
unproductive vulgarity. The two ailments complement each other.
The lower and middle classes, imprisoned by class snobbery, not
least of all their own, see no possible advancement for themselves.
The best emigrate, while the rest abandon themselves to the

pleasures of those who have no thought for the future.[19] The only genuine cure, it is widely believed, is some thoroughly democratic reform of British education that will break down the old distinctions and the paralyzing inhibitions that result.[20]

More concretely, it is widely believed that in Britain labour is less productive and management less enterprising than in almost any other advanced country. A severe critic notes:

> The one lesson which recent economic history has taught time after time is that British industry always performs far worse than it is reasonable to expect.[21]

In recent years, comparative studies for particular industries have seemed to indicate an alarmingly low level of productivity in Britain by comparison with the Common Market countries.[22] It also seems that foreign firms in England almost invariably do better than their domestic competitors, whereas British firms abroad generally do worse.[23] Management is also sometimes blamed for not often enough translating Britain's scientific and technological superiority in several fields into superior marketable products.[24] It often seems true, moreover, that the disappointing performance of British exports is less a result of inferior products than of poor marketing and unreliable delivery and service.

Similarly, British labour is said to make an ample contribution to the general Schlamperei of industry. As mentioned earlier, while British wage costs per unit of output are still within the general European range, the growth of output per man hour since the war has been strikingly less in Britain than in France or Germany. Doubtless this reflects the relative lack of capital investment in new machinery, but it is hard to believe that labour's obstinate resistance to new methods does not bear considerable responsibility. In recent years, to be sure, wages have gone up sharply everywhere—less, in fact, in England than in France and Germany. But Britain's comparatively slow rise in productivity means that advancing wages either cut profits and discourage investment, or push up prices and generally lessen the competitiveness of British industrial products.[25] As we have seen, British products have lost ground, not just abroad, but most spectacularly in their own home market. Indeed, if it were not that British tariffs on competitive manufactures have been higher than either

Table L1

ARITHMETICAL AVERAGE OF TARIFFS OF UK, EEC, AND USA (PRE-KENNEDY ROUND)

	UK	EEC (CET)	US
All non-agricultural products	18.4	11.7	17.8
Raw materials and energy	6.3	1.5	8.1
Semi-manufactured products	18.0	10.7	16.5
Industrial equipment	19.4	11.7	17.0
Other products	20.4	14.4	21.3

Source: Sidney Wells, *Trade Policies for Britain,* London, 1966, p. 123

Britain's relatively high industrial tariffs will persist after the Kennedy Round cuts are fully in effect.

Table L2

INDUSTRIAL TARIFFS AFTER THE KENNEDY ROUND (1972)
Average Tariff on manufactures, per cent *ad valorem*

US 11.2, UK 10.2, UK (preference) 1.2, EEC 7.6, Japan 9.8

Table M

PERCENTAGE OF INCOME DEDUCTED AS TAX IN DIFFERENT COUNTRIES

INCOME	first £10,000	£10,000-20,000	above £20,000
UK	43	88	96.25
Belgium	36.4	42.1	46.2
Spain	33	37.8	42
Sweden	52.8	61.6	71.8
France	41.2	51.1	57.4
Holland	49	59.6	60
Switzerland	21.3	22.6	23.6
Italy	24.7	31	60
Germany	50	50.1	55.5

Source: Sir Edward Beddington-Behrens, "Need for Incentives at the Top", *The Times,* February 2, 1967, p.13.

those of France or Germany, British manufactures would probably have lost out even more at home.

That British industry has consistently been comparatively lethargic seems evident enough. But why should this be so? In wide areas of industry where government is important, management frequently blame the allegedly unenterprising and inexpert attitudes of the Civil Service.[26] Critics looking for something more specific than wholesale condemnation of the culture and society often cite the British tax structure as perversely devised to discourage growth in corporations and initiative among managers. Although there are loopholes, it does seem broadly true that the tax rates fall most severely on precisely those people who earn high salaries for their managerial or professional services. Indeed, some argue that the English tax system seems positively to favour the "idle" rich and positively to discriminate against the productive manager.[27] It is easier to avoid death duties in England than America, but it is much harder for private individuals to accumulate capital from high earnings. A straight comparison of rates between the US, continental Western Europe and Great Britain certainly supports the belief that, in Britain, managers at the top levels are paid less to begin with and allowed to keep much less of what they earn than in either the US or Western Europe.[28]

Whatever the effect of the tax system on individuals may be, its incidence upon corporations does not seem designed to encourage the growing and efficient. Some economists have long argued that the European value-added tax encourages growth far more than the English system which taxes corporate profits.[29] Under the continent's value-added tax (TVA), firms are taxed at a fixed rate on the value they add to goods they process—roughly the difference between the price of the materials they buy and the price of the goods they sell. As a result, those firms who process their goods the most efficiently, i.e., at least cost to themselves, earn greater profits without having to pay any more tax than a less efficient competitor. The result is a premium on efficiency. Under the British system, however, taxes are levied not on the value added but on the profits themselves—with the result that the more efficient of two firms making the same product will pay more tax. Because it is in part a tax on the use of labour, TVA encourages capital intensity, and hence, it is argued, desirable investment.[30]

Similarly, the continental way of financing the welfare system seems better designed to encourage productivity. On the continent, workers' benefits are financed chiefly by a large payroll tax. As a result, the tax system encourages continental firms to limit the use of manpower and to invest in labour-saving machinery. In Britain, on the other hand, the payroll tax is strictly limited.[31] Once again, those who earn the greatest profits on their turnovers, presumably the most efficient, are the most heavily taxed, since corporation tax has to be kept at a level sufficient to help finance the welfare system.

Another structural rather than moral explanation for Britain's slow growth, comes from Professor Nicholas Kaldor, the celebrated Cambridge economist and government planner.[32] According to Kaldor's theory, Britain suffers from a chronic and fundamental labour shortage. Britain's economy, he argues, reached "maturity" early and, unfortunately, at a rather low level of productivity. "Maturity" comes when labour in all sectors—manufacturing, agriculture and service—receives the same wages and hence, with immigration cut off, there is no pool of cheap labour for expanding industry to draw upon. Kaldor maintains that economies of scale in manufacturing industry are the main engine of fast growth. Hence a country such as Britain, which is unable to provide the labour needed for an expansion of the manufacturing sector, must accept a low rate of growth. Professor Kaldor's most celebrated innovation, the Selective Employment Tax, is, among other things, designed to create artificially an adequate labour supply for productive industry by forcing workers out of services.

Kaldor's thesis enjoys considerable respect, but among economists probably the most favoured explanation for Britain's slow rate of growth is the recurrent deflationary "Stop-Go" policy, practised by all British Governments since the mid fifties.[33] The policy is designed to maintain the value of the pound in the international exchanges. "Stop-Go" cools down demand in the domestic economy by such devices as high interest rates, further credit controls, import surcharges and increased general taxation. With the home market depressed, imports fall and industry may be encouraged to export.[34] But, since many economists believe that the investment necessary for steady growth can only be expected in a climate of sustained and growing general demand they naturally lay a heavy burden of blame for the economy's slower postwar growth on these recurrent deflationary cycles.[35] Many believe that the depressing effect of the "Stop-Go" on growth, make the whole policy ultimately self-defeating. Smothered demand means less investment. Less investment means declining productivity and thus British goods become less and less competitive at home and abroad. The trade gap grows and the balance of payments crises are more frequent.[36]

Deflation is never a popular policy. Why have Governments of both parties, in spite of their announced intentions, been driven back to it again and again? Evidently, because they believe it necessary to defend the exchange rate of the pound. Hence the frequent charges that Britain's domestic industrial growth is being sacrificed to maintain the country's great international financial position—a burden not incumbent on the less pretentious nations of the continent. That the Government should follow such priorities is frequently blamed on the supposedly excessive political influence of the City bankers—a privileged special interest carrying on in the elegant world of international finance at the expense of the British workers and industry generally. These views, for obvious reasons, are probably an ineradicable element of British political folklore, and the City has been under persistent attack for many years.[37]

2. *Financial Problems and Remedies*

The City of London is certainly a prominent and singular feature of Britain's economic landscape. It is, in fact, a great complex of commercial institutions, the heritage of the days when London was the financial and trading centre of the world as well as the capital of an Empire on which the sun was ever shining. The City's international business has managed to survive the Empire in spite of the relative decline of Britain's industry and trade position and the crushing capital losses of two world wars.[1] Thus the City remains the world's greatest financial and trading centre outside New York. Its activities do indeed express England's "outward-looking" perspectives. Britain's banks, for example, are still far more international, with many more branches abroad than those of any other country, including the United States. Indeed an informed estimate gives British banks roughly 6000 overseas branches and American banks not 300.[2] Besides its banking, the City is a great centre for insurance and various forms of merchandising and brokerage. The City's earnings make a vital contribution to the balance of payments, an estimated £170 million to £185 million in 1963.[3]

The City's earnings are real enough. What of the belief that they are made by a privileged minority at the expense of the economy in general? The charges frequently heard generally intimate a number of separate points. To begin with, powerful figures in the City, allied with the foreign "gnomes", are supposed generally to impose bad advice on successive Governments and induce them to follow policies they would not have followed otherwise. Secondly, it is suggested that the City's advice stems from special interests contrary to the general interests of the economy—more specifically that it is the City's interest and not the nation's to maintain the international role of the pound.

How just are these charges? It is possible that the advice of key figures in the City has been too conservative, along the deflationary lines traditionally favoured by bankers everywhere. It may be that good bankers are generally men with canny, quick reactions to immediate situations who wisely suppress in themselves any way-ward tendencies towards imaginative, theoretical views. As a result, their advice on general economic questions may often be wrong. But bankers are not the only ones to give bad advice and governments are generally free to reject it.

Disappointed left-wing economists often blame the City for the Labour Government's unwillingness to devalue earlier, during the severe exchange crises of 1964 and 1966,[4] rather than when absolutely forced to do so in November, 1967. But, to begin with, it seems rather unfair to ascribe the Government's decisions to the City. It is not unusual for responsible governments to be reluctant to devalue because they believe the country's good faith is engaged. Furthermore, plenty of economists opposed devaluation in 1964 and 1966, with arguments that were persuasive if not unanswerable.

Classically, devaluation, lowering the official exchange rate, helps a balance of payments disequilibrium by raising import and lowering export prices. But the effects on the flow of trade may be slow in coming. Moreover, the consequent price changes may result in a substantial and not necessarily desirable redistribution of purchasing power within the country. Furthermore, devaluation succeeds only if other countries do not devalue in turn. And finally, the favourable effects in themselves are only temporary. They can provide time during which a country can take measures to improve its competitive position by increasing its growth and productivity and stabilizing its incomes and prices. It is these measures that count in the long run, and if governments take them in the first place, devaluation may be unnecessary.[5] The Labour Government did take severe measures in July, 1966. A great many people at the time believed these measures would be adequate without devaluation. That the measures failed can be blamed as much on bad luck—the continued closing of the Suez canal, for example—as on any initial inadequacy in the measures or any lack of skill by the Government in carrying them out. These questions must always be controversial. But the Labour Government's position in resisting devaluation was at least economically respectable and had many defenders outside the orthodox centres of the City.

In any event, it was the Government, headed by an ex-economics don from Oxford, that made the decisions not to devalue earlier than 1967. It seems harsh to blame the bankers because their allegedly limited vision seemed more convincing to Labour's Government than the ideas of its own left-wing economists.

What of the charge that the City's financial interests are somehow opposed to the "industrial" interests of the economy generally? Even assuming that the prolonged resistance to devaluation and, in general, the attempt to maintain sterling's international role has been harmful to Britain's domestic economy, it is by no means clear that sterling's world position is of any benefit to the City's own international activities. The City might well be better off if the pound were strictly a national currency like the German mark. No doubt banks earn some commission from dealing in sterling, but, in theory, the merchant banks, shippers, insurance underwriters and various kinds of brokers owe their customers to their skilled services and not to the currency in which they happen to deal.[6] The prestige of Britain's running a major reserve currency is imponderable but perhaps important. But it can certainly be argued that, for the City, sterling is a far greater curse than boon. The greatest immediate threat to the City's international business comes from the growing restrictions of capital movements the British Government has imposed to protect the balance of payments. And, in the long run, the City's vast brokerage and shipping business cannot flourish if British trade declines.

Perhaps it is more just to blame the City for its traditional skill and interest in mobilizing and directing funds abroad to more promising, or at least exotic, fields than domestic British industry. But England has always looked abroad for investments and had not two world wars forced the liquidation of so many external assets, there would be very much less worry today about the balance of payments.[7] Recent studies, however, do not suggest that the average immediate and long-run returns on exported capital justify the immediate damage to the balance of payments.[8] But these findings are controversial and tentative, and, in any event, most of the City's investments are, in fact, domestic. If domestic investment is not more attractive, it seems perverse to blame the City rather than the economy. In short, the argument that the City in some way has special interests opposed to those of the rest of the economy is not very convincing. If a few notable bankers give bad advice about sterling, it is only because they share the same illusions as the politicians, not because they have sinister special interests in maintaining the pound. And again, it is far from clear that the City has any genuine interest in maintaining sterling's international role. In short, whereas the economy may well pull down the City, it is unlikely that the City will pull down the economy.

But to return to our original question: why has maintaining the exchange rate of sterling over the years been such a burden to Britain—so severe that many observers find it the chief cause for the slow growth of the whole economy? Other advanced countries have had occasional balance of payments difficulties but resolved them without the deleterious general economic effects ascribed to the defence of sterling. The French economy, for example, went through a prolonged stabilization freeze at the end of the nineteen fifties and again in 1965-6; France's rate of growth remained, however, relatively high.[9] Why is the pound so much more of a burden than the franc, the lira or the German mark?

The pound, of course, is different from other European currencies in that sterling, like the dollar, is both a major international reserve and a major trading currency. Sterling is a reserve currency because a group of several countries, the Sterling Area, keep most of their monetary reserves as deposits in the Bank of England.[10] The pound is a trading currency because many people prefer to settle their accounts in sterling. It is estimated that roughly 25% of all international trade is still settled in sterling—nearly three times Britain's own foreign trade![11]

Running an international reserve and trading currency means, perforce, that a substantial proportion of the country's money is held by foreigners. The amounts involved are very large in relation to the size of the domestic economy. In December 1967 Britain's net external liabilities in sterling were £5,350 million.[12] Of this sum £3,079 million was held by foreign central monetary institutions. For an economy whose GNP is roughly £32,000 million, £5,350 million makes up a rather large tail for not so big a dog. The United States, which runs the world's other main reserve and trading currency, carried at the end of 1966 net external liabilities of $14,000 million, with a GNP of roughly $700,000 million.

Some of these sterling deposits, notably the official reserves held by other governments, are thought to be relatively stable.[13] But others, "hot money" in search of speculative profits or high interest rates, for example, constitute extremely volatile balances and move rapidly when confidence in the pound begins to weaken. And not even the most torpid and anglophile of foreign businessmen wants to hold sterling if there appears a serious possibility of imminent devaluation. Thus with so much money held by foreigners, the pound is obviously vulnerable to speculative currents. In addition, Britain's foreign trade remains very large, and the inevitability of large "leads and lags" attendant upon financing such a huge turnover means that there will be strong temporary fluctuations in the foreign exchange market. Leads and lags are said to run to hundreds of millions of pounds one way and another.[14]

For a country to maintain a fixed exchange rate in the face of these normal and special pressures requires intervention in the market to buy or sell the national currency when the supply is too great or too little for the official rate. To intervene, a country's central bank uses its monetary reserves. The bigger the reserves, the less likely that any speculative fluctuation will get out of hand and force devaluation. But Britain's reserves are and have been tiny in relation to her foreign and trade liabilities. Indeed, in June 1967, Britain's reserves, after subtracting her outstanding debts to the International Monetary Fund repayable in December 1967, came to only £825 million.[15] It is small wonder that the Government has found it difficult to maintain confidence in the pound over the years and was finally compelled to devalue in November of 1967. Devaluation, as noted above, is not in itself a solution, although it can provide a productive respite.

In short, with her large liabilities, heavy trade, and small reserves, it is not surprising if some people conclude that Britain is overextended. The British economy, with its frequently unfavourable trade balance and sluggish growth rate, seems increasingly an unsuitable base for a world currency, and, as we have seen, many believe the attempt to maintain the role has done the economy great harm. It is as if Britain's residual functions as financial head have become too taxing for her shrunken body.

There are the various schemes, much talked about in recent years, for reforming the whole world monetary system. A most helpful development for Britain obviously would be some general international agreement to increase the world's supply of reserves. Unfortunately for Britain, these schemes founder on international issues concerned more with the dollar than with the pound. The United States, although still in possession of large reserves, has been running a substantial payments deficit every year since 1957 and is not unnaturally concerned with increasing liquidity—America's primarily and everyone else's incidentally.[16] But the French, who deplore the continuation of American deficits, oppose any general increase in liquidity that would put off what they regard as the inevitable day of reckoning when the United States must control its external spending. Since the French have powerful support from the rest of the Six, who collectively hold the bulk of the world's uncommitted reserves, it will not be easy to achieve any general international agreement increasing liquidity to a degree sufficient to solve sterling's problems.[17] The one scheme the French might possibly accept, doubling the price of gold, has been unacceptable to the United States and is of no immediate benefit to Britain whose actual gold obligations exceed her gold reserves.[18]

If a universal reform easing sterling's burdens is unlikely there remains the possibility of some "regional" arrangement whereby sterling's reserve and trading role might be borne by a group of nations with larger collective reserves and a bigger domestic base. The obvious alternatives are a dollar-sterling union or the translation of sterling into a "European" reserve currency. Either arrangement could give Britain access to greater reserves and shift the burden of maintaining a major international currency to a broader base.

Either solution has strong arguments in its favour, to be taken up in a subsequent chapter.[19] Briefly, the former, the pound-dollar union, has the advantage of confirming long-standing, extensive and intimate ties—much strengthened in recent years. The latter, a "European" currency, might conceivably offer greater opportunity for British financial institutions to take a commanding position, but would appear to be far more difficult to bring about —particularly as it would essentially be a partnership to which Britain would bring the debts and the others the assets. Obviously, a decision for one solution or the other can only be taken in the context of the larger issues of Britain's future political and economic orientation. In any event, it does not now appear likely that Britain's inadequate reserves will soon be increased significantly by international action.

Why are Britain's reserves so low in the first place? Why, in spite of two devaluations and frequent deflationary cures, has she never been able to build up to the same level as, say, France or West Germany? Obviously, the bad export performance has not been helpful. It is sometimes suggested that the deflationary cures have never been severe or long enough.[20] A more popular theory holds that, in recent years, the British pound has been overvalued. As a result British goods have been overpriced abroad and imports underpriced in Britain. The remedy, devaluation, was finally adopted in desperation on November 18, 1967, when the official rate was reduced 14·3%—from $2·80 to $2·40. If ultimately successful, the 1967 devaluation should increase the demand for British products abroad and reduce the demand for foreign imports at home. The result should be an improvement in the trade balance and a gradual increase in reserves.[21] Success, however, is by no means certain. It depends, first of all, on other countries not devaluing in turn,[22] and then on the British economy's ability to meet the expected new demand for its exports without a corresponding rise in imports and prices. This depends on whether there is enough capacity, at full employment, to meet both the foreign and home demand for goods. This, in turn, depends on whether home demand can be kept down by tax and incomes policy and production shifted to exports.

The pitfalls are numerous. Devaluation means that import prices, if they remain at the same level in dollars, go up by 16·7% in sterling.[23] The tendency for import prices to rise, food for example, pushes up the cost of living and puts upward pressure on wages. Higher prices for imported raw materials tend to increase the price of British goods and thus offset somewhat the beneficial effects of devaluation. A rising demand for exports creates the need for more labour and thus builds up further pressure for wage increases.

The dangers of domestic inflation in such a situation are manifest. Yet as British prices rise, the effects of devaluation are lost. The solution lies in keeping down wages and home demand, so that British prices remain competitively low and the foreign demand for British goods high. Thus the trade balance can be turned about and reserves built up. Higher profits should, in turn, be channeled into investment to increase output and productivity, thus insuring that British goods remain competitive and allowing a gradual increase in home consumption to take place without inflation.

The Government's path is obviously thorny. Its ability to keep down wages in the face of higher prices for imports, higher demands for labour, and higher profits for industry can scarcely be taken for granted. It is entirely possible that the Government will prove unable to dampen home demand sufficiently and that home demand and export demand will exceed the productive capacity of British industry. Higher import prices and wage demands would be the logical result and could easily lead to a cost-push inflation, soon eliminating the advantage given to British export prices by the devaluation.

Of course, it is always possible to argue that demand for British goods is not much affected by price anyway. Another pessimistic, but plausible argument against devaluation holds that with the present inadequacy of world reserves, it is highly unlikely that foreign governments will permit any real improvement in Britain's reserve position. An improvement in Britain's reserves will mean a deficit for someone else. Those unfavourably affected will deflate, adopt trade restrictions or even devalue in order to stop their losses. Hence the demand for British exports will return towards its old level.

It is possible to argue that devaluation attacks only the symptoms, but not the heart of Britain's malaise. Britain's difficulties, it is true, stem from a relative decline in productivity in relation to the continent over the past few years. The cause of this decline may, in fact, spring less from the erratic demand caused by Stop-Go than from other factors like lazy management, an inadequate educational system or a reactionary tax system. Thus, British industry will not respond adequately to the opportunities prestented by devaluation. Productivity will continue to decline relatively and British goods will eventually be non-competitive until once again the pound is devalued.

In short, there are a wide variety of arguments, some of which question not only the difficulties of managing a devaluation successfully, but also its ability, even if successful, to do anything but palliate more fundamental diseases. There is certainly at least some truth in these arguments. Many people who support devaluation would certainly agree that it must be accompanied, not only by strong measures to control domestic demand, but by fundamental changes in Britain's society, culture and government policy.

3. *Other Burdens*

One widely held belief blames many of Britain's economic difficulties on her postwar foreign policy. Her failure to build reserves and to do as well as the continentals in general stems, it is said, from the heavy international burden she, alone of the European powers, has still been carrying. This belief, in turn, gives rise to a strong feeling that not only must Britain renounce or share the burden of sterling's international role, but that she must cut herself free from all the debilitating commitments and pretensions inherited from her great days as the world's leading imperial power —especially when these commitments involve the serious sacrifice of development at home. Such, it is often argued, are Britain's commitments in the Commonwealth and elsewhere to military support and economic aid, and, in general, Britain's close military partnership with America throughout the world. How justified is the belief that Britain carries heavier world burdens than her continental neighbours?

It is quite true that Britain has maintained more of a military commitment than any comparable European power. Britain has long sought to maintain an independent military establishment of great-power rank. She was a nuclear power long before France and indeed still has a substantial lead, although her position since the Nassau Agreement of 1962 depends increasingly upon American good will and assistance. At any rate, her defence expenditure in 1965-1966 was 6.8% of the GNP—higher ostensibly than France (4·8%) or West Germany (5·7%).[1] It is difficult, of course, to reckon the real cost of a military establishment to an economy since presumably specialist skills are created, employment is maintained, and there is a beneficial technological "fall-out" from the development of complicated weapons. Whether the technological resources that go into the development of complicated weapons could be of more use to the economy elsewhere and the degree to which such resources would exist at all without the military stimulus are all questions for which there is no easy or definite answer.

What seems less controversial is the cost to the economy of having large conventional forces stationed around the world. At the start of 1966, Britain maintained 94,000 men and numerous dependants in the Middle and Far East. In addition there were over three battalions in the Mediterranean and roughly 55,000 troops in Germany. What weighs so heavily on the British economy is not the general cost of these forces, but the cost in foreign exchange of having so many of them abroad. In 1965, the total foreign exchange bill for Britain's overseas forces came to £277 million—£100 million East of Suez, £92 million in the Mediterranean, and £85 million net in Germany.[2] Total net overseas current expenditure came to £456 million.[3] In 1964, a catastrophic year for the balance of payments, the exchange costs of overseas military expenditure were equal to three-eighths of the record deficit. In 1965, these same costs were double the deficit. Other European countries, their outside military commitments ended, do not have these expenses, although France keeps two divisions in Germany and the Germans have offset payments for allied troops on their soil.[4] While some in Britain defend her foreign military commitments as contributing to world stability and British influence and investment, critics in both parties have seen heavy financial costs, few compensations, and frequent ill-will—a striking example of Britain's over-extension into the outside world. The debate has gone on for several years in both parties. The cuts announced in January, 1968, however, do finally promise a drastic reduction of overseas military expenditure within a few years.[5]

Britain's foreign aid programme is sometimes regarded as a similarly unique burden, though with dubious justice. It is no doubt true that British private capital and trade have played a great role in the developing countries.[6] But Britain's official overseas aid is generally no greater than Germany's and has fallen well behind that of France. In 1962, the discounted value of British official aid was $211 million (0·27% of GNP); Germany's was $231·4 million (0·27% of GNP); whereas French aid was $908·4 million (1·32% of GNP) and American $3·069 billion (0·55% of GNP).[7] Even if it is true that the French give their aid in such a way that it brings maximum benefit to their own industry, nevertheless, the difference in amount and percentage is striking.[8] France's generosity, of course, is that of a country with its trade roughly in balance, with large reserves, no great monetary role, and substantially fewer troops outside the country, Germany, whose fundamental economic position is not unlike England's, has nevertheless enjoyed large reserves and impressive growth. While she does pay heavy support costs for foreign troops in Germany, she has no troops of her own abroad; while her foreign aid is considerable, it remains on an English rather than French or even American scale. In short, it might be argued that Germany has an international role far better suited to her economic position.

Indeed, over-extension is the general theme that emerges from this brief study. Britain's economic situation is such that with a large population in a small territory, she must import half the food consumed on the island. In general, she is a heavy importer of raw materials to feed her factories. Britain is thus constrained to earn enough from trade to pay for these vital imports. In this and many other respects, Britain's position is similar to that of West Germany. Britain must "export or die," yet in the years since the war, Britain, unlike Germany, has shown a serious decline in her share of world trade. In short, Britain has not, since the war, been responding successfully to her basic economic requirements—the need to earn enough from exports and services abroad to pay for imports. If the present trend continues, the future looks increasingly bleak.

The decline in Britain's share of world trade has paralleled an overall lack of domestic growth. An examination of the domestic economy suggests that, in a number of perhaps significant features, Britain's economy is closer to that of the US, whose growth has also been slow, than it is to that of France or Germany. Relative to Germany or France, Britain devotes a high percentage of her manpower to services, and gives a high proportion of her national income to the compensation of employees. Proportionately, the English spend more on private consumption than the Germans (though not more than the French). The British also spend more on public consumption, but devote much less to forming new assets.

There are numerous economic and cultural explanations for the British economy's lacklustre growth. A persistent theme in many of the explanations is that Britain has, in too many respects, still been attempting to play the role of a great world power when her economy does not allow it. No doubt, if Britain were to turn herself into a modern version of eighteenth-century Prussia, she might, as a prodigy of ascetic self-discipline, be able to play a big role with a small base. But the British economy, with high wages, high consumption and low investment, is the most self-indulgent in Western Europe. In short, Britain's economic and political policies since the war have not been suitable adaptations to her fundamental economic situation.

The extreme view would jettison all the old political and financial positions from the past and the great bulk of the domestic attitudes and institutions that grew up around them. Little England would triumph at last. These views have inexorably been gaining ground in England. After two decades, it seems clear that those who would preserve the grandeur of their country must find a more adequate economic base for their ambitions.

III.
Britain in Transit:
the Postwar Muddle

Future historians will very likely see the third quarter of the twentieth century as the period in which Britain haltingly took stock of her transformation from a world power of the first magnitude into a European power of limited resources. They will probably feel that Britain, compared with the rest of Europe, took rather a long time to come to terms with her problems. For since World War II every one of the great nations of Western Europe has faced the same painful discovery of reduced power and place in the world, and, broadly speaking, the same kind of crisis in national identity. Germany and Italy emerged from the war physically shattered and carrying a heavy burden of guilt and self-reproach. France, too, was in ruins and, despite de Gaulle's heroic rescue of her honour, the shame and ugly disunity of 1940 left wounds that would take long to heal. Moreover, France's precarious self-respect was soon to be shaken by a series of military disasters that would inexorably deprive her of a great empire.

By comparison the prestige of Britain's wartime victory concealed the extent of her decline; the gracefulness of her departure nearly obscured the end of her Empire. As a result, the British postponed facing their basic problems for almost a generation. Whereas the continentals, in those cold postwar years, huddled together and sought a new identity and self-respect in the ideal of European unity, British Governments, from the war's end until the early 1960s, refused to participate in and sometimes actively resisted Europe's federalist evolution. Not until Macmillan's time did any British government seriously deviate from Churchill's original

41

policy for the postwar era, the celebrated "three circles".[1] Britain was to continue to play three roles: a European power, the special ally of the United States, and the head of the Commonwealth. The chief rule of British diplomacy was to avoid ever being put in a situation where one role might have to be sacrificed for another. Naturally, therefore, Britain was not interested in a European union that would freeze her either in or out of the continent. Thus Britain's official contributions to the European enterprise were mostly rhetorical, and even then, generally from the statesmen out of office.

Churchill in opposition was especially well-equipped for these activities and indeed stirred all Europe with his eloquence. One of his most famous speeches was given at Zürich in 1946:

> We must build a kind of United States of Europe.
> If Europe were once united in the sharing of its common inheritance there would be no limit to the happiness, prosperity, and glory which its 300,000,000 or 400,000,000 people would enjoy.
> And why should there not be a European group which could give a sense of enlarged patriotism and common citizenship to the distracted peoples of this mighty continent? And why should it not take its rightful place with the other great groupings and help to shape the honourable destiny of Man?
> Therefore, I say to you, "Let Europe arise!"[2]

When Churchill in power showed no interest in Britain's joining Europe, the memory of these speeches caused considerable bitterness on the continent. But the disillusion came from not having listened carefully. The rest of the Zürich speech, for example, revealed clearly what Churchill felt subsequently called upon to state with more brutal clarity: "We are with them, not of them."[3] The union Churchill had in mind for Europe was to be built, not by Britain, but by a reconciled France and Germany. England, the Commonwealth, "mighty America", and, Churchill hoped, Russia, would be only the "friends and sponsors" of the new Europe. In short, even in rhetoric, Churchill's enthusiasm was carefully measured. Britain was to be a "sponsor", but not a participant.

One significant continental view of Churchill's policy can be found in de Gaulle's *Memoirs*. Throughout the war, the General

42

had tried to win the British to his plan for a European combination, based on France, to balance the super-powers on their periphery. When Churchill paid a moving triumphal visit to liberated Paris in November, 1944, de Gaulle pressed his familiar theme:

> You English, of course, will emerge from this war covered with glory. Yet to what a degree—unfair though it may be—your relative situation risks being diminished, given your losses and expenditures, by the centrifugal forces at work within the Commonwealth, and particularly, the rise of America and Russia, not to mention China! Confronting a new world, then, our two old nations find themselves simultaneously weakened. If they remain divided as well, how much influence will either of them wield?[4]

De Gaulle was especially worried about the settlement Roosevelt and Stalin would impose on Europe:

> The equilibrium of Europe ... the guarantee of peace along the Rhine, the independence of the Vistula, Danube and Balkan states, the creation of some form of association with the peoples all over the world to whom we have opened the doors of Western civilization, an organization of nations which will be something more than an arena for disputes between America and Russia, and lastly the primacy accorded in world politics to a certain conception of man despite the progressive mechanization of society—these, surely, are our great interests in tomorrow's world. Let us come to an agreement in order to uphold these interests together. If you are willing to do so, I am ready. Our two nations will follow us. America and Russia, hobbled by their rivalry, will not be able to raise any objection. Moreover, we shall have the support of many states and of world-wide public opinion, which instinctively shies away from giants. Thus England and France will together create peace, as twice in thirty years they have together confronted war.[5]

Churchill's answer was a more thoughtful version of what he had shouted in anger the preceding January at Marrakech: "How do you expect that the British should take a position separate from the United States? ... each time we must choose between Europe and the open sea, we shall always choose the open sea. Each time I must choose between you and Roosevelt, I shall always choose Roosevelt."[6] In Paris, a mellower Churchill defended his own and indeed postwar Britain's policy by observing that:

> ... in politics as in strategy, it is better to persuade the stronger than to pit yourself against him. That is what I am trying to do. The Americans have immense resources. They do not always use them to the best advantage. I am trying to enlighten them, without forgetting, of course, to benefit my country. I have formed a close personal tie with Roosevelt. With him I proceed by suggestion in order to influence matters in the right direction.[7]

De Gaulle's disappointed view: "The peace we French hoped to build in accord with what we regarded as logic and justice, the British found it expedient to approach with formulas of empiricism and compromise."[8] The British, as de Gaulle had occasion to remind them several years later, were not Europeans.[9]

De Gaulle was an early but by no means solitary sceptic about Britain's interest in European unity. Paul-Henri Spaak, with less controversial credentials as a good European than the General, once resigned as President of the Council of Europe's Consultative Assembly, with an angry attack on Britain's lack of support for the European Defence Community. If Europe were to be built, he concluded, it would have to be without Britain.[10]

The most bitter denunciations of Britain's European policies came, in fact, from European enthusiasts among the British themselves.[11] These formed a significant group, claiming at various times the apparent, if ambiguous, support of some of the most distinguished figures in the country. But in the nineteen fifties, these British Europeans had little effect on British policy.[12] Until 1961, every government was tepid and often hostile towards the whole idea of a close European union. Certainly no government was ever prepared to base Britain's future on such a union, or take the lead in creating it.

In the crucial postwar years that set the whole pattern of subsequent Western relations, it was not, of course, the Tories, but Labour's Foreign Secretary, Ernest Bevin, who directed Britain's foreign policy. Labour's policy went through roughly three stages, each corresponding to a different American phase. In the early days, while America was still flirting with the dream of a new "progressive" world order built around a Russian-American condominium, Bevin frequently found himself alone against Molotov in opposing Russia's ambitions, notably in Greece and Persia, with Byrnes looking on as a sort of benevolent and large-minded mediator. During this period, Bevin took the initiative in organizing a regional European defence arrangement, a policy leading in 1947 to the Treaty of Dunkirk between Britain and France.[13]

In 1947, with the Truman Doctrine committing the United States to the defence of Greece and Turkey, America began a policy of actively opposing Russian expansion. In 1948, there came the Marshall Plan and the Organization for European Economic Co-Operation, and in 1949, NATO. This fundamental switch in American policy constituted not only a triumph for imaginative American statesmanship, but also a victory for British policy. The United States, at last, was involved permanently on the European side of the Atlantic.

America's various European ties were organized in two quite distinct patterns—that of the Marshall Plan and OEEC on one hand, and that of NATO on the other. The OEEC reflected the ideal of an Atlantic Alliance built around two equal partners—America and a United Europe. NATO, on the contrary, was predicated on a direct relation between the United States and each of Europe's national states, without any intervening European Union. One was the relation often expressed metaphorically as an alliance with "two pillars". The other, the NATO relationship, seems to have been less inspiring to literary fancy. Perhaps a hen and her chicks would be the most appropriate metaphor. At any rate, both patterns continue to the present day.

From the beginning, British Governments clearly preferred the "Atlantic", NATO pattern over the two pillars pattern of the OEEC. True, in the Atlantic pattern America would always predominate, but that, the British felt, was a price worth paying for an American commitment to Europe's survival. Furthermore, the ties in so vast an assemblage could never be very tight. Britain's Commonwealth and American connections, and eventually Britain's own nuclear capabilities, would still assure her a major role—a "special" relationship within the Alliance. Meanwhile the presence of so many others would allow Britain room for manoeuvre in her relations with the Americans.

On the other hand, the two-pillars pattern, a European federation to match the American, had every disadvantage for Britain. In the unlikely event that Europe actually succeeded in uniting,

45

Britain would be confronted with the unpleasant choice either of being excluded from Europe or else impairing her independent world standing, Commonwealth connections and national economic independence. A federal European Union would end Britain's special position in the Alliance. With the continent united, Britain would either be absorbed or overshadowed. Thus while Britain was all for European co-operation, she was not interested in a European federation. Hence, she constantly stressed the necessary Atlantic dimension to European union. Bevin's own words in 1948 spelled out the basic British position:

> . . . the organization of all the Western European democracies, excellent and necessary as it is, can hardly be accomplished save within the framework of a larger entity. I am not content to confine either propaganda or speeches of action to the assumption that Western Europe alone can save itself.[14]

The British went so far in their enthusiasm for an Atlantic rather than a European grouping that they drew strong criticism from the American Congress itself: especially from the architects and enthusiasts of the Marshall Plan. The whole idea of that great venture was not only to save Europe from the communist flood, but also to provoke the Europeans to create, by their union, a self-sufficient economic and political unit capable of existing without indefinite American assistance.[15] The tension between these aims and Britain's policy was soon apparent. Thus, while the Americans in establishing the machinery of Marshall Aid were able to insist that Europe's economic problems be treated as a whole, British resistance killed off more radical proposals for integration along the lines of a European customs union.[16] In the same period, Britain so succeeded in watering down the institutions of the Council of Europe, the first of the actual attempts to build an organized European union, that even General de Gaulle found the Council a ludicrously inadequate instrument for forging the continent into a new nation.[17]

There were prominent Britons who criticized Labour's policy towards Europe at the time, but in retrospect the policy is easy enough to understand. The Government could hardly be blamed for being more interested in preserving the American commitment than in advancing visionary schemes for European unity. Furthermore, postwar leaders of both parties were suspicious of American enthusiasm for European federation. In the idea of the two pillars, the British were quick to see a more sophisticated version of the old American isolationism—as well as American naïveté in applying the lessons of their own federalist experience to divisions of vastly greater magnitude in Europe.[18] Britain's main interest was to ensure that the United States could not find an excuse, once again, to withdraw and leave Europe to its fate. Thus Britain continually resisted American efforts to encourage European federation—not only from a desire to maintain national independence, imperial connections, and great-power status—but from the fear that federalism for Europe and isolationism for America were reverse sides of the same coin.

Furthermore, the goal of European union, as an end in itself, quite naturally had less appeal for the British than for many other Europeans. Whereas every major continental power, with the ambiguous exception of France, emerged from the war with its old nationalist allegiances discredited, Britain had triumphantly confirmed the grandeur and durability of her own traditional loyalties and institutions. It was not surprising that there was lacking in England the same rather desperate eagerness to renounce national identity. In an odd sort of way, the German occupation had perhaps given the peoples of Western Europe a common experience, an intimacy among themselves, that made it easier for them to think of a new order in which they would work closely together and indeed become more like one another. Britain had been spared this painful education. The British could hardly be expected to embrace their disgraced friends and recent enemies quite so eagerly or expectantly.

If the British in general lacked any overriding enthusiasm for European union as an aim in itself, the Labour Party in particular found it not only irrelevant but often harmful to the actual goals in which Labour was interested.[19] Labour was more drawn to the internationalist idea of the United Nations than to the limited regionalist concept of a European union. Not only might a federal Europe provoke American isolationism, but, if Britain were bound up in it, the continentals might well constrain the Labour Party from pursuing its own cherished domestic and international goals. Internationally, Labour's imagination was fired by the vision of a new "multi-racial" Commonwealth bridging the gap between regions,

47

D

races and stages of economic development. This goal seemingly had little to gain from Britain's close association with unregenerate Belgian, Dutch and French colonialists. Not a few in the Labour Party still hoped that a socialist Britain might eventually act as a bridge between communist Russia and the West. Britain's freedom of action was unlikely to be improved by close association with the Catholic anti-communists of Europe's ruling Christian Democratic parties. Above all, the Labour Party was bound up in its vast programme of domestic reform. Socialism had at last gained the opportunity to rebuild English society. What Labour Government could be expected to renounce the hard-won machinery of the national state at just the moment when it could at last be put to good use? What kind of new society, Socialists asked, could be built in a federation with the right-wing, capitalist governments of France and Germany? In short, European union was not, in itself, an overriding goal for most of the Labour Party and there were many other factors restraining Labour's enthusiasm for a federal Europe.

The continentals, finding no lead from Britain, went their own way. In 1950, the Schumann Plan to place the coal and steel industries of France and Germany under a common "High Authority" became the first of the continent's major supranational initiatives. The plan had a rather *dirigiste* flavour, but the Labour Government clearly rejected for England any federal scheme that might hinder purely national planning.[20] The continentals went ahead and established the Coal and Steel Community without Britain and thus first brought into existence the non-British "Europe of the Six".

When the Tories came back to power in 1952, they soon dashed any hope that they might prove more sympathetic to European union. They had already made it quite apparent that they were no more willing to accept the supranational discipline of the Coal and Steel Community than was Labour.[21] The new Government's first major confrontation with the European federalist movement occurred over the ill-starred European Defence Community. The episode provides a classic illustration of Britain's unwillingness to co-operate closely with the continent. EDC's sponsor, French Foreign Minister René Pleven, envisaged nothing less than a common European Army. The whole scheme represented an ingenious "European" solution to the agonizing problem of German rearmament.[22] The Korean War had made a large new land army urgently necessary for Europe's defence. France, especially with her colonial involvements in Indo-China and Africa, was hardly able to put up enough forces. Neither America nor Britain was willing to contemplate a lasting commitment of a mass army adequate to match Russia. Inescapably, Germany would have to be rearmed. The French Foreign Minister saw in his European Defence Community the means to rearm the Germans without re-arming Germany. Individual national units would be kept small. The whole force would not be at the disposal of national governments as such, but under a common European command, directed, in turn, by a European political authority in which Germany was not likely to gain hegemony.

The political consequences of such an arrangement were immense. Once military power was organized on a non-national, "European" basis, a full range of European political and administrative institutions seemed inevitably necessary to provide the army with its goals, directives, funds, arms and provisions. Indeed, supporters of the scheme were busily drawing up and debating a constitution of the federal government of Europe.[23]

Ultimately, so great a loss of national independence proved too much for the French themselves to swallow. On one hand, General de Gaulle, reappearing from recent retirement, attacked the EDC as marking the end of French independence. With his notorious scepticism of the efficacy of a national structure, he saw the likely result of the EDC, not as the building of a new European super-power, but as the permanent domination of Europe by the non-European allies. The EDC, he believed, would destroy the independent political will of France. The supranational institutions that were to replace her would be weak, based on no authority profoundly rooted in the loyalties of the peoples of Europe. The result would be a vacuum, soon filled by the powerful state across the Atlantic. Thus, the European army would be an organization of mercenaries, directed by a foreign power. Indeed, de Gaulle predicted, the commander of the EDC would probably not even be a European, but an American.[24] Other French groups feared that in a purely continental structure, whatever the arrangements, Germany would soon dominate. The EDC would trap France in a German embrace. Without Britain there were not enough elements to establish an internal balance.

Both these arguments were greatly assisted by the policy of the British Government. The British gradually made it clear that they would never submit their forces to the proposed arrangements. That was hardly surprising. A Britain that could not contemplate putting her coal and steel under supranational authority, was unlikely to do so with her army, least of all under a Tory Government. Britain's reluctance to make any commitment to the EDC encouraged French fears that Europe's army would be dominated by Germany. British reluctance also seemed to confirm de Gaulle's thesis that the EDC was a clever Anglo-Saxon device to achieve German military rearmament at the minimum political price for the US and Britain. France, on the other hand, was expected to sacrifice her independence in order to prevent Germany from regaining hers. Britain, de Gaulle noted, had no intention of making a similar sacrifice. Only France, caught in the grip of self-abnegation, "neurasthenia" as he called it, could contemplate so servile a surrender of national independence.[25]

The French may not have accepted the EDC in any event and it might not have worked if they had, but it seems fair to say that Britain's reluctance to make any substantial commitments to an EDC force probably ensured that the French Assembly would eventually defeat the proposal, whatever the chances may have been for its passage otherwise.[26]

But Britain's motives are perfectly understandable. EDC was the most radical of all federalist proposals for linking together the nations of Europe. In the early 1950s Britain could still reasonably see herself as a world power, nuclear after 1952, whose concerns were hardly limited to Europe. The sacrifice of independence would certainly have been more real for her than for the France of the Fourth Republic. For those committed to the idea of a federal Europe, Britain's action was deplorably short-sighted. But is squared with the basic assumptions of bipartisan British foreign policy towards Europe — scepticism of Europe's federalist initiatives and fear of American disengagement.

And while Britain took no interest in federal military and political union, she was taking what appeared to be an effective role in encouraging more conventional forms of European co-operation. Indeed, it was Britain that rescued Europe from the impasse over German rearmament. Britain calmed continental fears of Germany by promising to station substantial forces on the continent as long as Britain was in NATO. At Anthony Eden's initiative, Bevin's old Brussels Treaty Organization—Britain, France and Benelux—was expanded to take in Germany and Italy, fitted out with some bureaucracy and an advisory parliamentary assembly, and re-christened the Western European Union.

Perhaps, as some bitterly argued, if Britain had made similar commitments in the first place, the French Assembly would have accepted the EDC.[27] In any event Britain would have joined it. There was all the difference in the world between giving a military guarantee and joining a common army. Neither Party, let alone the British public, was ready to advocate Britain's tying herself irrevocably into a European military union.

Possibly the Tories were right to treat the European army as a pipe-dream, but it is more difficult to defend their reaction to the continental initiative that led ultimately to the Common Market. The British Government not only disapproved of these developments, but failed, it seems, to understand even what they were about. While the continentals set about to build a great new regional state in Europe, the British, with rather arrogant irrelevance, lectured them about the dangers of trade distortion in a customs union. Against the political ideals of regional federalism, the British preached the economic ideal of universal free trade—and seemed surprised that the Europeans felt the British ideal had little to offer, as if, indeed, the political goal of a United States of Europe could be measured by the economic standards of nineteenth-century free trade! It is this profound failure of the British political imagination in the 1950s that seems responsible for much of Britain's embarrassment in the following decade.

The Common Market was conceived after the defeat of the EDC in 1954, when the Good Europeans decided to "re-launch" the European movement along economic rather than political and military lines. Following a memorandum of the Benelux governments, the foreign ministers of the Six met at Messina in early June, 1955, and ultimately voted a resolution calling for a European Common Market. They charged a committee to study the means not only to eliminate all internal tariffs and quotas, but also to create, throughout the Market, the fundamental economic conditions that would allow all parts to participate successfully in the benefits of open competition. Thus the committee studied a common external tariff, the harmonization of regulations and economic, monetary, and social policies, the free movement of workers, and the use of a development fund to develop backward parts of the proposed Community.[28] It was generally accepted that these aims would require strong Community institutions. In short, from the first, the Six were thinking not merely of the usual advantages of free trade, but of the integration of Europe into a single managed economy. This Committee, called the Spaak Committee after its Chairman, met throughout the rest of 1955 and, in April 1956, issued its notable report—the basis of a Treaty, negotiated throughout 1956, signed at Rome on March 25, 1957, and ratified by the national parliaments later in the same year. In January, 1958, the European Economic Community was born.

The significance of these developments seems to have been little appreciated in England. Britain sent a representative to the Spaak Committee who eventually withdrew. The Tory Government was preoccupied with other worthy goals, and especially with encouraging a new spirit of conciliation between Russia and the West. There was the general feeling that relations with Europe were proceeding satisfactorily. Arrangements for co-operation had been worked out with the Coal and Steel Community in early 1955, and with the birth of the WEU, British military relations with the continent had reached a new degree of intimacy. More fundamentally, however, the British Government, and indeed the public generally, never took seriously the political aspirations of the European Movement and of its artefact, the Common Market. Thus there seemed little sympathy or even comprehension of what the Europeans were after nor of how powerful were the forces sustaining them.

Britain's miscalculations led her into a disastrous effort to transform the Common Market into a free trade area, an initiative that resulted in the establishment of a rival European bloc, the European Free Trade Area (EFTA) and set the seal upon Britain's exclusion from Europe.[29]

Britain's motives were open enough. Once it was clear that the Common Market was to be established, the Government began to fear the dangers to British trade of being on the wrong side of the Market's common external tariff. The Government thus proposed a wider European "free trade area", envisioning an end to all tariffs and quotas on industrial goods within ten to fifteen years.[30] On November 26, 1956, Harold Macmillan, then Chancellor of the

Exchequer, explained to the Commons that Britain wanted an agreement that would supplement but not sabotage the continent's customs union, while associating England with it in such a way that she did not have to sacrifice either her economic interests or her vital links throughout the Commonwealth and across the Atlantic.[31]

The British free trade proposals touched off a great debate in Europe and many now familiar arguments were then heard for the first time. The British solemnly warned of the dangers of an "inward-looking" Europe, split into two blocs and pointedly began discussing the possibility of free trade with Canada. The French and the federalists warned of the danger of Britain's watering down the coherence of the Six. Within the Common Market Countries, England's role became a focal point in the struggles between the federalists, protectionists, planners and free-traders.

Serious negotiations started in the fall of 1957, after the Rome Treaty was out of the way. The basic protagonists were the British and the French. The latter enjoyed powerful support from the Common Market Commission while Britain could count on the sympathy of such groups in the Community as Erhard's supporters in Germany, who were more inclined to favour free trade than political integration. Britain's essential interests were to ensure first that her exports were not put at a disadvantage in Western Europe, and second that the network of Commonwealth trading arrangements was not significantly disturbed. The British position developed a theoretical economic rationale, namely, that free trade was of benefit to all, while a narrow, "inward-looking" customs union was "trade-distorting". Such unions created artificial barriers against the outside world and the members' increased trade with each other was not justified by genuine economic advantages. The results would be harmful to outside countries and, indeed, harmful to the members of the Union itself. The most efficient international division of labour and pattern of trade would be distorted by the arbitrary barriers imposed by the Union.[32]

The French argument, like the British, ran on both the level of national interest and economic theory. The French realized that they had to modernize their overprotected industry and that the competition of an open European market would be salutary if painful. But feeling themselves weak in relation to the industrial exuberance of Germany, they were anxious that they should compete on equal terms unhampered by the institutional factors which, in addition to their inefficiency, might render the French incapable of competing with Germany. The French therefore insisted on arrangements to guarantee roughly uniform conditions for competition, wages, welfare costs and tariff duties. They were also interested in the development of backward regions. With their predilection for planning, the French believed that central "European" institutions would be needed to bring about these uniform conditions. The French wanted, in short, a larger market in which competition would be controlled intelligently to secure the progress of the weaker as well as the stronger members. Hence they opposed any serious dilution of the Common Market by a free trade area because they saw it as undermining the safeguards built into the Rome Treaty to ensure the even development of the Common Market as a whole. Furthermore, the French insisted that a fair deal for them would have to include agricultural as well as industrial goods. If they were to buy cheaper German industrial products, then Germany should buy cheaper French food.

As the French saw it, the British were seeking all the advantages of a European customs union without any of the obligations the others had accepted in the interests of the whole—weak and strong elements alike. The British, on the other hand, saw the French view as nothing but old-fashioned French mercantilist protectionism. The economics behind the demand for equal conditions of competition was faulty. Didn't the French know that free trade would soon result in equalization of conditions?[33] The desire of the French to foist their agriculture on the rest of Europe was deplorable. Surely Britain could not be expected to abandon her traditional Commonwealth supplies of cheap food.

The British reassured themselves by condemning the French for backward protectionism. But, in doing so, they ignored the sound political logic behind the French position. France, to be sure, sought particular advantages for herself in the EEC, as did everyone else who joined it. But the French position also accepted the rationale behind the Treaty, which was that a common European economy might be the foundation for an ultimate political union. Thus the Common Market was inspired not by free trade, but by a different sort of economics, strongly tinged with the political ideal of federation. The object of the Common Market was to create a new kind of regional economic unit that would enjoy many of the characteristics of a national economy. By joining the Common Market, the Six were taking the first steps not simply towards a more effective international division of labour among independent states, but towards economic cohabitation in a single community. It was the political logic of nation-building and not the logic of free trade that dictated that the Six should favour each other over outsiders, that Germany should buy food from France and France manufactures from Germany, and that they should both contribute to the economic development of Southern Italy.

Against the political logic of federalism, the British continually countered with the economic logic of free trade. Not surprisingly, they got nowhere. Both sides had recognizable national interests intertwined with the competing ideals they presented to the rest of Europe. But the interests of French protectionism were combined with the regional ideal of European political union whereas the defence of Britain's traditional trading patterns was justified by the universal ideal of classical economics. For a Europe determined to unite, the French position was obviously more attractive. In opposing it, Britain struck at the very heart of the political aspirations of Europeans. What is so surprising is that the fundamental philosophical differences involved in the conflict were not seen more clearly at the time. Indeed, ten years later, they are barely appreciated now.

Britain's failure was really a failure of imagination. There were some, but not many, who saw the issues clearly at the time. One of the most interesting critiques of the British position comes from the distinguished Canadian economist, Professor Harry G. Johnson, himself a leading advocate of liberal free trade. Looking back on the negotiations, Johnson was struck by the startling "insularity of the reactions of British economists, and the grudgingness with which they tend to recognize the continental viewpoint", an attitude manifested in their unshakeable assumption that the "desire to create a unified economy is not a reasonable policy objective, but a delusion whose possessor should be treated with due gentleness." Johnson's further observations are worth quoting at length:

> . . . the most striking characteristic of the reactions of British economists to the Common Market and Free Trade Area schemes, viewed in the light of subsequent developments, was

the solid Britishness they displayed. With few exceptions, if any, the economists seem to have agreed with the Government's general line both that freedom of trade, and not freedom of factor movements or the co-ordination of economic policies and institutions, is the substance of economic co-operation, and that what had to be decided was the terms on which Britain would be willing to join with the Six. None, so far as I can recall, showed any very profound appreciation of the possibility that the Six might have quite a different conception of economic co-operation than the British, let alone any sympathy with this conception or willingness to consider its merits as against trade-oriented British conceptions. It has since become clear enough that the Six, or at least the French, do take their alternative conception of economic co-operation seriously. But recognition of this fact has tended to be more a matter of growing irritation with French perversity than of British self-questioning: while the fact that Britain has been trying to muscle in on a scheme whose earlier development she had formerly been steadily resisting, has been conveniently forgotten. The celebrated *Times* headline, "France the Wrecker", epitomizes this attitude; a headline more in accord with the historical evolution of events might well have been "Britain the Uninvited Guest".[34]

The free trade negotiations of 1957 constituted the first of the great diplomatic duels between Britain and France over the organization of Europe. It is interesting to speculate on the different reactions during the fifties of these two great European countries both faced with a cruel reduction in their world positions. The Suez Affair saw them acting together. Both were deserted by their American ally and forced to acknowledge their decline into dependent, second-class powers. The French, although distracted for some time by the agonies of their dying empire, turned resolutely to Europe. The British, on the contrary, sought busily to restore their torn Atlantic connections. Ironically, at the same time in America the Common Market was reviving all the old enthusiasm for European political union. Thus the United States increasingly urged Britain to join Europe at the very moment that the British were preoccupied with moving closer to America.[35]

But it was not so much American pressure as a remorseless logic of circumstances that was steadily forcing Britain towards Europe. The Suez debacle in 1956 shattered the illusion of independent world power. By 1958, it was clear that there would be a European Common Market without Britain, a community that might even develop into a European federal union. Britain was not only being pushed out of the European "circle", but might ultimately come to be displaced in her special relationship with America as well. A united European group would surely be of more importance to the Americans than Britain.

The change of Presidents in Washington, from Eisenhower to Kennedy, removed from the White House the figure who, more than anyone else, symbolized that wartime camaraderie of soldiers and bureaucrats in arms that formed so much of the substance of the "special relationship". The Prime Minister and the new President soon formed close personal relations of their own, but it was apparent that, for the new generation of American leaders, official Anglo-American relations would be more practical and less sentimental. In hard terms, Britain had much less to offer than a unified continent. The unseemly collapse of the Paris Summit Meeting in 1959 had brought to a disastrous close one of Macmillan's favoured roles for Britain, the wise and honest broker at the summit with Russia and the United States.[36] The new freeze that followed suggested that British enthusiasm for peacemaking had possibly been premature. At any rate it was unlikely to be a particularly promising role for the future. The new administration in Washington was itself far more vigorous in approaching the Russians than its predecessor had been. Henceforth, Russia and America would play alone without their British nanny.

Meanwhile, on the domestic front, the early successes of the Tories began to turn sour. After a euphoric spurt in the mid-fifties, the economy had to be checked between 1955 and 1957 by severe Government measures to deal with a declining balance of payments. In 1957, bank rate reached 7% for the first time in decades. The reflation of 1958 and 1959 had to be checked in 1960 because domestic demand appeared to be outrunning the capacity of the economy. Imports rose faster than exports and, once more, there were difficulties with the balance of payments. Restrictions returned and, at the end of June, 1960, bank rate went back up to 6%. By 1961, the economy, after a short improvement, was again in difficulty.

Looking back over the fifties, Englishmen began to entertain the disquieting thought that something fundamental was wrong with their economy. True, it had grown faster than in a long time.[37] By 1960, national output per capita was 12½% higher than in 1955. But, as we have seen, Britain's continental neighbours had been growing at twice that rate. The depressing British pattern of Stop-Go was already familiar, and many observers began to doubt if there were any cure short of some drastic recasting of the economy.[38]

Accompanying these diplomatic and economic discouragements, there was abroad in England during the early nineteen sixties a widespread sense of cynicism and disillusion—especially among the clever and articulate young. Macmillan, far from insensitive to the need for imaginative idealism in politics, sought a new cause that could bring challenge, opportunity and fire to national politics. His solution was to lead Britain to the Common Market. In his announcement to the Commons on July 31, 1961, Macmillan reversed the whole postwar policy of Tory and Labour Governments alike. Britain suddenly appeared to take a major step towards Europe.[39]

But Macmillan's step was not as unequivocal as a Good European might have wished. Doubtless he had his own hesitations. From the beginning, moreover, he was met by a strong bipartisan diffidence and uneasiness—which he knew might easily turn into active hostility. Tactically his Government's situation was extremely complex. Any number of entrenched interests and loyalties might be aroused to oppose Britain's entry. Negotiations had to be conducted simultaneously on several shifting foreign and domestic fronts. The entire performance was an extraordinary balancing act, with Macmillan in the essential role. Everything depended on his courage and skill. Although he held his own in Parliament, his position among the general public was much weaker. Public support for joining was hesitant and volatile. Throughout the whole year and a half of negotiations, polls never revealed a stable majority for or against. By late 1962, the portents were suggesting a swing against the Conservatives.[40]

The study of British opinion during the negotiations reveals two interesting points: the indecision of the general public and the strong European enthusiasm of the Establishment.[41]

If leading Britain to the Common Market was a revolution, it was a revolution led from the top, from the ruling cliques of the Establishment itself. Nearly all the serious papers supported the

Government. It was Lord Beaverbrook, the perennial leader of un-fashionable causes, who led the journalistic opposition. The chief pro-Market public-relations organization, the Common Market Campaign, was compact, distinguished, efficient, non-partisan, well-financed and had easy access to the corridors of established power. Its leaders were Lord Gladwyn, a Liberal City banker who had just retired as Ambassador to France, and Roy Jenkins, a rising Labour moderate MP, later Home Secretary and Chancellor of the Exchequer. The arguments and techniques of the group seemed obviously aimed at informed rather than mass opinion and were a far cry from such great popular economic crusades of the past as Corn Law repeal or Imperial Preference. The chief opposition counterpart, on the other hand, the Anti-Common Market League, was obscure, amateurish and poor.[42] It appealed to the mass public, partly, no doubt, because it was not taken seriously by anyone else.

There are many plausible explanations both for this sharp dis-tinction among the activists as well as for the apparent apathy among the masses. Why were the established classes so dispropor-tionately in favour of joining? Federalism generally appeals most to a cosmopolitan upper class, rather than to the local masses. Some elite groups anticipated that a Europeanized Britain was the post-war solution that would be most favourable to their interests and tastes. The possibilities of Britain's running Europe presumably appealed more to those who already ran England. Furthermore, while many of the pro-Market arguments put off both the expert and the mass reader, they struck just the right tone of technicality and progressivism to appeal to a general educated audience.

The gulf between general and elite opinion does not, of course, prove anything about the quality of the arguments on either side. While one could deplore the presumed apathy and prejudice of the general public, one could also conclude that the views of the masses really were less fickle and more profound than those of the more educated public.[43] It may well be that the hesitancy of the general public to commit themselves to Macmillan's daring but dubious venture was the appropriate response for a great people who realized instinctively what their Government avoided telling them whenever possible: that England had reached a profound crisis in her search for a new identity and purpose. A moment of choice had come that would probably mean the end of the dreams and loyalties people had for a century been taught to cherish.

It would be wrong, in any event, to assume that the case against Britain's joining was as weak as it was unfashionable. The Anti-Common Market case was powerful and not without distinguished advocates. It reflected both political loyalties strongly held by most people in England and also genuine hazards and sacrifices involved in merging the British economy with the Common Market. What were the arguments for and against Britain's joining the EEC?

The arguments that are said to have influenced Macmillan in 1961 had long been familiar in Europeanist circles in England.[44] Only by leading the Europeans could Britain gain enough weight to be a major force in world affairs. Only by extending herself into a continental home market could Britain keep up her great positions in finance and technology. Only by a "cold shower-bath" of competition in a large competitive market would British industry be stimulated to efficient growth. On the other hand, should Europe be forged without her, Britain would be left isolated, weak and threadbare. Without Britain's political weight and skill, to be sure, the prospects for a stable democratic union in Europe were much reduced. But if the whole enterprise did fail and Europe reverted to chaos, Britain would suffer as twice before in this century.

The Anti-Market case was similarly both economic and political. The economic arguments were the most precise and were backed by the authority of some of the nation's leading economists. These professionals and their students tended to be sceptical of presumed advantages that were as numerically indeterminate as "economies of scale" or "cold shower-baths of competition", while they found it easier to measure the likely short-term loss to trade.[45] Their economic objections turned around the probable effects on the balance of payments and on the prospects for long-range economic growth. Rough calculation of the effects of joining indicated that, in the short run at least, changes in the balance of trade would be unfavourable. Britain would lose preferences averaging 10% on the third of her exports that went to EFTA and the Commonwealth. In return, tariffs averaging 10-15% would be dropped on the sixth of British exports that went to the EEC. Furthermore, imports from the Six, mostly competitive manufactures, would increase. The Common Market's protectionist agricultural policies would not only seriously hurt Britain's traditional Commonwealth suppliers, but raise English food prices. The resulting increase in the cost of living would push up wages and prices and squeeze profits. These immediate adverse effects would be reflected in the balance of payments and would soon require compensatory deflationary measures, made less effective, to be sure, by the Common Market's freedom of capital movements. In such an unfavourable atmosphere, the British economy would never get off the ground to meet strong new competition. The cold shower-bath would be followed by shock and paralysis. Britain would languish and become a mere offshore island of a European economy whose vital centres lay elsewhere. The attitude of many economists at the time, even many in favour of joining, was well summed up by Sir Donald MacDougall: "Looked at as a purely commercial deal, and ignoring the indirect consequences, it is thus by no means obvious that entry into the Common Market would be a good proposition for Britain. It might well tend to worsen the balance of trade."[46]

The political opposition was more diffuse, but no less powerful.[47] In Macmillan's view, Britain was going into Europe not to lose her independence, but to gain power. Like de Gaulle, he saw no reason to take federalist pretensions of the Brussels bureaucracy too seriously. In a Europe of States, Macmillan believed Britain's stable political traditions would lend strength to the shaky democratic governments of the continent. Britain's leadership would make Western Europe "outward-looking" that is, pro-American and sympathetic to the Commonwealth. Opponents attacked every one of these expectations. The federalist framework of the Community, and the general right-wing capitalist bias of the Six would, they believed, impose great limitations on the British Government's ability to plan its own economy. Britain would be swept up into a political system dominated by alien ideals and practices. Britain would not swing the continent; the continent would dominate Britain. British politicians and civil servants would be baffled and ineffective in the continent's entirely different legal and administrative traditions. The colonialist, right-wing, capitalist, anti-communist policies of the continent would become the policies of Britain—to the detriment of herself, her Commonwealth and the world in general. Opponents of joining naturally made much of Britain's ties with the old dominions, the new "multi-racial" Commonwealth, or the economic allies who had stood by her in

61

EFTA. A most popular charge saw the Common Market as a "rich man's club" in a hungry world. Britain, it was felt, had sterner duties.[48]

Behind the more elaborate anti-Market arguments lay the fundamental unwillingness of many British to jettison so many of their old loyalties and prejudices to seek a common future with Europe — at least on any terms the Six were likely to accept. Some of these feelings were part of almost every Englishman and when they were added to the quite genuine economic pitfalls and thorny political problems, they formed an extremely formidable obstacle to the whole-hearted pursuit of a European policy. While Macmillan, with his customary dexterity, was able to keep his forces in order and dampen the immense potential opposition in the country, he ended up making so many concessions to the opposition at home that he had very little chance of succeeding with the Six on the continent. Thus in spite of all the official protestations to the contrary, it is doubtful that the Brussels negotiations ever were near success.[49] The agricultural concessions Britain asked for alone made it impossible for France to agree without a quite unreasonable sacrifice of her own economic interests — national interests, in truth, more in harmony with progress towards European union than England's.

It is highly unlikely, on the other hand, that Macmillan, even if he had accurately judged the situation, could have made Britain's entry any more appealing to the French. Conceivably, if Macmillan had offered to build with France a joint nuclear deterrent and weapons system, the French might have been tempted. But de Gaulle too had to measure his political ambitions against the underlying economic strength of his country. Without the agricultural policy, a vital French economic problem would have remained unresolved. With Britain in the Common Market, the French would probably never have achieved the agricultural agreements of 1965. As it was, they came only after the most prolonged and bitter struggle with the Germans who, for the same reasons as England, preferred to import cheap food from outside Europe.[50]

In any event, it is rather idle to speculate on what would have happened if Macmillan had offered nuclear co-operation or modified his economic demands. For it is highly unlikely that he would have been able to do so without losing the domestic battle upon which his whole position depended. Macmillan had probably pushed his Party and the country about as far towards Europe as it was possible to go. Furthermore, Labour by then was committed to opposing the whole venture and not unlikely to win the on-coming General Election.[51] By the time of de Gaulle's veto in January 1963, Britain's step towards Europe had become very shaky indeed. In short, de Gaulle was presented with a situation in which British public opinion was deeply divided, the Government's position precarious, Labour opposed, and the application to join loaded with qualifications fatal to France's economic plans. His veto was not surprising. What was surprising was the astonishment of the British. And whatever France's particular motives, the official French view was widely appreciated, if not exactly shared, among many devoted to the creation of a European Union. It was quite unlikely that the rest of Europe would band together to bring irre-sistible pressure on the French, however sympathetic they appeared to Britain in private.

In short, while it may be true that a less qualified British bid to join Europe would have succeeded, Macmillan's Government, even if willing, was unable, because of deep domestic divisions, to make a more straightforward application. Thus the Government's domestic struggles cost it the foreign war. In this sense, it is prob-ably true that the vital struggle in the campaign to get Britain into Europe goes on primarily in Britain.

In announcing his veto in 1963, de Gaulle went out of his way to suggest that Britain's internal evolution might well lead her some day to make an offer the Europeans would have to accept:

Lastly, it is highly possible that Great Britain's own evolution and the evolution of the world would lead the British to the continent, whatever may be the delays before complete realiza-tion. For my part, this is what I am inclined to believe, and that is why, in my opinion, it will be in any case a great honour for the British Prime Minister, for my friend Harold Macmillan, and for his Government to have perceived this so early, to have had enough political courage to proclaim it and to have had their country take the first steps along the path that, one day perhaps, will bring it to make fast to the Continent.[52]

Has not that evolution taken place to a remarkable extent? Three and a half years later, not a Tory but a Labour Government took the lead in bringing Britain to Europe. In certain respects, the

63

E

situation in 1966 was remarkably unchanged from 1961. The British economy was once again in serious difficulty after a much-heralded attempt to promote growth and productivity. The old economic arguments, pro and con, were roughly the same. British trade had continued to grow more rapidly with the EEC than with the Commonwealth.[53] The old problems of agriculture and sterling remained. The new Prime Minister did, to be sure, make more of the fear that Europe's industrial technology would soon be hopelessly surpassed by the United States.[54] Only enlightened Government co-operation within a common economy could, he often said, save Europe from eventually becoming a backward area. Meanwhile, many of the old political arguments against joining had been diminished, ironically, by General de Gaulle himself. The General had at least temporarily quashed the federalist pretensions of the Common Market Commission. Membership in the Communities did not seem to have restrained unduly the French government's domestic or international freedom of action. De Gaulle's foreign policy could scarcely be called right-wing, colonialist, or anti-Russian.

And three years after the 1963 veto, still no alternative to Europe had caught the imagination of the British public. Enthusiasm for the "multi-racial Commonwealth" had declined steadily. While there was undoubtedly strong sentiment for "Atlantic" ties with America, the notion of an institutionalized junior partnership with the United States enjoyed a limited appeal, further constrained by the agitation over technology. And many British suspected that their own lack of enthusiasm was more than reciprocated by the great majority of Americans. Many, to be sure, were coming to believe that Britain should shed her extraneous foreign commitments and rebuild her own economic and political future by some thorough-going internal reformation. But the final desertion of the Labour Government's National Plan in July 1966, suggested that Britain could not resolve her economic problems by herself.

In any event, by 1967 Britain was once again seeking to enter the Common Market. The old problems remained. Could Britain bring herself to be sufficiently "European", whatever that might mean, to make herself irresistible to the continent? Could she avoid those inhibitions abroad that public opinion demanded at home? Were there any attractive alternatives to Europe?

The French reaction in 1967 suggested that the question of Britain's joining Europe might be unresolved for many years. De Gaulle's obdurate refusal to admit Britain on any terms other than his own and his relentless exposure of the ambiguities in Britain's position at least had the advantage of driving Britain to face up to the fundamental questions. These basic questions about the kind of future Britain wants for herself and for the world will remain long after the immediate problems of joining or creating this or that international arrangement have been resolved. If, for example, Britain gains Europe, what will she do with it? It is this fundamental indecision about her role and purpose that has been troubling Britain since the war and so often made her policies ambiguous and self-defeating. But how can the British resolve this problem? What, in fact, are the basic alternatives for Britain? What are the prospects and the commitments involved in each?

IV.
Britain in
Europe: the Elusive
Alternative

1. *Some Basic Questions*

By the middle of the 1960s, the general enlightened public in England appeared to have reached an overwhelming consensus that the most promising path for Britain's future lay with Europe in the Common Market. The Labour Party, once opposed, was making a far less qualified bid for membership than had the Tories in 1961. All the same, the domestic opposition to joining the Common Market still included some of the most distinguished of Britain's economists, armed with arguments which seemed, if anything, more formidable than before. And the renewed French objections to Britain suggested that the continental opposition was far from over. Britain's path to Europe was still hazardous. The harsh Gaullist glare evaporated the early optimism and illuminated so many difficulties that many former enthusiasts began to wonder if joining Europe was, after all, a possible or even a congenial future for Britain.

Any answer to these doubts must concern itself with three fundamental and related questions. First of all, is union with Europe the best or even a possible solution to Britain's present economic and political problems? Secondly, are the Six interested in having Britain as a close partner? And thirdly, is Britain herself genuinely interested in what Gaullists and federalists alike see as the ultimate goals of the whole European enterprise—the building of a strong union capable of standing on its own and playing a major independent role in the world? These are not easy questions to answer, involving as they do not only innumerable hazardous calculations of interest, but deep and often highly emotional loyalties and reactions.

Britain's present uncomfortable situation in Europe stems, as we have seen, from her own early diffidence towards the goals of the continental Good Europeans. Anyone familiar with Britain's history cannot be surprised. While Britain is obviously a part of Europe, her own world role has depended on the continent's divisions rather than its union. In spite of the profound European roots of English civilization, the traditional Englishman's definition of his nation has been as much extra-European, indeed counter-European as European. The most notable extensions of Britain's personality and power have not been into Europe but to the far-flung provinces of a world Empire and Commonwealth. The white dominions and even India were more important and familiar to Englishmen than were France, Germany or Italy.

But in spite of this past, public opinion does appear to have evolved towards Europe. There is a new generation, it is often said, that no longer dreams the old exotic imperial dreams and is eager to get on with its continental cousins. To many Englishmen, it has appeared objectively true, even if emotionally unwelcome, that an inexorable logic of economic and political interest impels post-imperial Britain into Europe.

2. *Britain's Case for the Common Market*

What are these forces and arguments that constitute the case for Britain in Europe? The last chapter touched briefly on the arguments in their historical context. It seems true, for example, that the initial motives leading Macmillan to revise the Government's policy towards Europe were more political, at least in the broadest sense, than economic. In retrospect, Macmillan's motives also seem rather strikingly negative. By 1961, the Government had concluded that the Common Market, for better or for worse, was functioning as a reality and, whatever the difficulties, Britain would be better off inside than out. Any dangerous tendencies a united Europe might display could be more easily fought from within. And with de Gaulle facing a revolt over Algeria and Adenauer waning in Germany, Macmillan is said to have believed that Britain's more intimate presence in Europe was badly needed to support the continent's alarmingly precarious democratic and constitutional forces. Britain could not detach herself from Europe's fate. The inevitable logic of geography meant that if Europe reverted to chaos and the whole common enterprise collapsed, Britain would inevitably suffer along with the rest.[1]

There was, to be sure, some consideration of the positive benefits Britain could bring to Europe, although these views tended to be rather unflattering to the Europeans. British Socialists believed they would greatly strengthen the faltering European Left and thus cure the continent of its right-wing capitalist predilections.[2] "Outward-looking" Britain would call the continentals to their philanthropic responsibilities towards the underdeveloped countries. Similarly, many British as well as American Atlanticists convinced themselves that England's presence in the Community was needed to keep Europe firmly allied to America. Britain's steady Atlantic orientation would counterbalance de Gaulle's disconcerting penchant for adventurous international friendships and theatrical quarrels and, above all, would discourage any German attempt to turn eastward and seek unification through neutralism.

Another important set of considerations had to do with Britain's continuing relations with the United States. The rise within the Atlantic Alliance of a European bloc, Britain left outside, would inevitably displace Britain as NATO's second power and lead to a deterioration of the special relationship with America. But if Britain were to become a leader of the new Europe, her European and American connections would reinforce each other and she could easily retain her role as second Western power.

It must be confessed that all these political arguments, seen in retrospect, do not reveal much British enthusiasm for the European venture in itself, or for what many people regard as its overriding goal—the creation of a powerful European grouping capable of acting ultimately as a self-sufficient major power in the world. This is a subject to be returned to presently.

While those who led England to Europe's doorstep in 1961 were said to be thinking primarily of the political opportunities of the new Europe, the arguments presented to the public tended to focus rather heavily on the economic side. And since 1961, both sides of the economic case have remained in the forefront of attention and indeed developed considerably. The early pro-Market economic case, like its political counterpart, reflected not merely admiration for what the continent had done, but also fear for the effects on England of being left out. Membership in the Common Market would not only avoid tariff walls, but also encourage British trade and stimulate economic growth. The improvements in trade, to be sure, were admitted to be long-range rather than immediate. Even by 1965, British exports to the Commonwealth were still substantially greater than to the Common Market, 28·4% of the total as opposed to 19·1%. But exports to the Commonwealth were growing very slowly—a mere 28% since 1958, whereas exports to the EEC had, in the same eight years, increased by a stunning 101·9%.[3] Proponents admitted that it would hurt Britain to give up her Commonwealth trade preferences, but in a world where the industrialized rich countries seemed to trade increasingly with each other, Britain's best opportunities for the future lay on the continent—particularly if Britain's entry would unify the separate elements of the EEC and EFTA.[4] Conversely, as the Community's members progressively eliminated their tariffs with each other, English trade would find the Community's common external tariff a more and more serious barrier to the rich and growing continental market. The customs union was effectively setting up a new preference system among its members a great deal more promising for Britain than her agreements with the Commonwealth.[5] In short, it would probably have been better if the Common Market did not exist at all, but since it did, Britain was better off inside than out.

On a more positive note, the Government believed that joining Europe would bring great advantages to domestic productivity and growth. British industry would suddenly be exposed to vigorous competition. The shock would be salutary to lazy British management.[6] For the efficient, there would be great opportunities in a rich, large-scale market. Labour would be more tractable and it would be easier to establish a reasonable incomes policy. Others have advocated joining the Common Market not so much because they believed membership, in itself, would particularly help the British economy, but rather because it would lead to much needed domestic reforms probably otherwise unacceptable in Britain. Many people have looked forward to the continental "value-added" tax as a greater incentive to industrial efficiency than Britain's tax on profits. Europe's heavier payroll taxes have been thought to be

69

an effective inducement to the more rational use of labour. Europe's income taxes have been eagerly anticipated by those who believe in the incentive effects of lower rates of high incomes.[7] And joining the Common Market would, some argued before November 1967, induce the British Government at last to go through with a long overdue currency devaluation.[8]

Big business in Britain has been strongly in favour of joining, a phenomenon sometimes explained by the presence in Britain of giant corporations in comparison with the continent.[9] With their large resources and big-scale views, and with the City of London's formidable facilities for marshalling finance, British companies expect to take the lead in the continental reorganization and rationalization of Europe's national industries—a rearrangement encouraged by the big new market and by the steady pressure of competition from the American giants. Thus top British management would extend its sway into Europe.

The general European problem of competing with big American firms is another important argument greatly used in recent years. It is said that, while the present national markets may be large enough for the average industry, they are not large enough for industries requiring a heavy investment in research, notably the computer and aerospace industries. As a result, American aircraft projects, for example, are said to have an obvious advantage over separate European national projects. Aside from having a government with greater resources, American firms can count on a much greater market for their aeroplanes and thus spread out the costs of research and development over a larger volume of production.[10] While it can be argued in reply that only the richest and largest countries should indulge themselves with vast and hazardous aerospace projects, the space and electronic industries thus engaged are said to be vital for scientific and technological development.[11] The whole industrial system benefits from their "technological fall-out." Unless the Europeans persist in these activities, it is argued, Europe will eventually become an underdeveloped American technological colony. Her brains will "drain" away to the United States and her industries will have to be content with the crumbs falling from America's table. Britain, with Europe's greatest technological capacity and heaviest expenditure for scientific research, stands to benefit especially from the larger assured market and wider sharing of costs.[12] While technological sharing is possible without joining the EEC, as the Concorde project with France illustrates, co-operation would doubtless be encouraged and possibly made more systematic by the general fusing of economies and central planning implied in the whole idea of the Common Market.[13] Meanwhile, in science and technology, as in so many other respects, the British are top-heavy.

To some, finance seems another field where Britain, built up beyond the resources of her national economy, could save her institutions by attaching them to Europe. The City of London is increasingly threatened by the restrictions necessary because of the pound's recurring weakness. A "European" solution might translate sterling from a purely British into a common European reserve currency. This presumably would not mean merely that the Common Market countries would give Britain their reserves and, in return Britain would give them her debts![14] But the Common Market is perhaps evolving slowly towards a common currency and it is not impossible to imagine a new world monetary system organized along regional bloc lines rather than the more universal or unitary system favoured by the Atlanticists. Each side of the Atlantic world could have its own reserve currency system. Fixed exchange rates would be normal within each of the two systems. But between the American and European blocs, an occasional revaluation might well be the best way to correct a persisting balance-of-payments deficit on one side or the other.

From the point of view of the Good Europeans, some such bifocal arrangement would fit into the broad logic of the "two-pillars" concept of Europe's relations with America that they favour. Such a system would also eliminate what some believe to be the unfair advantage which comes to Americans, who, because they operate a reserve currency, are able to buy up more and more European industry while running simultaneously a very large deficit in their balance of payments.

The chief difficulty in reducing the role of American capital in Europe's affairs is that, for the moment, the Europeans have no alternative institutional means for organizing enough local capital for their own industrial expansion.[15] But England has all the institutions for a large capital market, indeed has them to excess. What could be a more natural marriage? What would be a better way for Britain to escape from a world financial role too extended for her domestic economy while still preserving the justly renowned institutions that are the heritage of that role?

Sterling is a kind of metaphor for what many people feel instinctively is England's basic problem. There remain too many institutions and skills which, while they embody much of what is finest in English life, are on too large a scale for the shrunken dimensions of post-imperial Britain. Many people see Britain saved by extending herself into Europe. There alone, they believe, can England regain the dimensions appropriate to the scale of her institutions, skills and habits. The alternative is an increasingly lonely and threadbare isolation in which the country will be forced to throw away its best furniture because it is too grand for the tenants of a cottage. There is widespread fear that an isolated Britain would lose not only her institutional grandeur, but those aspects of her national character that make her a great nation. In a broad sense, many people want Britain to go into Europe to restore her own morale. There is a great new power rising out of Europe, a power filled with promise and danger. Britain—to save her own soul— must take up the opportunity at her doorstep.

Many people, of course, disagree—either because they are uninterested in grandeur or because they judge that joining would have highly undesirable economic and political consequences. What are these consequences? Why does any reasonable Englishman oppose his country's entering the EEC?

3. *The British Case Against the Common Market*

It has already been noted that the economic case against joining has had behind it the authority of some of Britain's most distinguished economists.[1] Their arguments have essentially been based on the assumption that the immediate effects of entering the Common Market would be so disastrous for the balance of payments that, in consequence of such weakness at so critical a moment, irreparable damage would be done to the long-range development of the economy.

The main threat to the balance of payments comes from the EEC's agricultural programme. For Britain and the Common Market have radically different agricultural programmes that reflect basic economic and social differences between the two.

Both subsidize farmers, but by radically different methods. Broadly speaking, in Britain the taxpayer pays the subsidy, while in the Common Market it is the consumer. In Britain, food enters duty-free and the consumer enjoys the low world price. The government subsidizes the farmers directly out of taxes. Cheap food helps keep down the cost of living, hence wages and production costs. The system appears to make sense for a country like Britain that needs to import half its food, if the detriment to the taxpayer of subsidies is less than the benefit to the consumer of low prices.

Many Common Market countries, on the other hand, have large farm populations and surpluses. The prospect of a common market in agriculture was part of the basic deal that brought France into the Community. In January 1962, after years of wrangling, the Six finally agreed in principle on a common agricultural system. Its actual establishment took four more years of argument, including a crisis so bitter that it nearly broke up the Common Market.[2] What resulted is a system which is almost the exact opposite of Britain's. A tariff keeps food prices high enough so that European farmers can compete and earn a reasonable profit. Such a protective system probably makes at least social and political sense in an economic grouping that has many farmers and is agriculturally self-sufficient. Neither of these conditions, of course, describes Britain; but if she joined the Common Market, she would nevertheless presumably have to adopt the continental system. The results would be highly undesirable.

To begin with, the continent's entire arrangement is profoundly irritating to a country whose whole economic tradition preaches the virtues and glad benefits of free trade and the wicked folly of agricultural protectionism. After 120 years, Britain would be going back to the Corn Laws!—and for the sake of inefficient German, French and Italian peasants! More concretely, the system would raise British retail food prices substantially—by 1966, experts estimated from 10 to 14%.[3] Higher food prices would hurt the poor, raise wages and prices generally, make British exports less competitive. In addition, as the system now works, Britain would have to pay a disproportionate contribution to the European Agricultural Guidance and Guarantee Fund—the Common Market's fund to modernize agriculture. All this would affect the balance of payments adversely.

In 1967, before devaluation, it was generally agreed that the whole agricultural policy would cost Britain from £175 million to £250 million annually in foreign exchange.⁴ Devaluation, of course, would increase the sterling cost. There is no disputing that the Common Market's agricultural system, whatever its merits for Europe, would be a bad deal for Britain.

Were Britain in the Common Market, the exchange losses from the agricultural policy would have to be made up from somewhere, but not, it seems, from any immediate rise in sales of British manufactures. On the contrary, since Britain's home market has been more protected by high tariffs than the EEC, most studies suggest that, if anything, joining would immediately worsen Britain's trade balance in manufactures.⁵ The prospects appear to be even grimmer when account is taken of the likely effects of higher food prices on British wages and export prices. In short, it is highly unlikely that the huge payments deficit resulting from agriculture would be made up by industrial trade.

On May 1, 1967, *The Times* presented a lengthy anonymous article which reckoned that a conservative estimate of the overall cost of joining to the British balance of payments would be a staggering £600 million annually.⁶ The trade loss alone was set between £455 million and £530 million. The article anticipated further annual losses from adopting the continent's value-added tax (a minimum of £200 million), and the freeing of capital movements within the EEC (a minimum of £100 million).⁷ There was no reason, according to the article, to count on a compensating inflow of American capital. Americans would be more likely to invest on the continent where plants would be more centrally located and still have free access to Britain.

These estimates in *The Times* article were, of course, far from incontestable. A few days later in the Commons, for example, the Prime Minister argued that Britain's position would be aided by several compensating factors. He expected capital to flow from America, and even from the continent itself. The agricultural programme was unfortunate, but spread out over five years, the resulting increase in the cost of living would be minor.⁸ British agriculture would expand its output, world food prices would rise anyway, and very likely the Common Market's would fall. The EEC's agricultural arrangements, moreover, were scheduled to be renegotiated in 1969 and Britain's projected share of the burdens,

74

which at 35% was twice that of any other country, might well be reduced substantially. Other features, like the value-added tax, by encouraging more efficient producers, might ultimately make British exports more competitive, whatever the immediately unfavourable effects.

Nevertheless, the Prime Minister did apparently concede that membership would involve an annual exchange cost of £500 million, although he sought to put the whole matter in another light. No one, he said, expected Britain to join without a reasonable transition period. Thus the effects would be spread out over several years. If the transition period were five years, for example, the annual cost would be only £100 million. And as the Government's expected annual growth rate of 3% meant an actual increase in British production of £100 million annually, joining the Common Market would require deploying to exports, each year for five years, only one tenth of the country's anticipated annual increase in production.[9] This would not be a crushing burden when measured against the advantages that could be expected.

On the positive side, the Prime Minister saw a new large market giving a tremendous boost to those technologically advanced products in which Britain excels. In the long run, it would be a great stimulus to growth and excellence, a growth that could not take place in a purely national market.

This argument, that a large rich market is the key to growth, has been the fundamental answer to all the short-term calculations of loss. To grow, Britain must be allowed on equal terms into what is for her the most promising large-scale market. A contemporary *Times* leader put the fundamental assumption succinctly:[10]

> The truth is that the industrial structures that develop in a very large market have a natural advantage in complexity and resources over those which develop in a smaller market.

British industry must either get into that very large market or decline. In the modern world, size was the key to growth, the short-term costs of readjustment to the new market notwithstanding.

Whatever the basic correctness of this view, the short-range difficulties for Britain have appeared sufficiently formidable to lead many economists to doubt whether any long-range advantages would ever come into play. From the moment the Labour Government came into power, it had been wrestling with a recurring exchange crisis, leading first to a severe deflationary squeeze, then collapse of the National Plan and a cessation of growth, and finally, by the end of 1967, to a forced devaluation accompanied by another round of deflationary measures. Few people expected the devaluation package to be a magical cure. If all went well, not anything to be taken for granted of course, it would most likely be 1969 before British payments came back into balance.

Any country in such precarious condition could not take lightly the prospect of having to pay out an additional £500 million a year in foreign exchange, even at the gradual rate of £100 millions more each year—a figure, after all, double the average annual trade deficit from 1962 through 1965. The prospect might seem daunting to any country, but Britain's exchange difficulties would be greatly complicated by the international exposure of her currency and the paucity of her reserves. Could sterling, so weak already, hope to stand the strain?

Sterling's problems would be compounded because joining the Common Market would involve a commitment to free capital movements among the member states. Thus the Government would open the door to what might become a persistent flow of capital from the domestic economy and would renounce one of the major means for heading off a run on the pound.

Furthermore, it was generally believed that devaluation was impossible for a country already in the Common Market.[11] If Britain joined and the balance of trade ran further against her, as it would certainly do in the short run, the Government would have no alternative policy to deflation. In such a climate and with the economy in such a fundamental state of weakness, was it realistic to expect British industry to respond to whatever opportunities the new market offered?

Many economists feared, in short, that if Britain entered the Common Market in so feeble a state, she would be far more likely to decline than grow. It was unconvincing merely to cite the overall growth in the Common Market and expect that England, once inside, would share in the general prosperity. While the economy of the EEC as a whole might have been expanding rapidly, growth had not taken place evenly throughout. Belgium, for example, had been in the Common Market since the beginning and had not enjoyed the same rapid growth as the others.[12] The general pattern of economic development in an expanded market tended, if anything, to increase the differences between advanced and retarded areas. Areas that were already flourishing grew even faster whereas the decline of languishing regions accelerated. Such developments were all the more difficult to control as governments gradually lost the means to plan their own national economies. In a continental market, whole countries might become backward regions as capital flowed elsewhere.

Britain was not, after all, in particularly favoured circumstances in relation to the industrial centres of other European countries. She was, in fact, an off-shore island on the edge of Europe, with a labour-shortage, high welfare costs, and a very mature industrial system.[13] Industrially, Britain might well become to Europe as Wales, Northern Ireland, or Scotland have become to England. And, within Britain herself, there might be a further distortion of economic development towards the south-east. In summary, critics saw the expectation that joining the large market would lead to growth and rejuvenation as a sad and dangerous illusion.

It is, of course, true that the devaluation of 1967 could ultimately have a decisive effect on Britain's economic prospects as a member of the EEC. If, as some have predicted, Britain's trade begins to show a healthy surplus by early 1969, enabling sizeable reserves to accumulate, and if British industry mounts a successful programme to expand productivity and output, then it is certainly true that Britain will be in a far better position to meet the burdens of the agricultural system, the shocks of increased competition and the opportunities of a big new market. But, as we have seen, all this will take time—the trade balance itself is not even expected to turn until the last quarter of 1968, and that is by no means assured. It is also true that since Britain's tariffs on manufactured goods are, overall, nearly twice as high as the Common Market's, any elimination of tariff walls would presumably give more of a premium to competing continental goods in England than to English exports among the Six. It would also enhance the position of some manufactures from outside Europe. Hence, if Britain unexpectedly joined the Common Market in 1968, British goods would very likely lose some of the comparative advantage anticipated from devaluation. In addition, the rise in food prices from the agricultural policy would also, of course, make it more difficult to maintain that control of wages and productive costs thought to be essential if devaluation is to succeed.

77

In short, devaluation has by no means brought an immediate improvement in Britain's situation and, even if ultimately successful, cannot be expected to start doing so until 1969.[15]

4. *The French Case Against Britain*

If the economic case against joining is powerful from Britain's point of view, how must it appear to the continentals? Why should they be expected to show enthusiasm for so sickly a new partner particularly when recent experience among the Six demonstrates how especially susceptible the partners are to each others' diseases? As usual it was President de Gaulle who spelled out the bad news. In his Press Conference of May 16, 1967, the General discussed the probable effects on Britain of participation in the Community's agricultural system:

> If she submits to the rules of the Six, her balance of payments will be crushed by the levies and she will, on the other hand, be forced at home to bring the price of food up to the level adopted by the Six, to raise her workers' wages correspondingly and to charge correspondingly more for her manufactured goods which will be that much more difficult to sell. She clearly cannot do this. But, on the other hand, to bring Britain into the Community without her being really bound by the agricultural regulations of the Six would amount automatically to disrupting the system and therefore to upsetting completely the balance of the whole Common Market and robbing France of one of her chief reasons for being a member.

The French President turned to sterling. Noting the Community's requirement for free capital movements among its members General de Gaulle thought the risk too great both for Britain and for the Six as well. Sterling's "peculiar position", as long as it lasted, would continue to keep Britain outside the Common Market:

> Indeed, the fact that the organization of the Six is bringing down all trade barriers between them necessarily entails that their currencies must have a constant relative value and that, if one of these were to be shaken, the Community would put it right. But this is only possible because the Mark, the Lira, the Florin, the Belgian Franc and the French Franc are in a

thoroughly strong position. On the other hand, although we need not despair of seeing the Pound maintain itself, the fact is that we cannot be certain for a long time to come that it will succeed in this. We shall be all the less certain since, in relation to the currencies of the Six, Sterling has the special character of what is known as a reserve currency, which means that a great many States in the world, and particularly in the Commonwealth, hold enormous Sterling balances. Of course, one may attempt to draw a distinction between the fate of the Pound as a national currency and as an international one; it may also be claimed that, once Great Britain would be inside the organization, the Community would not be obliged to answer for what might happen to Sterling. But these are purely exercises of mind.

When all is said and done, monetary parity and solidarity are essential rules and conditions of the Common Market and can assuredly not be extended to our neighbours across the Channel unless Sterling presents itself one day in a new position, with its future value seemingly secure, freed, like the others, from its reserve currency role and with the burden of Great Britain's debit balances inside the Sterling Area having been eliminated. When and how will this come about?

Whatever may be thought of de Gaulle's motives, it must be confessed that he had put forward a telling case. In the discouraging state of the British economy, how could Britain be expected to endure an additional £500 million debt on her balance of payments? With her frightful recurring exchange crises, Britain has become the financial leper of Europe. Why should the continentals take on so sickly a giant?[1] In short, de Gaulle in his Press Conference said only what some of Britain's own best economists had been saying for a long time. Britain in the Common Market would be a danger both for the Market and for herself until the fundamental disequilibrium of the balance of payments had been overcome. Doubtless there were numerous possible cures for Britain's difficulties. But simply leaping into the Common Market was not one of them. Somehow Britain had to cut her foreign exchange commitments and increase her domestic productivity to the point where exports were sufficiently competitive to balance imports even when the economy was growing rather than stagnating. France herself had faced a similar situation when de Gaulle came to power in 1958. De Gaulle found the solution through devaluation

79

F

and Draconian measures to keep down costs and increase productivity. He took strenuous measures to cut France's losses around the world and bring her commitments into line with the realities of her position. Thus he made France a far stronger influence in the world and an active and vigorous force in the new Europe. Was it unreasonable to expect Britain to perform a similar exercise in self-mastery?

In his Press conference of November 27, 1967, the General made it clear that devaluation, in itself, had not appreciably altered his view of the economic obstacles to Britain's joining the Market. Britain's agricultural policy and the precarious state of her currency, coupled with its heavy international liabilities, effectively ruled out any immediate entry.

But for General de Gaulle, there has always been a more fundamental problem in Britain's entry, the problem of whether or not Britain was genuinely interested in what he saw as the overall political aims of the Community:

> The idea, the hope which, from the beginning, led the Six continental countries to unite was undoubtedly to form an entity that would be European in all respects, that is to say, that it would not only carry its own weight in trade and production, but that it would be capable one day of dealing politically with anyone, for its own sake and on its own. In view of the special relations of the British with America, together with the advantages as well as the liabilities arising for them out of these relations, in view of the existence of the Commonwealth and of the privileged relations they have with it, in view of the fact that the British are still assuming special commitments in various parts of the world, which set them fundamentally apart from the continental peoples, it is easy to see how the policy of the Six, providing they have one, could, in many cases, be associated with that of the British. But it is not possible to see how the two policies could merge, unless the British resumed complete freedom of action, particularly with regard to defence, or unless the peoples of the continent gave up the idea of ever building a European Europe.[2]

De Gaulle's view was bitterly resented by the British Government. Yet it reflected not only a strong body of opinion in Europe but surely had considerable substance to it. By mid-1967, Britain's evolution towards the European circle appeared far from complete, her devotion to the ideal of a great power in Europe far from assured. True, the Prime Minister had at least begun to talk about what Britain could offer rather than get out of Europe. In this respect the second bid to enter the Community no doubt marked a considerable improvement over the first. But Wilson's argument that without Britain's resources, especially in technology and finance, Europe could never achieve a position of economic and political parity with the United States was continually being undermined by the actions of the Government itself. In technology, to be sure, the Labour Government had gradually given considerable substance to the idea of European technological co-operation.[3] But the Government appeared absolutely unwilling to consider any basic shift in its defence policy from an Atlantic to a more European focus. Yet defence is so intimately connected with technology that, for a large number of informed persons, it seems quite unrealistic to consider close co-operation in one and not the other.[4] Nevertheless, when in May, 1967, the Opposition leader launched a small trial balloon in Parliament about a Franco-British nuclear force to be held "in trust" for Europe, the Government's ostensible reaction was embarrassed shock—no doubt for the benefit of its own left-wing with its manic preoccupation with disarmament.[5] But surely, if there is to be a Europe which is a great world power, it must not deny itself forever the *sine qua non* of modern military defence.

There is something profoundly unrealistic in the notion that a uniting Europe, with such vast resources, should continue indefinitely to rely on the American nuclear umbrella. Granted that there must remain a basic alliance between Europe and America, is there any reason that the military relationship should continue to be so grotesquely out of line with the relative economic and political positions? It is difficult to see how Europe, so vulnerable and so satisfied, would ever be anything but the most cautious of nuclear powers. How should a significant European nuclear force be a greater threat to world peace than the weak national forces of England and France? If China is to be a nuclear power, then why not Europe?

Yet in this field where Britain was still pre-eminent, there was no lead for Europe either in 1962 or in 1967. Quite the contrary. Britain's role in the non-proliferation treaty negotiations in Geneva scarcely would have suggested to the sceptical that she had any great concern with the defence needs, technological development, or ultimate political position of Europe.[6] Indeed, Britain's whole defence policy—support for the war in Vietnam, fervent enthusiasm for NATO, and dogged hanging on East of Suez, has been essentially based on the Atlantic special relationship with America. There does not appear to be much room, within this policy, for the development of a separate European deterrent. Indeed the logical outcome of Britain's position calls for Europe to remain a permanent military protectorate of the United States, a prospect that the British often appear to greet with greater enthusiasm than the Americans themselves. This is, of course, a perfectly respectable concept of Europe's future, but it is not one that appeals much to those who dream of restoring Europe to a major role in the world.

Similarly, in the discussion about the reorganization of the international monetary system, Britain has continued to support the present "Atlantic" system, dominated by the United States— Britain again enjoying a junior but "special" relationship—rather than to work for a bi-polar system that might reflect the immense financial and trading position of Western Europe. Britain has continued thereby to support American demands for more uncontrolled liquidity, in spite of Europe's strong opposition.[7] So far there have been few ideas from Britain for a regional reserve system based on a European currency, a not illogical expression of the two pillars concept and a not unpromising solution for sterling.

In short, in the great questions that have to do with the future role of a united Europe as a major political force in the world, Britain has seldom seemed on the European side. Britain does indeed have a great deal to offer Europe, but instead of showing any imaginative enthusiasm for developing a regional bloc, a bifocal Western world, she has remained wedded to the old Atlanticist pattern embodied in NATO, a pattern that presupposes a single Western bloc and ensures domination by America. In 1967, as in 1944, Britain seems to prefer the realities of the special relationship to the possibilities of European unity. Britain's real diplomatic initiative has been reserved not for building Europe, but for acting as a superfluous go-between in the attempts at mutual accommodation between America and Russia. For a Europe that still groans under the ministrations of Yalta, Britain's predilections have not made her seem a very reliable member of the European club.[8]

When all is said and done, it is hard not to agree with Lord Avon, who, speaking in 1952 of the possibility of Britain's joining a European federation, concluded: "this is something which we know, in our bones, we cannot do."[9] If Britain's anti-European policy does not emanate from the bones of the British, it seems very much of a piece with a world-view popular in Britain, a view dominated by the logic and vision of universalist free trade and world government. These are surely worthy ideals, but as long as they predominate in the national mind, Britain will always be incapable of a profound sustained commitment to the ideal of European political union. Somehow, if Britain wants to join Europe, the English imagination must turn away from its old idols. Quite apart from the usual British views on the grand issues of world strategy, it would be some slight sign of evolution if the contemporary British showed more concern for the problems of building Europe and less for the necessity of diluting it. Europe's main problem at the moment is that it is not nearly "inward-looking" enough. Britain's much vaunted internationalism is hardly a virtue to those who are concerned with building a coherent region. It might help if the British took to looking at the European enterprise less as an exercise subject to the principles of classical free trade and more as a possibility for exciting breakthroughs in international economic planning.

Indeed, even at this late date, the British give little serious study to the conflicting principles that have informed the whole European movement. The field has been pretty much left to the doctrinaire federalists. As a result, "practical" Britons retain a primitive and uniformed view of the great issues and ideals that have been bound up in the postwar drive to build Europe. One of the most glaring consequences is the surprising lack of knowledge in Britain about the policies and visions of General de Gaulle. Because de Gaulle is known to scoff at the inflated political pretensions of supranational technocracy, he is frequently dismissed as an antediluvian nationalist out of the seventeenth century. The British, left on the sidelines by their own insularity, continually berate the French as bad Europeans, as if it were not the French who have been the leaders of Europe ever since the Common Market came into being. To be sure, France has used her European vocation to enhance her own position greatly. It is indeed a sign of the intelligence of de Gaulle's policy that he has managed to reconcile the interests of France with the growth of Europe. Would that the British could make the same claim for their postwar statesmen!

There is something extremely unattractive and demeaning in the constant belittling of General de Gaulle in Britain. The assertion, constantly repeated and apparently seriously held by large numbers of people, that de Gaulle's policy towards England is dominated by petty jealousy and wounded pride—"the French have never forgiven us for not having surrendered in 1940"—perhaps reveals more about the contemporary character of England than it does about France. It somehow smacks more of C. P. Snow's Senior Common Rooms than de Gaulle's Elysée.

5. Britain's Prospects in Europe

If Britain seriously wants to join Europe, there is a good deal to be said for trying to come to terms with General de Gaulle. Successive British Governments have resisted this elementary truth and never properly taken the trouble to understand what de Gaulle wants. They have had, it must be said, little help from the rather doctrinaire, anti-Gaullist Good Europeans in Britain.[1] Much of the British opposition to de Gaulle lacks substance. While there are certainly sharp differences between France and England on the kind of foreign policy an independent Europe should maintain, it seems odd for the British to criticize de Gaulle for his views on the constitutional organization of the new Europe. For his views are almost exactly the same as England's. Both want a confederal "Europe of States". Neither has been enthusiastic about the supranational aspirations either of the Brussels bureaucrats or the federalist enthusiasts for a sovereign European parliament. While France and Britain may disapprove of each others' foreign policies, neither is willing to see the conflict settled by the Germans!

De Gaulle bases his opposition to supranationalism on two assumptions, neither of which should seem exceptional to Britain. De Gaulle's first assumption about Europe holds that an effective federalist government is, at this stage, impossible. If such a government did somehow exist, de Gaulle argues, it would be a weak non-government. Lacking any national base and thus any deep popular roots, it would be incapable of formulating any strong policies or of rallying the peoples of Europe behind them. Hence a federal government would be quite unable to resist the domination of European affairs by outside powers. If, in the present era, the national states of Europe were effectively destroyed, federalism could only replace them with an impotent hybrid.

But, as his second assumption, de Gaulle believes it may be possible to build slowly a European grouping of states who act in effective concert with each other, because they are collectively informed by a growing sense of mutual identity and interest, because, having agreed to find their futures together in Europe, they have come closer to each other than to friends outside. Thus, a common European identity and interest may slowly be nourished and formulated by a continuous intergovernmental conversation through a network of shared institutions grouped around the Common Market. In this Europe of States, each partner retains its sovereign independence, modified only by the habits of co-operation and a certain shared identity. The strongest and most resolute give the lead, the others follow as they like. All this, somehow, is very English. It sounds almost as intangible as the Commonwealth. Indeed the constitution of the European Union is perhaps the one issue on which there is and always has been total agreement between Britain and France.

On the other hand, the conflict between the two on what sort of foreign policy a united Europe should follow is profound. Whether or not Britain should take to a Gaullist world policy is discussed at some length in the next chapter. It suffices to say here that until Britain does reach an entente with France, she is unlikely to be a member of the Common Market. Britain's probable exclusion is justified, ironically enough, because the Europe of States both she and France favour cannot hold together with two contradictory major powers. Its network of voluntary co-operation is inevitably fragile in its early stages. It would be impossible to maintain if any one of the principal powers within it is not devoted to the whole enterprise, or if the membership is so heterogeneous that it is difficult to find any common personality or policy. That is why an Atlantic England could so easily be fatal to Europe, as indeed could a Europe of thirteen partners. Whatever the relative merits for Europe of de Gaulle's independent and Britain's Atlanticist policies, it seems clear that any European grouping cannot contain them both. The present Europe of the Six rests on a fundamental entente between France and Germany, a tie that has been strained but never broken. If it were, the Common Market would come to an end. Germany does not always follow France, but neither does she actively oppose her. On those few occasions when she has, over the MLF or the EEC's agricultural policy, Europe has come close to breaking up. In the end, Germany has always given in. On the other hand, France has gone to great trouble to frame her policy towards Russia and Eastern Europe in such a way that it ostensibly serves German interests.

It has become fashionable, particularly in the United States, to argue that European union is a dead cause. But, in fact, the work of union does proceed, even if undramatically. The EEC appears to be inching towards a coherent economic union. De Gaulle does provide a hectic, but not ineffective political lead. His role, as he sees it, is to point the way, without waiting for the others to follow. His ideas do, in fact, have a growing influence in shaping the way Europeans look at their position and its possibilities. If they do not follow de Gaulle in everything, neither do they set off by themselves in another direction. And on many issues, the Six are, in fact, coming to act more and more as a coherent bloc.

In short, the fabric of a European unity does exist at this stage but is inevitably fragile. The presence of another large power, headstrong and unconvinced, might well tear it to pieces. If Britain got into the Community with her present orientation, she might well wreck it. In other words, until Britain and France reach a basic entente on world policy, they cannot live together in the only kind of Europe, a Europe of States, either of them would find acceptable. Whether such an entente can or should be considered by Britain remains the fundamental issue of Britain's world policy.

If Britain and France cannot live in the same union, could a Europe of States be constructed with Britain and without France? What chances would Britain have if, despairing of ever getting past the French veto, she actively sought to break up the present Six and to replace France? The moment, if there ever was one, has very likely passed. To some extent, the issue was decided in those fatal free trade negotiations in 1957. For several years after the war, Britain could have had the leadership of Europe for the asking. She was concerned with other things and Europe has moved on. Inertia and their own impressive achievements are likely to keep the present Six together.

Britain should not overestimate her popularity on the continent. Many people on the continent may favour having Britain in the Community, but their enthusiasm is sapped by the force of the Gaullist arguments, and they certainly would never consider destroying the EEC for the pleasure of being led by Britain rather than France. Years of hostility to the idea of European integration and constant lecturing about "right-wing inward-lookingness" have created an abiding distrust of Britain's motives in trying belatedly to join the Common Market, most particularly among the devoted partisans of federal European unity. This suspicion cannot be dispelled by a few enthusiastic speeches on European technology from the Prime Minister or the Foreign Secretary.

Not only do Britain's past record and perspectives undermine her present standing on the continent, but she is not much assisted by her reputation for being the American Trojan Horse. It is all very well to invoke the idea of Atlantic partnership as an essential dimension to European Union. Britain gives the impression, nevertheless, of trying to practise political bigamy. There is a deep psychological truth in the Gaullist argument that Europe will never find herself until Europeans stop looking to Washington before they look to each other, a point felt not only in Paris but occasionally in Washington itself. Britain's Atlanticism involves something considerably more than the general proposition, accepted after all even by de Gaulle, that Europe and America must remain allies. It is hard for many continentals to believe that the English, always closer to America than to the continent, will not represent a foreign voice in their affairs. Thus England's kind of Atlanticism seems a threat to a Europe struggling to find its own identity.

For all these reasons, Britain is not likely to enter a Gaullist Europe of States without coming to some fundamental understanding with France. It is always possible, of course, that the French may decide to gamble on Britain's ultimate conversion rather than risk alienating England from the continent forever. God or his own people may bring down de Gaulle and replace him by a weak Government that will renounce the Gaullist dreams. But, even if Britain were to enter the Common Market, the same basic question would remain. If Britain were to gain Europe, what would she do with it? Is Britain genuinely committed, in de Gaulle's words, "to allowing Europe to construct itself by itself and for itself, in such a way as not to be under the dependence of an economic, monetary and political system that is foreign to it?"[2]

In summary, both from her own point of view and the continent's, there are substantial objections to Britain's joining Europe. The strain of joining may be too great for the country's ailing economy and the economic risks too great for the Six. Britain's lack of a firm commitment to Europe, or, at any rate, her active opposition to Gaullist policies, pose great dangers to the fragile fabric of the existing European construction. All this is not to say, however, that in the end Britain may not genuinely evolve into Europe. The pro-Market case is basically a sound one—for the long run.

Historians will probably agree that a Europe of States was the only practical route towards building a European Union. After all, the building of a voluntary union cannot be treated realistically as an end entirely separate from the general policies that the entity is meant to pursue. Sensibly the Europeans have begun formal co-operation within the economic field, where the aims seem the least controversial and divisive. In other areas like defence or foreign policy, the differences and suspicions among the Six have been far too great to hold within a single community, at least if it is to be based on consent rather than force. The result is de Gaulle's Europe of States, co-operating more and more closely in economic affairs and perhaps slowly evolving common perspectives in other matters.

Whether de Gaulle's Europe of States can be a permanent as well as a transient arrangement remains to be seen. As the work of union slowly proceeds, the growing interdependence of the European economies has already in some respects made national planning more difficult among the Six.[3] Whether effective European planning can be carried on within the structure of the Europe of States is uncertain. Perhaps new institutions can be created. Or perhaps there will be a retreat from planning and governments will abdicate from the rational control they have, in France particularly, come to exercise over their economies. Perhaps it will prove impossible without a regional government to build a regional economy. It is always possible that internal contradictions and external diversions will cause the whole enterprise to break down.

The idea of Europe may yield before the political logic of national-ism and the economic logic of internationalism. It is also possible that the growing tensions and pressures unleashed by America's programme to end her payments deficit will prove too great for the bonds of the European Community to bear. These are the great issues that will determine the future of Europe. Britain, with her economic resources and great tradition for economic speculation and institutional inventiveness, could make a decisive contribution to Europe's success. Indeed, some people even believe that it is from Britain that the catalytic federal impulse for Europe may someday come, even some people who currently agree with General de Gaulle. What could be the foundation for such an odd combina-tion of views?

The study of Britain's economic problems, as we have seen, suggests how fundamentally unbalanced the country is in com-parison with almost any other major power. Britain is too big for her island. There almost seem to be too many people, too much industry, too much finance and possibly too much talent for the narrow base of food and raw materials. No wonder the economy is always in a precarious state—a great head managing by its wits to get by with a tiny body. The condition of sterling seems some-how a metaphor for the position of the whole country. An economy one-seventh the size of the United States and with less than half the reserves of France supports a currency that handles one quarter of the world's trade.[4] In the past, both free trade and imperial preference were doctrines to enable Britain to escape from the dis-abilities of her limited base. Neither seems politically possible in today's world of giant regional states.

Many of the objections to Britain's joining the Six are based on the assumption that the Common Market will remain more of a customs union than a federal state. The free flow of goods and especially money exposes Britain to all the dangers of a large economy and few of its advantages. Sterling's position, for example, might, as we have seen, be seriously weakened by the end of the currency controls within the Common Market. But if sterling were merged with a European currency, backed by French and German reserves, that great amalgam of financial skill and connection that make up the City of London could function on a far more secure basis than it ever can while attached to an overpopulated island whose watchword must be "Export or die!"

89

Similarly, if British industry has special structural problems that make growth unlikely without intelligent government intervention, then it is quite true that the obstacles imposed by the EEC on national planning are a serious disability. But these restrictions seem a logical necessity if Europe is to develop into a single economy. The natural cure, in the Europe of the future as in the America of the present, is for the area disadvantaged by the working of economic laws to seek help from the federal centre. It may well be in Britain's national economic interest to see developed a strong central political authority capable of planning effectively on a European scale.

It is the way with heads that they want themselves firmly attached to their bodies. It may well be Britain's natural policy to build a federal Europe. That surely is a programme that will provide a new role and purpose for Britain.

But there remains nothing inevitable in such an evolution of British opinion. The intellectual and emotional links with America are strong and the military and economic advantages of the Atlantic connection are not to be taken lightly. Even if the Commonwealth seems to be fading, the old ties still persist and humanitarian interest in the Third World is perfectly genuine. There are plausible arguments for finding Britain's future in her present national context, made economically viable by intelligent domestic reform, and a judicious pruning of international commitments. While it may be true that going into Europe is the only way to save the habits and institutions associated with the grandeur of the imperial past, there are many people in England who have no wish to continue those traditions and that character. In short, there remains a strong political and cultural opposition in England to joining Europe. If that opposition was more silent in 1967 than in 1961, it was probably because, like many of Britain's continental critics, it had come to rely on General de Gaulle.

But de Gaulle's obduracy has had its benefits. For he has posed the real issue with a clarity the British were unlikely to have achieved by themselves. The Government has been ruthlessly caught out in the old vice, so well illustrated in Macmillan's bid, of trying to have all things all ways. In one sense Macmillan's anti-Market critics were right and he was wrong. It would not be possible to remake "inward-looking" Europe in Britain's image.[5] De Gaulle has made it clear that Britain cannot have it both ways. If she wants to become a part of the new Europe, she must become "European". De Gaulle's Europe will not become British.

Whether this is a sacrifice Britain is willing to make, only time will tell. Certainly, it would be a considerable aid to evolution in Britain, as it has been for each of the Six, to be inside the institutional framework of the Common Market. Thought usually follows practice and ideas grow from habits. But the guardians of the Europe of the Six appear to believe, probably rightly, that its structure is still too fragile to survive the full entry of a new power, at once so large, so troubled and so unconvinced. True friends of Europe should sympathize with France's objections, even if they do not share them completely. It would, in fact, be a tragedy if Britain's premature entry spoiled what Europe has accomplished. The dangers are real enough so that even Britain's best friends must have secret doubts.

Under the circumstances, there is a good deal to be said for Britain's accepting some transitional association with the Community, a kind of insulation for both, allowing time for economic adjustments and the mutual evolution of institutions and opinion. It might be possible to negotiate a non-voting status lasting until Britain was ready to accept the full application of the regulations accepted by the others. Indeed General de Gaulle has been suggesting this course for some time and the Kiesinger-Brandt Government has been trying to promote it. In any scheme Britain might reasonably expect to have some kind of non-voting representation on the Council of Ministers and among the Permanent Representatives. But unless some such arrangement can be worked out, Britain will probably not soon be involved in the Common Market. The further evolution of Britain towards Europe will depend to a great extent on the evaluation of public opinion in Britain. England will have to decide to join Europe; she is not already in it. It is a mistake to call the Common Market a Club. It is a Church. Britain will have to become a convert to the creed of Europe. Whether this evolution can and should take place is the great question in Britain's future. Needless to say, only the British themselves can answer it.

V.
Britain in
Atlantica: the Reluctant
Alternative

1. *Imperial Relations*

If outgoing and top-heavy Britain must join a bloc, and the price for the Common Market is too high, an Atlantic association with America appears the natural alternative. For many in Britain, the "North Atlantic" tie with the United States should remain the fundamental axiom of British military policy, even if Britain were in the Common Market. It is the prevalence of this view, among other things, that has made Britain's entry into Europe so difficult. Some people, increasingly dismayed at the apparent price and prospects of entering Europe or opposed from the first to joining it, now argue that Britain's best hope for the future lies not with Europe, but with Canada and the United States. Some look forward to a day when Britain and America will merge into a common "Atlantica",[1] and a few, perhaps, even play with the notion of Britain's becoming the "fifty-first state". Most "Atlanticists", however, seriously contemplate little beyond the transformation of the present institutions of the Atlantic Alliance, today mostly military, into a community with broader economic and perhaps a few political dimensions.

These "Atlanticist" views have expressed themselves in a number of formulas over recent years; among the most recent is the proposal by several groups in Britain, the US, and Canada for a North Atlantic Free Trade Area—or NAFTA, as it has come to be called.[2] These new proposals come at a time when the rise of the continental bloc, strongly influenced by France, has led to such tensions in the present military alliance that many fear it has little future unless reinforced soon by further inducements to co-operation among its members.

It is hardly surprising that many in Britain should look for a future close association with America. De Gaulle is not far wrong in believing that the course of postwar British policy was set when Churchill decided, in 1944, to concentrate more on cultivating influence with America than on building Europe.[3] Governments of both parties have generally given the North Atlantic tie with the United States first priority. Much of British policy has, in one way or another, concerned itself with enlisting and maintaining America's interest in world military and economic problems and with influencing that interest in directions satisfactory to Britain.

As discussed at length in Chapter III, Britain has worked not only to keep America involved in Europe's affairs, but also to organize that involvement within the general "Atlantic" pattern, significantly modified, to be sure, by Britain's "special relationship". Within this NATO pattern, Britain's position as America's special relation has bolstered her precedence over the other states, while her role as chief secondary power has given her leverage against too overpowering American leadership. In short, a satisfactory special relationship is more easily maintained within a structure including several other allied powers with less intimate American connections.

It is, incidentally, not without interest that the absence of too intimate federal ties is one of the chief arguments of those who favour NAFTA over the EEC.[4] Neither is it uninteresting that much of the initiative for NAFTA comes from Canadians—a people possessed of an equally ambivalent disposition towards increased intimacy with the United States.

The rise of a nascent European Union grouped around the Common Market has raised the chief threat to Britain's strategy within the Alliance. Britain resisted the whole European development but it has occurred anyway. Since Britain has not been able to stop it, she has been trying to join it. But the whole lesson of Britain's various applications has been that she is unlikely to be accepted until she comes to terms with Gaullist France. Whatever that really means, it appears to suggest that Britain must give up her present world role and the views behind it and pledge herself instead to accepting the ideal of a politically independent Europe disengaged from America's world burdens. It means, in short, the end of the postwar special relationship with America. How much has it been in Britain's interest to keep up the close military and political connections of the special relationship? How do its advantages and the satisfactions of this partnership measure against the advantages of joining the new Europe?

It is difficult to assess the political and military value of the special relationship because it is difficult to tell exactly what it is. Whole books have been written about it,[5] but its nature necessarily remains rather elusive. Naturally, the close wartime partnership with its network of acquaintances and common practices was central to what followed.[6] Britain's remaining world-wide commitments made her the logical collaborator in American postwar strategy. Britain's early role as a nuclear power created the basis for a military intimacy never extended to the other Western allies.

Ironically, Britain's acquisition of nuclear weapons, perhaps the most concrete foundation of the special relationship, was carried out in defiance of American wishes. Britain, after having made her pioneering nuclear research available to the US in the beginning of the war and having agreed to the atomic project's being carried on in America, found herself gradually excluded from the whole enterprise. In 1946 Congress passed the McMahon Act which registered its determination to guard the terrible secret of the bomb for America alone, and in 1948, Congressional pressure, using Marshall Aid as its leverage, forced the British to renounce whatever special concessions remained as the fruits of their earlier open-handed collaboration.[7]

Needless to say, this American policy towards its special ally was not warmly regarded by the British. From an American point of view, however, the policy was a logical extension of America's desire to prevent proliferation and to maintain military hegemony within the Western Alliance. The British reacted by going ahead with their own nuclear programme. On October 3, 1952, Britain exploded an atomic bomb and by 1957 had exploded a hydrogen bomb as well. Britain's development of a V-bomber force gave her a sizeable nuclear deterrent of her own. As a result, the pattern of the Atlantic Alliance was significantly altered. Britain's nuclear role gave her special status over the others. Again, she was America's special partner.

The logic of this development was not lost upon the French, who in 1955 began themselves to develop an atomic bomb—less as a weapon in a hypothetical war against Russia than as a passport to the Anglo Saxon inner circle of the Atlantic Alliance.[8] But France has never gained admission to America's inner councils and her failure has poisoned the Alliance.

How valuable has her nuclear intimacy with America been to Britain? It has made Britain privy to some American research and strategic planning. The latter doubtless provides vicarious satisfactions, but the former does not seem nearly so important to Britain as the necessity to find more resources and a bigger market to support her technology. Indeed, from the point of view of specific national advantage, a survey of British-American collaboration throughout the world since the fifties does not immediately make clear how the partnership has been helpful to the English.[9]

In the Far East, the US has involved her ally in two wars, Korea and Vietnam, neither, it might be said, of any special interest to Britain. The prolonged American quarrel with China has certainly not facilitated Britain's trading hopes in that direction, and since the outbreak of the war in Vietnam, Britain's close identification with America has probably greatly increased the danger to Hong Kong. America's enthusiasm for building up Japan, moreover, has encouraged a powerful trading rival—not only in Asia but throughout the world. In Britain's own major Asian military operations, the struggle against the insurgents in Malaya and the "confrontation" with Indonesia, she received no direct American help. Moreover, in the ANZUS pact of 1957, Britain was unceremoniously excluded from a military alliance with two of her own dominions.[10]

In the Near East, the British might not be blamed if they felt, at best, only tepid enthusiasm for postwar American policy. If that policy has served anyone's interest, it does not seem to have served Britain's. It was in this "theatre", in fact, that the special relationship nearly came to an end. At Suez in 1956, Britain temporarily joined with France and both suffered deep humiliation. But whereas the French appear henceforth to have turned resolutely to Europe, Britain returned to America.[11] It was foolish, the British apparently decided, ever to attempt a policy directly opposed by the Americans. Britain's strength lay in her influence on American policy. Macmillan made great and highly successful efforts to rebuild the old relations.[12] But Macmillan also was the

95

G

Prime Minister who sought to take Britain into the Common Market. The special relationship was not much help in Europe, as Nassau made apparent.[13]

The supporters of this special relationship are not so much inclined to defend it by reckoning up particular instances of national advantage as by invoking general concepts of world order and responsibility. Britain, it is argued, policed the world and by and large kept the peace throughout the nineteenth century. Now the Pax Britannica has been succeeded by the precarious Pax Americana. But Britain, with her great experience, still has a major role to play in helping America keep the peace. According to this whole view, the world is seen as divided up into "spheres of influence" that fill otherwise dangerous "power vacuums". If the West retreats from the Third World, there will be chaos and someone else—Russia, China, Indonesia, Nasser or Castro—will move in and take over. Thus, for example, Britain cannot move out of Malaysia or the United States out of Vietnam. Peace will be endangered and "vital interests" imperilled. This is essentially an imperial view inherited from the last century.

In its contemporary version it often takes the form of anti-communism. Communists, it is argued, come like scavengers onto nations just beginning their development. They impose not only an undesirable political system but prolonged economic backwardness. The West's profound moral obligation and practical interest combined oblige it to protect backward countries from communism until they reach their economic "take-off" point and hence are able to stand on their own.[14]

American officials sometimes speak of America's role as establishing a new world "equilibrium" of power, a system to replace the old balance that has been shattered by the self-destruction of Europe and the end of its empires. American strategists of this school envision a world order based on a series of overlapping economic and military groupings designed to bring political stability and economic progress to the various regions of the world. But a stable world system can only be achieved, they believe, with the active, sustained involvement of the United States, supported by its European and Japanese allies. Great nations, they say, must always exert themselves to bring order to the natural turbulence of international life, all the more in an age when the decline of European empires, the ambitions of the communists, and the aspirations and quarrels of the new nations have turned the Third World into a gigantic Balkans. To shrink from an active role in shaping the new world order would be, according to this view, to resign from the responsibilities imposed by history and, indeed, to condemn the world to ultimate catastrophe. Such diffidence today represents the same kind of irresponsibility towards shaping events that infected the European democracies before World War II.

To call this an imperial view is not to condemn it nor to deny it nobility, sincerity or relevance. The view of the world as an arena of power obviously has fitted the facts of international life during whole periods of history. The notion that those who have great power should exert it creatively is not an ignoble or irrelevant precept. This imperial theory of international politics, however, is not particularly popular nowadays among many Western Europeans. For that matter, because of opposition to the Vietnam War, it is under bitter attack in the United States as well, where it is central to the intellectual debate between "hawks" and "doves".

The main alternative theory to imperialism is what might be called the nationalist theory of world politics, upheld nowadays in America by such figures as Walter Lippmann and Senator Fulbright.[15] Its greatest champion, of course, is General de Gaulle. According to this nationalist view, the imperialism of the past two centuries must come to an end. It was based on a transient period of Western technological and social superiority that allowed small numbers of white men to dominate huge masses of apathetic Asians and Africans. Today, it is argued, as France learned painfully in Indo-China and Algeria and as the United States is learning in Vietnam, the cost of maintaining Western military control over foreign countries has increased far out of proportion to any conceivable advantages. In short, the Third World is no longer politically apathetic or military ineffective. There are no more power vacuums. The West and the Russians must reconcile themselves to having local indigenous forces settle their own affairs and forge their own nations. The new nations thus should ordinarily be left alone to resolve their inevitable internal conflicts. No matter what kind of governments ultimately result, the advanced countries have so much to offer that they can count on being able to maintain mutually profitable relations in any event, provided they refrain from taking sides in domestic political conflicts.

It is not difficult to adapt this Gaullist view of world politics into a persuasive strategy designed for Britain's own national interests. It could be argued that, whether or not America's imperial view is appropriate for America, it is not appropriate for Britain and, indeed, actually prevents her from playing the useful world role that might otherwise be hers. According to this argument, Britain's useful military contributions are coming to an end as the last of the independent new states are launched on their way. Beyond these terminal obligations Britain lacks the means for a continuing major military role in the Third World, whether or not she approves of what America is doing there. Since Britain cannot really continue to make a substantial contribution to Commonwealth defence, it might be more sensible for her to adopt the French views about non-interference. The French, after all, came to these views after having lost two major colonial wars. Their doctrine of non-interference at least makes the best of their weakness. Britain's identification with American policy, on the other hand, has put her in the unrewarding position of supporting unpopular imperial theories without herself having the means to play an imperial role. Thus she had shared America's unpopularity, but none of her power. Britain's close alliance with the United States has won her few friends in the Third World. If it has helped protect investments in some places, it has seriously endangered them in others. In short, it is at least questionable that close military association with America East of Suez has been the most appropriate policy for a Britain eager to go on playing an important role among the coloured Commonwealth countries and in the underdeveloped world generally.

British statesmen often seem to hanker for a mediating role in the Third World. But as Britain's rather humiliating efforts in North Vietnam ought to have made apparent, it is difficult to sustain simultaneously the roles of impartial mediator and close ally.[16] It could be that Britain's greatest potential contribution to world order, and indeed to the cause of the West, may not, in the long run, lie in the military field.

This debate has continued for several years in Britain. The drastic defence cuts of January, 1968, appear to constitute a major and probably definitive step towards ending Britain's present military role East of Suez.[17] But the more general struggle between competing imperial and nationalist views of world politics is obviously not going to be settled for a very long time, in England or America.

Nor is it certain that the principal world powers will always hold their present views. The popularity of the imperial view in the United States may not be enhanced by the experience in Vietnam. On the other hand, a more united and hence stronger Europe might be less inclined to take so non-interventionist an attitude towards world affairs. Many Europeans are, however, likely to retain indefinitely their present deafness to American appeals for collaboration in various military ventures in the Third World. Europeans will not quickly forget that not long ago it was the Americans who were regularly lecturing them on the evils of colonialism. Rightly or wrongly, many Europeans are unlikely to see in situations like Vietnam a moral imperative to help the Americans. Furthermore, morality, in this instance, combines conveniently with interest. Europeans, committed to neutrality, can expect to make further inroads in areas under governments angered by some American policy or other.[18]

But a great many Britons, in this respect, are different from most Europeans. Whatever their country's actual national interests, the imperial way of thinking comes naturally to many people in England. It is this instinctive British way of thinking that forms the real foundation of the special relationship with the United States. For Britain to renounce this imperial view, whatever the conceivable commercial and political advantages, will not be easy for a nation with her traditions. Yet if she will not, she cannot, in all likelihood, expect to enter de Gaulle's Common Market.

For many people in Britain, going into Europe on these terms will hardly seem worth the price, once that price comes to be understood. Many of those who have seen this dilemma most clearly are today among ardent proponents of an Atlantic solution to Britain's future. But the Atlantic partnership cannot, they fear, be sustained indefinitely on purely military and political grounds. Europe appears to offer great economic attractions and while economic gain may not, in the end, determine Britain's choices, any feasible alternative to Europe must at least offer a reasonable prospect for escaping from England's present unhappy economic predicament and gloomy long-range prospects. Thus the proponents of an Atlantic England have been busily promoting the advantages of a North Atlantic Free Trade Area—both as a much-needed reinforcement for the military alliance and as a solution to the problems of the British economy.

2. *Atlantic Prospects for Trade and Industrial Growth*

People in Britain who advocate an Atlantic economic bloc as an alternative to the Common Market have linked themselves with like-minded groups in both the United States and Canada. As a result of their collaboration, there have been several trans-Atlantic studies and schemes.[1] In August, 1965, for example, Jacob Javits, United States Senator from New York, floated one of the earliest specific American proposals for an Atlantic free trade area. Initially, it was to include the United States, Britain, and Canada, but remain open to the OECD countries, including the EEC and the rest of EFTA, Javits' plan called for a twenty-year advance to completely free trade in manufactures. For the less developed countries, there was to be an associate membership which would allow them to retain special protection for their own infant industries. Finally, the Senator's proposal contemplated considerable financial support to modernize Britain's industrial plant. Javits' scheme seemed chiefly animated by concern for the plight of England after her rejection by the EEC in 1963.[2]

The Senator's ideas appeared to arouse little immediate general interest among the English. But further proposals for a North Atlantic Free Trade Area, or NAFTA, have been echoed in financial circles in Britain and the USA, supported by some noted economists, and studied actively in Whitehall itself.[3] These proposals form part of the whole North Atlantic "option" for Britain. Unquestionably, many who are willing to entertain these schemes see them clearly as a second-best alternative—to be taken up in desperation if the European option seems hopeless.[4] After General de Gaulle's discouraging Press conference in November, 1967, at least some renewed British interest in the North Atlantic option is not unlikely.

Some distinguished economists and businessmen, however, have preferred this option from the beginning. It has had special appeal among those particularly concerned with advancing the cause of world free trade. Some economists, for example, have argued that the whole postwar universalist approach to trade, epitomized in the most-favoured-nation principle that underlies the GATT agreement, has now reached a dead end. According to this view, the Kennedy Round has shown clearly that tariff reduction on a world-wide basis, extending the same benefits to all as one, is no longer practicable.[5] The Kennedy Round's tactic of seeking tariff cuts by universal agreement, it is said, only means that the continentals, dominated by France, have been given a veto over all liberal American trade initiatives. It is said that the Common Market, with its common external tariff has in fact, split the free world into separate trading blocs. It is time for the like-minded countries to form their own bloc—a grouping of liberal trading nations like the US, Canada and Britain, possibly the rest of EFTA, and perhaps even Australia, New Zealand and Japan. In this new world of regional blocs, Britain belongs with these countries—with the US, not with the continent; with NAFTA, not the Common Market.

Not the least advantage of NAFTA, it is said, is that its aims would be genuinely economic rather than essentially political. Economics would be the master rather than the slave of politics. Free trade would be allowed to work its magic without distortion by federalist goals and the apparatus of central direction would be minimal.[6] In addition, there is a whole series of arguments (examined at length in Chapter VI), that have to do with the benefits of NAFTA to the underdeveloped countries.

The arguments are forceful, although they seem to be based on the questionable hypothesis that the Common Market countries are more protectionist than the US, Britain or Canada. But, as mentioned earlier, the Common Market's industrial tariffs are, in general, substantially lower than those of either Britain or the US. Indeed, by 1972, when the Kennedy Round cuts are fully in effect, it is estimated that the average EEC industrial tariff will be only 7·6% as compared with 11·2% for the US, 10·2% for Britain (1·2% for the Commonwealth preference area, however), and 9·8% for Japan.[7] In any event, the NAFTA proposals, whatever their merits, have attracted distinguished adherents and, at the very least, raise trans-Atlantic issues that must somehow be dealt with.

What are the economics of the North Atlantic option? How, for example, would British membership in some large free-trade area with the United States and others, but not the EEC, affect British exports and imports? Would the predictable effects compare favourably with those reckoned for joining the Common Market?

In terms of short-run effect on the balance of payments, NAFTA, which does not saddle Britain with the continent's agricultural support programme, has an immediate advantage over the EEC. As we have seen, generally accepted estimates reckon an annual cost of £185-£250 millions to the balance of payments if Britain has to participate in the Common Market's present agricultural support programme. NAFTA, on the other hand, would include at least two suppliers of cheap food, Canada and the US, and presumably would not include agricultural products anyway. Thus, unlike the EEC, NAFTA would not disrupt the traditional Commonwealth suppliers of food.

Some enthusiasts for NAFTA, however, claim that it would offer better opportunities for trade in manufactures as well. Here, as usual, there are formidable hazards in calculating how a change in tariff rates might change the pattern and volume of international trade, a reckoning further complicated by the diversionary effects of trading blocs. Wells' study, using 1960 trade flows, concluded that if there were a vast free trade area that included the US, UK, Canada, the EEC, EFTA and Japan, the British trade balance with the US would deteriorate by $50 million, and with the EEC by $80 million. Wells' categories are difficult to use for determining the relative trade effects for Britain from joining a NAFTA without the EEC as compared with joining the EEC itself. Wells himself decided that, for industrial trade, the immediate effects from NAFTA would probably be somewhat less unfavourable than the immediate effects from joining the Common Market. In either case, he believed that the magnitude of the shifts would not be large.[8]

Maxwell Stamp Associates' recent pro-NAFTA study, based on 1965 trade flows, comes to more optimistic conclusions. If British prices remain stable in relation to American, a NAFTA of Britain, Canada and the US should, by 1972, "create" a new demand in America for British manufactures totalling $243 million. In return, American manufactured imports in Britain would rise by only $186 million—a net improvement in Britain's bilateral trade balance of $57 million, or nearly 30%.[9] On the same basis, Britain would enjoy a net improvement in her balance with Canada of $49 million.[10]

The study estimates that the "trade diversion" effects of NAFTA would be even greater than the "trade creation" effects listed above. With steady prices, Britain would win $304 million in the North American market from the EEC; and, if Japan were not a member, an additional $292 million from displacing Japanese exports.[11] These results, as shown by Stamp's table below, compare favourably with the Stamp estimates from joining the EEC.

Table N
EEC and NAFTA COMPARED—US $ Million
(increase in trade resulting from UK membership)

UK	NAFTA	EEC
Export Increase (trade creation)	292	316
Export Increase (trade diversion)	552	191
Import Increase	189	286
Net Change	655	221

Source: Maxwell Stamp Associates, *The Free Trade Area Option*, p.46

To put these forecasts into perspective, however, it should be remembered that Britain sent 20% of her exports to the EEC in 1965, roughly double her exports to the US—$2744 million as opposed to $1454 million. The British trade deficit with the US, moreover, was $432 million as opposed to $44 million with the EEC.[12]

Stamp's forecasts, as noted, are based on 1965 trade figures. When an attempt is made to allow for the Kennedy Round cuts, the estimated increase in net British exports to the US from trade creation in NAFTA falls from $57 million to $41 million.[13] Presumably the Kennedy Round should also substantially reduce the trade diversion potential of NAFTA, though this calculation is not made in the Stamp study.

These relatively optimistic forecasts, however, are based on the assumption that British prices will not rise more rapidly than American prices in the face of higher demand. Stamp estimates that if, by 1972, British prices in NAFTA had risen relatively only 25% of the cut in tariffs, the expected net change with the US from trade creation would be cut from +$57 million to −$4 million and the gain in Britain's total North American trade would be cut from +$103 million to +$31 million.[14] When the Kennedy Round cuts are taken into account the effects of such a British price rise are even more severe. In fact, the Stamp study estimates that Britain's new imports from the US would exceed her new exports by $72 million.[15] Again, the negative effect on trade diversion would be correspondingly severe.

How realistic is it to assume that British prices will not rise relative to American? Or how realistic is it even to assume that, by 1972, their relative rise will be no more than 25% of the tariff cut—in other words, less than 3%? Devaluation in November, 1967, should, of course, aid appreciably in maintaining British prices at a competitive level. Devaluation gives an automatic price advantage to British exports and a disadvantage to foreign imports. The relative advantage would perhaps be more completely retained while entering into free trade with America, whose existing tariffs on manufactures are slightly higher, than in entering the EEC, where industrial tariffs are substantially lower.

But as Wells points out in his study, the chief problem facing Britain in the North American market lies in her relative lack of spare capacity which makes it extremely likely that a sharp increase in demand will lead to a sharp rise in prices.[16] This consideration, in fact, was important in leading Wells to be sceptical of any substantial short-run trade advantages and to argue that the real benefit of either form of association would lie in its stimulus to the growth of British capacity and productivity. To quote from his study:

> Thus unless there are dynamic advantages to be gained from the better use of resources, greater specialization, and the jolting of inefficient industry out of its protected rut, integration will intensify and not ease the nation's balance of trade difficulties.[17]

Between NAFTA and the EEC, what then are the relative prospects of settling the long-range difficulties of the British economy and encouraging its steady growth?

For many, the chief advantage of NAFTA over the EEC is that it would provide the advantages of a large market without saddling England with European agriculture and other federalist commitments. It is significant, however, that NAFTA's large market has aroused remarkably little enthusiasm from top industrial management, which has, on the other hand, been one of the strongest forces pushing Britain towards the Common Market.[18] Some observers attribute this phenomenon to the peculiar perspectives of the big industrialists. On the one hand, British industrialists are said to fear competition from the bigger American companies.[19] On the other, they are supposedly enticed to the Common Market by the prospect of extending their corporate and financial power over the smaller firms of Europe. British management's conquest of Europe should be possible, it is believed, because, except for the

Dutch, the continentals have never developed the giant industrial corporations typical of Britain and the United States. The giant corporation is an Anglo-Saxon invention, testifying as much to the political as the managerial skills of the race.[20] Top British management feels that with its organizational skills, reinforced by the capital-gathering facilities of the City, British corporations would soon be able to take over their smaller continental rivals. This is the opposite, of course, of what would happen if the British economy were somehow yoked to the American. Thus the British tycoon's lack of enthusiasm for NAFTA.

But while the British domination of the continent's corporate industrial structure might prove gratifying to top British management, some economists fail to see corresponding benefits to British industry and economic development as a whole. These economists argue, privately at least, that if there must be some sort of larger economic union, America has more to offer. Naturally, top management prefers the take-over possibilities of economic union with Europe, but its interests in this matter are those of the governing élite and not of the British economy as a whole. British management is better at taking things over than running them. NAFTA, which allegedly would result in heavy American investment and participation in British industry, would bring to Britain the managerial skills that are so badly needed.

But why should NAFTA bring American capital to Britain as well as American goods? Britain, with nearly 55 million consumers, is said to be alone a sufficiently rich market to attract American firms to invest. Furthermore, conditions are such that investments in Britain have a comparative advantage over equal investments in the US. British labour is well trained, and its cost is lower. Furthermore, the relatively under-capitalized state of British industry means that marginal productivity from investment of new capital should be better than in the US.[21] Hence, American firms, attracted by a large market, cheaper high-quality labour, and a relatively under-capitalized industrial plant, would hasten to invest in Britain.

Enthusiasts for greater American participation in British industry draw on the widely shared view that American management is generally more efficient than British. They can point to recent studies that suggest that American firms in Britain earn higher profit on their invested capital than comparable British companies.

105

The better performance of American firms in Britain seems to arise less from any superiority in product than from a notably greater efficiency in the process of manufacturing—a superiority most easily accounted for by the access of the Americans to the productive techniques and research and managerial talents of the parent companies in America.[22] In short, closer economic ties with the United States, with more direct investment from America, would bring British industry a much needed transfusion of new capital and technique, leading to genuine economic growth, whatever its unsettling effects on entrenched British management.

None of these assertions is unchallenged. To begin with, there is general alarm in Britain, as in all Europe, over the growing American presence in European economies. These fears may seem exaggerated when the size of the American stake in Europe is compared with European investments in the US. At the end of 1966, for example, while American firms and individuals had assets in Western Europe of $19·1 billion, Western Europeans held $18·3 billion in the US. It must be admitted, however, that since the American economy is much larger, the proportion and hence impact of foreign investment is a good deal less. More important yet, while $13·9 billion of the American investments were "direct" for overseas branches and subsidiaries of American firms, most European investment in the US was portfolio investment, generally yielding profit but not control. In fact, in 1965, only $6·1 billion of European investments in the US were direct.[23] Thus American money tends to mean visible American power. British managers and workers are understandably reluctant to take orders from foreign masters. The British managerial establishment in general is not eager to find itself integrated into a system whose centre of power is abroad, even if it might thereby boost efficiency.

Much of the fear of American investment is connected with the widespread concern for the future of advanced technology in Britain and throughout Europe generally. One of the most impressive assets of modern Britain has been the high quality of its scientific research, resulting in several of the more significant discoveries of the century, including, for example, penicillin, radar and jet propulsion. While American firms in Britain do seem, in fact, to spend generally at least as much on research as their British counterparts, it appears common sense, some say, to anticipate that American firms will cut back research that duplicates what they can do at home.[24] Whatever the general situation, research may well decline in those particular areas that are critical for major technological advance.[25] "Rationalizing" British production into a North Atlantic economy might well wipe out exactly those industries, like aerospace, said to be vital for advanced technological development in the economy as a whole.[26] As advanced research in the genuinely exciting fields shifted increasingly to America, the "brain drain" would increase and the centres of creative vitality in Britain would dry up.[27] Whereas, in Europe, Britain could expect to be pre-eminent in scientific research, in NAFTA the logic of comparative power and resources would gradually make her an industrial, political and even intellectual dependency of the US.

The American Government has not diminished these fears by its tendency to see commerce and technology as weapons of political policy. The British were given a strong lesson in 1946 when the McMahon Act suddenly and brutally denied them the fruits of the nuclear research to which they had initially contributed so much.[28] As we have seen, the US agreed to resume collaboration only after Britain, without American help, had built her own nuclear capacity. The American government has grown even more determined in its opposition to proliferation and has, on notable occasions, gone so far as to forbid American companies in France to sell equipment for the French nuclear programme.[29] Americans, of course, justify their opposition to proliferation on the grounds of high policy, but some Europeans are more cynical. Their cynicism and resentment are fed by the energetic efforts of the Defense Department to sell American military equipment to the Allies.[30] In the present world, the development of military weapons and the general development of technology are so intimately connected that unless Europeans find a way to maintain their own defence industries, many believe they will fall back irrevocably from the vanguard of technological advance.

There are rejoinders to all these arguments and fears against America. It must be admitted, nevertheless, that while heavier American investment would in many ways be a blessing to Britain, it might also carry potential dangers, especially for Britain's long-range technological growth. The disparity in size is bound to provoke fear of too close association and Britain would seem more

107

likely to be the forgotten "off-shore island" of America than of Europe.

Quite apart from whether much more heavy American investment in Britain might be desirable, would joining NAFTA promote it? Why do American companies invest abroad? Presumably it is thought important to get behind different tariff walls into rapidly growing markets.[31] For example, much American capital is thought to have come to Britain in order to get within the Commonwealth preference area, or EFTA, or in the expectation that Britain would soon be in the Common Market. If Britain turns away from Europe into a rival North American bloc, a good deal of American investment may be deflected from Britain and go instead directly to the continent. If NAFTA encompassed both the Commonwealth and EFTA, American firms, with a direct access of their own to these markets, might, it is feared, lose a large part of their incentive to invest in Britain at all. Indeed, joining NAFTA might turn out to be Britain's best defence against the evils of American investment! Paradoxically, the best way to attract American investment to Britain may be for Britain to join Europe. In investment, as in other areas, the special relationship often appears to defeat its own purpose.

The strong American measures taken at the beginning of 1968 to control capital movements, of course, throw doubt on the prospects for any continuing heavy investment from America to Europe. No one can safely predict how long these controls will last or what their effects may be. It seems unlikely, however, that heavy American investment will resume as long as the American balance of payments continues to remain so unfavourable. That condition, on the other hand, is likely to remain at least as long as American foreign military expenditures continue at their 1967 rate. It is possible that the era of great American investment abroad is coming to an end. It is also possible, of course, that the US will seek to restrict its future investment to a limited number of countries with which it feels particular political and economic affinities. Some such policy was suggested by the discriminating character of the restrictions of investment as between one country and another, although the American government denied any such intention. In any event, there clearly seems a greater element of risk than formerly in any economic strategy that counts on heavy capital investment over the next few years.[32]

Indeed there is a strong wind of protectionism blowing in America, particularly through the Congress. Particular interests, general resentment of Europe and growing alarm and truculence over exchange difficulties may well combine to set off a spiral of restrictive and retaliatory measures. To many Americans, the Common Market appears less and less a federal European political partner and more and more an unco-operative commercial rival that discriminates against American goods. There is little American enthusiasm nowadays, for example, for schemes that would extend Common Market association to additional countries, for this merely increases the area within which American goods face discrimination without, it is believed, resulting in any compensating progress towards regional political integration. It seems to make little difference that, in fact, American trade practices are equally, if not more, discriminating.

Even if much of the present American indignation is misconceived, it is well to remember how precarious is America's dedication to liberal trade policies. A mercantilist view towards trade arises more naturally in a vast continental country with less than 5% of its GNP coming from foreign trade than in an island where the proportion is nearer 15%. This might mean, of course, that the United States would turn to a NAFTA for its possible political advantages—as a means for preventing wider association with the EEC and bolstering those allies that remained resolutely immune to Gaullist tendencies. These political considerations are discussed in a later section of this chapter. Economically, however, there seem to be relatively few commercial advantages for the US in a NAFTA without the EEC. The expected improvements in the British trade balance will, after all, presumably be achieved at American expense. The trade diversion from the EEC, while it might gratify American outrage at France, might also provoke retaliation in a market that is much larger and more promising than Britain, a market in which the US already earns a large trade surplus.[33] Commercially, a free-trade area among developed countries might well be in the enlightened American interest, but only if it included, rather than excluded the Common Market.

Perhaps it should be said that the arguments for a large free-trade area of developed countries, many of which in themselves have considerable merit, are not much improved by the strong anti-Common Market tone that frequently goes with them. It is sometimes said that the EEC could not join NAFTA because the Community's Common External Tariff is essential to maintaining its economic cohesion in the face of the outside world. According to this view, the Common Market is, by its very nature as a nascent political federation, less amenable to "liberal" trading initiatives than established states like the US or Britain. As noted above, the argument would be more convincing if it were not that the Common Market's tariff in manufactures is substantially lower than the comparable tariffs in Britain, Canada or the US.

In summary, the long-range advantage of Britain's joining a close economic association with the United States would seem to depend on a resulting American investment of capital and talent sufficient to make a drastic improvement in Britain's productive efficiency. Otherwise British industry may well not be able to compete. But heavier American investment might be a mixed blessing and it is by no means clear that a North Atlantic Free Trade Area would attract it. Thus the purely economic case for NAFTA is controversial, as is, of course, the case for the Common Market. Unlike the latter, however, NAFTA has yet to arouse much enthusiasm among British industrialists or politicians.

3. *Sterling, the Dollar and International Liquidity*

Whereas British industry has been slow warming to the whole NAFTA idea, it has received strong support from important groups in the City of London. The interest is not surprising; the City always had close personal and institutional relations with American banks. The relations have grown closer and more official as in Britain's recurring exchange crises, the pound has come to lean more and more heavily on the dollar. The Bank of England has come increasingly to count on supplementing its own precarious reserves with massive support from the American Federal Reserve.[1] America, moreover, has taken the lead in organizing a world-wide pooling of reserves. These arrangements have generally worked smoothly and quickly—among men with strong ties of mutual esteem, confidence and experience. And until the devaluation of 1967, they saw the pound successfully through numerous crises. It is difficult to imagine how the pound would have survived in its world role as well as it has without this American support. It was possible to hope that this special relation between the two reserve currencies, by providing the pound with the reserves it so notoriously lacks, would allow Britain to maintain her world monetary position without constant disruption of her domestic economy.[2]

From this point of view, the British have had every reason to strengthen and extend existing ties. A formal economic association, like NAFTA, would serve to confirm and extend the ties that bind the two currencies together. Britain in the Common Market, on the other hand, might attenuate the proven trans-Atlantic banking connections, for the sake of dubious long-range opportunities for collaboration with relatively backward continental bankers—not the sort of proposition that tends to recommend itself to the City men caught up in urgent day-to-day business.

These expectations have naturally been affected by the November 1967 devaluation. American support, of course, was vital for the success of the devaluation itself and in holding the new level. Nevertheless, America's reserves did not save the pound in November and, some people have come to believe, may not ultimately save the dollar either. While these gloomy perspectives are far from universal, they at least suggest the wisdom of questioning the long-range prospects and advantages of further monetary co-operation between Britain and the United States. General de Gaulle has made it clear that Britain's monetary "special relations" are a major obstacle to her entering Europe. Are the trans-Atlantic prospects for monetary co-operation brighter for Britain than the European? These questions are part of the yet more fundamental issue of how the world's monetary system should be organized. In the continuing quarrel over the future of the monetary system, Britain has tended to side with America and against France. Does this position represent Britain's genuine long-range interest? Or the world's?

To begin with, it should be said that while American support for the pound has been crucial, a concrete illustration of the value for Britain of its special relationship with the US, American charity has not been entirely disinterested. For several years running, America has herself been faced with a large deficit in her balance of payments with the result that the position of the dollar, like that of the pound, has come increasingly to depend on the co-operation of other countries. Thus it is very much in the American interest

111

to foster arrangements whereby the reserves of other countries are automatically placed at the disposal of a "reserve currency" to tide it over exchange difficulties.[3] Indeed America, like England, has been forced increasingly to rely upon the reserves of others.

The deterioration of the American position has been spectacular. From 1958 to 1965, America's reserves, mostly in gold, dropped from $22·54 billion to $15·45 billion. Against these reserves in 1965, foreigners held net short-term liabilities of $16·34 billion.[4] Thus, by the middle of the 1960s, America's reserves were fully committed to backing the convertible dollars held by foreigners. With the heavy exchange costs of the Vietnam War, the considerable action taken in 1965 to limit American investment abroad proved insufficient to end or even diminish the deficit. Indeed the American balance of payments deficit in 1967 reached $3·6 billion. Gold reserves dropped $1·17 billion, $925 million following British devaluation, to a low of $12·065 billion.[5] Strong measures taken at the beginning of 1968 will doubtless have more success than earlier curbs, but as long as American military commitments remain at the present level in Asia and Europe, the room for manoeuvre is limited. Measures against investment and tourism abroad are unpopular and, if successful, may provoke countermeasures by foreign governments. In any event, these troubles have long since begun to affect the standing of the dollar as a "reserve" currency—"good as gold." America's creditors have become increasingly restive about holding so much of their reserves in dollars. Likewise American domestic opinion may grow increasingly disenchanted with the restrictions, long familiar to the British, that attend countries that take on the responsibility of maintaining world "reserve" currencies.

How did the dollar and the pound ever come to hold their singular roles as "reserve" currencies for other countries? The use of sterling "balances" as a reserve has been a long-standing practice in the Commonwealth countries of the sterling bloc, made natural, in the past at least, by the considerable integration of their trade and finance.[6] The balances, in large part, stem from Britain's wartime debt.[7] The dollar's position as a reserve in place of gold arises from the situation at the end of World War II. The United States held most of the free world's gold. Europe needed American food and fuel to stay alive. The tattered European economies looked chiefly to America for the equipment to rebuild their industrial plants. In the early years, there was naturally an enormous imbalance of trade between the Old and New Worlds— the "dollar gap"—filled by American aid and investment. Since dollars were the most needed currency and since America had most of the West's gold, it was only natural for Western Europeans to hold dollars as reserves in place of gold. Gradually, as Europe recovered, the dollar gap closed. Nevertheless, Europeans continued the practice of holding dollars as a reserve and trading currency. As America has continued to invest and give aid abroad, Europeans have come to hold more and more dollars. Since international trade has been increasing much more rapidly than the gold supply, these dollars held abroad have become an indispensable element in world finance. Without these dollars held by foreigners, there would not have been enough international "liquidity", i.e., enough universally acceptable money to finance the world's growing trade and ensure the possibility of everyone's having a satisfactory level of reserves.

The disadvantages of having an international medium of exchange tied to the economy of any single country are obvious— both in theory and in practice, particularly if that country plays a large and controversial role in world affairs. For pounds and dollars to be held as reserves, others must have them and thus, to increase liquidity in the world, Britain and America must between them run balance of payments deficits. Otherwise, the supply of international money does not keep increasing fast enough for world trade. But these reserves of pounds and dollars are, in fact, a form of indebtedness by Britain and the United States to other countries. Americans spend the dollars abroad, and the Europeans agree to hold them. Naturally, the bigger the debts, the more restive the creditors. Persistent balance of payments deficits suggest eventual devaluation. Thus the American government has faced growing difficulties in financing its balance of payments deficits.

These difficulties have been countered by a number of ingenious devices. In the early sixties, for example, the American Treasury began issuing the so-called "Roosa Bonds", medium-term US bonds payable in foreign currency rather than dollars. Several other arrangements of an *ad hoc* nature were developed in this period to ease the financing of the American deficit, e.g., so-called currency "swaps" and the early repayment of past loans.[8] The new cooperative arrangements among central bankers for bolstering each other's currencies against speculative runs, so vital in the pound's recent crises, are a similar development of this period of ingenious but haphazard inventiveness. It is not surprising, however, that the continuing US deficit should have led to renewed interest in more fundamental and comprehensive revisions of the international monetary system. By 1963, the American Treasury itself seems to have decided that the deficit was likely to go on for some time and that more fundamental reforms should be discussed. Any such reforms are, of course, of profound interest to Britain because of sterling's international role. The issues raised by ultimate structure of the world monetary system, moreover, point to the very heart of the question of Britain's future role and alignments.[9]

Revision of the world's monetary system leads to all the vexing questions of world "liquidity", much debated by economists and, more recently, by bankers and politicians as well. The chief antagonists in the political, as opposed to the academic debate, have been the United States and France. Essentially the American government seems to be looking for some new way to keep running deficits, only with less difficulty. The official Americans point out that the actual trade balance of the US shows a great surplus and argue that the American balance of payments deficit, in fact, springs from the special political and economic burdens the United States has assumed as the leader of the free world. The deficit, in other words, springs not from trade, but from war in Vietnam, military aid to beleaguered governments, and vast economic aid programmes to underdeveloped countries.[10] If heavy American investment abroad is also partly responsible, American officials point out the advantages of that investment to those who receive it. Finally they note that in the present international monetary system, world liquidity depends on dollars being used as a supplement to gold. Therefore, the argument runs, it is in the interest of everyone to support the dollar by holding without question the increasing flow of dollar liabilities put out by the American Treasury to finance its deficits. These deficits are in the interest of everyone in the free world. They are, after all, backed by the tremendous strength of the American economy. If the world's monetary system is reformed, it should be in some manner as to increase liquidity and thus make it easier for the US, and incidentally the British, to finance their beneficial deficits.[11]

The official French position disagrees with the American on nearly every count. The heart of the problem is that the French profess little sympathy with the American activities causing the deficit. They are opposed to the war in Vietnam and unsympathetic with many of the regimes propped up by American aid—especially as they regard this aid as a lever for maintaining American political and often economic hegemony in large areas of the ex-colonial world. Finally, they are sceptical about the benefits of American capital investment in Europe. Their basic position is that by agreeing to hold an unlimited amount of dollars, Europeans are, in effect, financing a detestable war in Vietnam, American colonialism in general, and American economic domination of Western European industry. They regard the argument that the world monetary system depends on Europeans holding dollars as a form of blackmail. They are naturally suspicious of schemes to increase liquidity, generally regarding them merely as a means for allowing the US to continue running its deficits. Therefore, they have consistently resisted a major increase in liquidity through a reformation of the world's monetary system until such time as the US ends its deficit by ceasing the policies that cause it.[12]

Many academic economists have tended to see the force of French objections to the continued financing of American deficits by Europe. They also share, however, a general concern to find some adequate means to replace the American deficit as a source of international liquidity, increasing sufficiently for the rise in world trade, and general economic activity. What sort of alternate system might be developed to provide enough liquidity, and what does it have to do with Britain's future role and alignments?

The concept of international liquidity is elusive and the issues it raises complex. Essentially, liquidity refers to the available supply of internationally acceptable money. Without sufficient means of international payment, trade and investment might be constrained, either by the actual lack of money to finance the transactions, or, more probably, by government policies that slow down trade and capital movements in order to conserve scarce reserves. Liquidity requires a sufficient pool of monetary reserves, spread out among the trading nations, so that countries temporarily in deficit are likely to have enough reserves to avoid having to adopt those drastic restrictive measures that injure their own development and world trade in general.

The supply of international money has to be considered in rela-

115

tion to the level of prices and the volume of world trade. As prices and volume rise, it is presumed that the supply of money should increase as well, in order to preserve "international liquidity." In the days of the gold standard, when gold was the only reserve asset, the real value of reserves was increased by adjustment of the price level for goods and labour. This was a process not without pain, as falling prices also brought down wages and profits, reduced employment and made life hard for debtors. Sometimes the "automatic" process of adjustment was prolonged, and several depressions in the nineteenth century were blamed on the sinister workings of the gold standard.[13] Today, the generally accepted commitment of governments to maintaining a high level of employment makes a return to the classical gold standard impossible. In our present-day economies, since wages seldom fall and large-scale unemployment cannot be counted an acceptable means of economic adjustment, the price level cannot be expected to adjust itself downward. Instead, some means have to be found to keep the reserves adequate for rising prices and increasing business.

The need for international liquidity is, if anything, greater since the war than before. For throughout the postwar period, there has been a growing determination to maintain fixed exchange rates. To maintain these rates while pursuing domestic full employment calls for currency reserves large enough to allow a country to correct its trade deficits gradually, without having to resort to deflationary policies severe enough to cause large-scale unemployment. Britain, as was discussed earlier, is thought to have been particularly handicapped by a shortage of reserves.[14]

Students of these matters differ over whether there is already a serious shortage of reserves throughout the world in general. Sir Roy Harrod, in arguing that the situation is already dangerous, observes that world reserves, as a percentage of annual imports, have dropped from 107·1% in 1937/8 and 88·6% in 1948 to 56·8% in 1963.[15] Jacques Rueff, who takes a similarly alarmed view, notes that while other prices have doubled, the price of gold has not changed since 1934.[16] As a result, gold is a far smaller proportion of total reserves than before the war: 26·4% in 1963 as opposed to 99·6% in 1937/8.[17] Its declining place has been filled chiefly by the dollar balances, and marginally by sterling and drawing rights at the International Monetary Fund.[18]

Not all experts are alarmed about the quantity of reserves at the moment; but even those who are relatively complacent agree that the present system is becoming unworkable. The distinguished monetary expert, Professor Robert Triffin, observes:

> The survival of the gold-exchange standard has now become dependent on the *political* willingness of foreign countries to finance, through their own monetary issues, the deficits of the countries whose national *currency* is accepted by them as international reserves. Compliance with such a system becomes more precarious every day, not only because the growing illiquidity of the reserve debtors throws increasing doubts upon the ultimate exchange value of such unguaranteed claims, but also because central banks are being called upon to finance debtor countries' policies in which their own governments have no voice, and with which they may profoundly disagree.[19]

If these academic experts are right, the present system must soon end, either through rational change or catastrophe. The whole elaborate *ad hoc* structure built to maintain the dollar and the pound will ultimately be insufficient. If the present system is likely to change, it would seem prudent for those planning Britain's future to take a long look at the various possible reforms to determine not only the possible structural changes most in Britain's monetary interest but changes that are also broadly compatible with her other goals and allegiances. In monetary matters, as in so many others, any number of arrangements are possible. The problem for Britain is to integrate her policy for monetary reform with her whole broad strategy for the future. What kinds of solutions have been proposed?

Theorists suggest reforming the present international monetary system in one of two ways—either by some new general agreement increasing the supply of reserves or else by going over to "floating" exchange rates, a free market in currencies that would, in theory, settle problems with the balance of payments automatically and do away with the need for reserves.

A simple rise in the price of gold would be the most direct method of achieving the first solution—an increase in the world's monetary reserves. It is the shortage of gold that has made necessary the present reserve role of dollars and sterling, but if an ounce of gold were worth $70 rather than $35, then there would be, in effect, twice as much gold available. Sir Roy Harrod has been an advocate of this remedy as a helpful first step leading out of the present frustrating impasse over genuine reform.[20] Further support comes from the distinguished French monetary expert, Jacques Rueff, whose influence with General de Gaulle is thought to be considerable.[21] Reuff, however, envisages an increase in the price of gold not merely to supplement dollars and sterling, but to retire them altogether as reserve currencies. The large "windfall" profits coming to the United States could somehow be used to buy out the dollar balances held as reserves. Rueff further suggests that the "windfall" profits coming to other large holders of gold like France might be used to fund sterling's debts.[22]

Many experts, like Triffin, find the idea of doubling gold's value technically impractical.[23] The American Government has traditionally disliked such proposals, among other reasons because they would, as a side effect, benefit several countries the American Government does not like, such as South Africa, Russia, China and France. The British Government has been unenthusiastic because its obligations payable in a set quantity of gold are greater, in fact, than its gold reserves. Thus if gold's value were doubled, the increase in Britain's debts would be greater than the increase in her assets.[24] Beyond these particular calculations, there is a general aversion in many quarters to the whole idea of basing the world's monetary system on a fortuitously variable supply of precious metal.

The "modern" approach to increasing liquidity lies in creating some artificial new unit of international exchange to supplement gold and thus supersede the present reserve currencies—sterling and the dollar. A new international reserve unit would presumably avoid the difficulties of a currency tied to any single national economy. The new unit could be backed by a mix of various national currencies, or, more radically, an entirely abstract currency issued by some sort of central world monetary authority.[25] The rules and machinery of this authority would comprise a sort of world central bank, acting not only as a clearing house, but also deciding how much liquidity to create and how much credit to extend to nations in deficit. Such a scheme would only carry on further in the direction of the present International Monetary Fund—itself a scaled-down version of a grander scheme imagined by the great English economist, John Maynard Keynes.[26] The IMF holds as its assets deposits subscribed by its members in debt.

Despite Keynes' intentions, the IMF was set up on a scale far too small to make it the chief creator of new world liquidity. It was soon surpassed as a provider of new reserves by dollars and pounds. New plans for an artificial currency are, in a sense, resumptions of the schemes that lay behind the IMF.

The difficulty with all such arrangements is that they need some multilateral political body to decide how large reserves should be and how much credit should be extended to debtor nations. While an international monetary system should be designed to provide adequate leeway to nations to adjust to the unavoidable cycles of trade, it should not presumably be so constructed that certain favoured nations can run deficits indefinitely, their profligacy financed by all the others.

It is this last point that worries the European central bankers in general and the French in particular. At the present time, for example, the two major debtor countries, the United States and Britain hold a majority of voting rights in the IMF.[27] They are naturally not inclined to discipline themselves too severely. The French, on the other hand, have been uninterested in schemes for increasing liquidity through the IMF until its control structure was organized to give the Six a veto on the creation of new reserves. The modest agreements of August 1967 were achieved only after the Six collectively were given a veto over the creation of new drawing rights. That veto probably means that the effective increase in reserves will be minimal. The French fear of political mechanisms subject to the control of the big debtors leads them to favour "automatic" systems based on the "objective" value of gold rather than artificial creations easily manipulated. Thus, although they may come to agree to a small increase in liquidity through the IMF, they are unlikely ever to agree to anything large enough to satisfy America's needs.[28]

The search for an "automatic" mechanism has led some well-known economists, Professor Harry Johnson for example, off in another direction—towards ending fixed exchange rates and going over to a "free" market for currency.[29] In such a market, governments would no longer intervene with their reserves to maintain a fixed exchange rate and national currencies would automatically "float" to their own relative levels according to changes in supply and demand. In theory, the system might almost eliminate the need for reserves and thus solve the problem of liquidity.[30]

A free market would also tend automatically to bring appropriate pressures to bear on economies either in excessive deficit or surplus and thus by-pass the difficulties of multilateral political control. An American balance of payments deficit, for example, would lead to an international over-supply of dollars and a consequent drop in the dollar's relative value. This would automatically have the advantages of devaluation without the danger that other countries could retaliate by following suit. Other countries could only restore the original ratio of the dollar to their currency by buying or investing more in the US. Otherwise, American exports would be cheaper and imports more expensive. Thus the trade balances would shift and the balance of payments would have an inherent automatic tendency to right itself.

According to Professor Johnson, the floating system he suggests would be greatly to America's advantage. For, in his opinion, the dollar is overvalued and the result is both an advantage to continental exports and a powerful inducement to American capital to invest in Europe. Hence, gold flows relentlessly from American to European reserves to support the dollar at a level which really gives more advantage to Europeans than Americans. In a free-floating system, the dollar's relative value would fall unless the heavy outflow from the US were matched by a corresponding high rate of inflow to the US from Europe. It would, in this sense, be up to the Europeans to decide whether they wanted to keep the dollar at its high value.[31] If they did, they would have to support its price by buying or investing in America. The present arrangements, according to Johnson, are doubly bad for they not only cost the US gold and trade advantages, but they give the Europeans increasing control over American policy:

> ... the Europeans have cleverly exploited the naïve American devotion to the US price of gold and sense of responsibility for the dollar's role in world trade and finance ... to the point where the smaller and poorer Common Market calls the tune to which the US economic giant must dance.[32]

Ideas like Johnson's are occasionally heard outside academic circles, particularly in the American Congress and Treasury. Congressman Henry S. Reuss, for example, who is Chairman of the International Exchange and Payments Sub-Committee of the Joint Economic Committee of Congress, in February, 1967, after suggesting that American tourists be forbidden to enter France and American investment be prohibited in countries that "capriciously" and "destructively" demand gold for dollars, went on to observe:

> If the Europeans demanded all the US gold reserve, with the last US gold gone overseas, the dollar would then become *de facto* a floating exchange rate dollar; with the strength of the American economy, I should think the dollar would be a very desirable currency to hold, and it's quite likely that the dollar might even appreciate in value. If it fluctuated downward in terms of other currencies, this could be a *de facto* amendment of the Bretton Woods philosophy of 1944, and would be one way of our attaining at that time balance of payments equilibrium.[33]

The Congressman appeared to overlook a critical fact: America's balance of payments difficulties are not caused essentially because Europeans capriciously demand gold for dollars, but because the United States spends abroad more than it earns. The view that foreigners are morally obliged to hold dollars to show their faith in the strength of the American economy suggests that foreign traders and bankers should act like loyal citizens in wartime who buy government bonds as a token of their patriotic faith in national victory. Lamentably, however, foreigners tend not to share the Congressman's views about international trade. The relationships are purely commercial and thus entirely different from those of a private citizen with his own government. Foreigners buy another people's currency because they need it to do business. Bankers hold a foreign currency as a reserve because they have faith in its steady value. Persistent deficits inevitably undermine confidence. The parallel between domestic and international deficits is entirely specious. While a government may be able to run an internal budgetary deficit indefinitely, international deficits are of an entirely different order. In its international transactions a country is in the position not of a central bank, backed by the sovereign's control of the domestic economy, but of a private bank which, regardless of its total wealth, cannot honour its obligations if its liquid assets are insufficient. As long as the US goes on spending more abroad than it earns, there will continue to be downward pressure on the dollar and very likely a continuing loss of reserves. There is no point in blaming the situation on the malevolence of foreigners.

121

In any event, since foreigners are reluctant to hold dollars, what alternatives are available to the US, aside from cutting the outward flow of dollars for official and investment purposes? One classical solution would be to devalue at once. With the security of still large reserves and the enhanced competitiveness of American exports, the deficit might be stopped. Alternatively, the US could, as the Congressman suggested, wait for the reserves to be exhausted and then, of necessity, go over to a floating rate. A variation would be to release the rate at once, while using the remaining gold reserves to prevent the dollar from fluctuating wildly because of "speculative" and seasonal oscillations. But every solution of this kind is likely to face great difficulty if the present level of American foreign expenditure is not reduced.

Anything that lowers the exchange value of the dollar increases the dollar price of foreign commitments. An orthodox devaluation, for example, by lowering the relative value of the dollar, would lead to an immediate increase in the foreign exchange cost of foreign aid and defence: but the compensating beneficial effects of the lower exchange rate might well be slower in coming. On the most optimistic view it would take some time for home and foreign markets to adapt to the new attractiveness of American goods and for trade and private capital flows to compensate for the rise in government expenditure. The initial effect of this solution might well be to worsen the balance of payments deficit. Similarly, with a floating rate, it might require a dramatic fall in the value of the dollar to maintain overseas government expenditure while trade gradually adjusted.[34] Even if it worked in time, this adjustment of trade would, in effect, be shifting the burden of the deficit from foreign holders of dollars to the American consumer and his standard of living. Devaluation usually hurts the domestic consumer, though, within limits, it might have a relatively small disruptive effect on the domestic American economy because of the low ratio of foreign to domestic trade, and large unused capacity. A drastic increase in the already substantial American trade surplus, however, might lead to protectionist measures by those unfavourably affected.

Meanwhile, the drastic short-run decline suggested here, either of the gold reserves, or of the rate, would make foreigners even more reluctant to hold dollars. Needless to say, the general disruption of world trade and finance attendant upon such experiments might have repercussions that neither the United States nor anyone else would enjoy. In short, it is not easy to see how a floating rate could solve the American payments deficit, unless, of course, there were a drastic cut in spending. Thus, if the American strategy is to find some new device whereby Europe continues to finance part of America's overseas political policy, exchange rate adjustments do not seem to be the answer. Indeed, they might be as ruthless a device for cutting back America's world involvements as General de Gaulle's gold standard.

There is, of course, another whole line of argument against floating rates in general that sees them as a solution that would be extremely difficult to manage technically and highly disruptive to world trade. Sir Roy Harrod, for example, admits that while floating rates are an intellectually attractive solution to exchange deficits and reserve shortages, they are nevertheless completely impractical to operate. To begin with, Harrod believes it would be impossible, at the present time, to run a floating system without official intervention to stabilize the continuous oscillations resulting from the "leads and lags" of trade, the considerable oscillations in the currency market caused simply by variations in the timing of movements for trade.[35] Harrod believes that, with floating rates, these swings would be even larger because traders would always have to take into account the possibility of revaluation. Hence, Harrod concludes, floating rates might well require more official intervention and thus even greater reserves than with fixed rates.[36]

A floating system, moreover, would be unbearably complicated. With a large number of separate national currencies simultaneously oscillating against each other, "cross-rates" would introduce formidable complications, scarcely conducive to the facility and serenity of international transactions.[37] These objections, well-founded or not, are alone likely to prevent the general adoption of floating rates.

Grouping the world's currencies together into two blocs, with fixed exchange rates within each bloc and a floating rate between them, might, according to Harrod, be a more acceptable alternative that would include some of the benefits of flexible rates.[38] The system would certainly be easier to operate. On the other hand, as Harrod observes, it would scarcely do away with national balance of payments crises and the need for monetary reserves. Each country within the bloc would still have its own separate balance of payments, not necessarily co-ordinated with the others, in the bloc and would thus still need adequate reserves to maintain its fixed exchange rates with the others.[39]

Another claim sometimes heard for a freely floating exchange system is that it would automatically solve the problem of "cost-push" inflation. This variety of inflation, wages pushing up prices, has infected most advanced capitalist economies since the war and seems the inevitable accompaniment of the simultaneous commitment to full employment and growth on the one hand and a relatively free market for wages and prices on the other. But the failure to stop prices from rising beyond international competition leads inevitably to exchange difficulties and, if unchecked, compels devaluation. The usual remedy is some sort of governmental initiative to regulate prices and incomes—by persuasion and coercion. A floating exchange rate would theoretically make a prices and incomes policy unnecessary. As prices went up, the currency would go down and the whole system would have an inherent automatic tendency to bring trade into balance without the government's having to act.

It is this feature of floating rates that particularly recommends them to Professor Harry Johnson, a leading advocate both of floating rates and of NAFTA. He has closely related reasons for advancing both these causes. He is against fixed exchange rates because, in his opinion, the attempt to maintain them leads inevitably to more and more government interference in the economy. He is sceptical, moreover, about the possibility of a successful incomes policy and sees "no evidence that it will work especially in large and competitive economies".[40] Governments committed to fixed exchange rates are thus, he believes, constrained to take more and more active measures to improve their exchange position. Direct measures are taken to spur exports, discourage imports and prevent the outward flow of capital. All this leads inevitably, Johnson believes, to more and more clumsy distortion by governments of national and world economies. He thus fears the trend towards rigidly fixed exchange rates:

> So long as they continue in this direction, we must expect international adjustment to be increasingly handled by governmental interventions in international commerce and finance.[41]

Professor Johnson's basic views naturally make him unenthusiastic about the economic effects of a European customs union like the Common Market that inevitably distorts the "normal" patterns of trade, especially in agriculture. He is quite aware, of course, that the Common Market, in the eyes of its continental creators, has never found its essential justification, strictly speaking, from economics. For many Common Market zealots, it is, in a manner of speaking, a fortunate accident that its customs union has apparently enhanced the economic prosperity of its members. The avowed purpose of the whole enterprise, however, has always been "mercantilist"—the creation of a co-ordinated Western European political power—an ideal not less espoused by the Gaullists than federalists. Johnson understands Europe's aims, but feels they are not England's. A liberal free trader, he hopes to keep England away from the embrace of the continental heirs of Napoleon through the appropriately liberal device of a free trade area. Significantly, for him a chief advantage of NAFTA is that it would require minimal conscious co-ordination of economic policies by its member governments.[42] Thus the two fundamental elements in Professor Johnson's grand strategy, floating exchange rates and a North Atlantic Free Trade Area, find a common element—the avoidance of the mercantilist, politically-oriented *dirigisme* typical of a continental tradition stretching from Colbert to de Gaulle.

Professor Johnson's arguments are ingenious and powerful, but they are rather special. They are, in fact, an interesting illustration of the practical affinity between universalist internationalism in economics and national particularism in politics. Internationalist free trade economics provide the arguments to justify Britain's holding aloof from a regional political association with her closest neighbours. But in the long run, as Professor Johnson himself has sometimes admitted, the political logic of regionalism seems to be triumphing over the economic logic of universalist free trade.[43]

In summary, it seems questionable that any of these universalist solutions to a world monetary system will succeed, for each introduces technical or political consequences unacceptable to one or another of the major financial powers. The United States and Britain oppose raising the price of gold. Both favour a major increase in liquidity through some international organization like the IMF, a solution that seems, for understandable reasons, unacceptable to the Europeans, at least until the American deficit is ended. A floating system is unpopular with many because its unpredictableness is thought to be bad for trade. Certainly it is unacceptable among states, like those of the Common Market, who are moving towards a unified economy. And even if adopted by the US, a floating dollar would increase the real price to America of her overseas commitments.

One hard truth does seem to emerge: the United States is in no position to impose a universalist "world" monetary system without the co-operation of the continental countries. Their increasing weight springs not from some particular set of artificial voting arrangements, but from the realities of trading and monetary power. The external trade of the Common Market is greater and growing faster than that of the economically narcissistic US.[44] The EEC's monetary reserves are half again as great as those of the United States and, more importantly, they are not held at the pleasure of creditors. In short, when the Six act together, they restore something like Europe's pre-war significance as a major world economic centre. If they work in concert, ultimately there must be established a world monetary system that reflects their collective power. In economics, as in politics, the arrangements that reflect the overwhelming economic dominance of the United States in the late forties will have to yield to the realities of twenty years after.

If the major financial powers can neither agree on some sort of world central bank to regulate liquidity nor are willing to hazard floating exchange rates, it may well be that the ultimate reorganization of the world monetary system will see a financial expression of the "two pillars" idea—a dollar bloc and a European bloc. Inside each bloc there would be fixed exchange rates and, at least in the European group, a growing co-ordination of economic policy.[45] Between the two blocs, there would be looser ties and, if not an actual floating exchange rate, at least the possibility of occasional revaluation. The degree of co-ordination that seems essential to rigidly fixed exchange rates perhaps cannot be maintained except in areas, like the EEC countries, with especially strong incentives for intimate co-operation pointing towards political union. Outside such areas, an occasional revaluation may perhaps be the most sensible means to maintain equilibrium with the minimum of domestic sacrifice and distortion.

One strong factor favouring such an arrangement is that it can develop without any particularly dramatic alterations in the present system. The EEC countries are, in fact, moving slowly towards a monetary union. They are not likely to permit any drastic overhaul of the IMF or some successor that will greatly increase liquidity. The American deficit, if it continues, will eventually lead to devaluation and may, as Reuss suggests, lead to a floating rate for the dollar. Thus the two blocs would arise, in fact, from what is not an altogether improbable course of events.

It is sometimes assumed that, in such a world system, Britain would fall within the dollar bloc.[46] It is true that the *ad hoc* arrangements developed to support the faltering dollar have given a support to the tottering pound as well. To this extent, the "North Atlantic" ties have given Britain succour during her recurring bouts of exchange sickness. But these aids are a narcotic rather than a cure. There is, at best, a limited future for an alliance between the two overstretched reserve currencies. It should be noted, for example, that even in the sterling crises from 1964 to 1966, however beneficial the initiative of the Federal Reserve, the rescue of the pound required massive support from the European central banks as well.[47] The devaluation of November, 1967, made it clear that the dollar cannot support the pound indefinitely. The dollar has troubles enough of its own.

In the long run, there might be great advantages for Britain in the European bloc. As noted earlier, the chief obstacle to Europe's freeing itself from the "hegemony" of the dollar lies in the structural financial weakness of the Europeans themselves. The Common Market countries, for all their commercial importance and enormous monetary reserves, nevertheless still are thought to lack the machinery to finance their own trade and capital requirements. The inefficiency of the European capital market is notorious.[48] Indeed, there is something preposterous in the whole idea of the American dollar as the chief medium of intra-European trade. If such arrangements give the American economy the power to force others to finance its deficits, if American investors are thereby unfairly assisted in buying up large bits of continental business, the fault surely lies at least as much with the continentals as with the Americans. Without the dollar in its present role, the European economy would collapse. Thus, if the Europeans want to end whatever unfair privileges the American gain from their financial "hegemony", if they want, in short, their own regional reserve and

127

trading currency, then they must create it, along with all the financial apparatus.

The French have recognised the logic of the situation and are belatedly making some efforts to develop the financial machinery of Paris.[49] Important financial centres do, of course, exist in Germany and the Low Countries. No doubt, it is unwise to underestimate the ingenuity of the French or the other continentals in these matters. Nevertheless, an indigenous European financial system, adequate to Europe's trading and capital requirements, may be a long time coming if it depends on the present members of the Common Market. But the necessary financial apparatus and skills do, in large measure, already exist in Europe—in the City of London.

At the present time, the City seems too big for England. Its capital-raising functions are increasingly restricted by the pound's weakness. If Britain turns inward, joining neither the European nor the American bloc, the slow decline of the City's international position seems inevitable, in spite of the considerable ingenuity of its denizens. If Britain joined with America, as the Atlanticists urge, then it seems inevitable that both sterling and the City would become absorbed into the colossus that would dominate that bloc. But Britain in Europe would give the City the chance to be the financial centre that the Europeans will need if they are ever to replace American finance and the dollar with some structure and medium controlled by themselves.

In summary, closer financial links between the US and Britain may supply useful assistance in those moments of recurring exchange crisis. Even this aid, however, can no longer be provided by America alone. For while the US brings to a partnership the incomparably vast American economy, it does not, in fact, possess either reserves or a favourable balance of payments. Neither does the partnership appear to bring Britain much opportunity, for clearly New York and not London will dominate an Atlantic bloc. Two reserve currencies in one bloc would be superfluous; two financial capitals would be unlikely. London would be not the New York of Europe, but the San Francisco of Eastern Atlantica.

4. America's Perspectives

When all is said and done, it is hardly realistic to consider

Britain's option to join a closer form of Atlantic association without considering the likelihood of serious American interest in such projects. While it might seem, as we have noted in Section 2, that a NAFTA offers only questionable commercial advantages to the United States, it is often argued that America, a country whose foreign trade represents only 8% of her GNP, generally decides her trade policy in terms of her political rather than economic goals.[1] Broadly speaking, there is a good deal to be said for this view. Americans, for example, are uniquely concerned with the dangers of "conferring the benefits of American trade" on unsuitable countries—a mercantilist luxury not usually indulged in by European countries for whom foreign trade is a vital part of their economic life. It may be, however, that America's growing balance of payments difficulties will make her more mindful of economic goals and limitations. At any rate, it must be asked whether a scheme like NAFTA is likely to seem commensurate with America's long-range political interests. On the surface, at least, there would seem to be some impressive support in America for Atlanticist schemes like NAFTA and certainly for continuing the present Atlantic pattern in military affairs. NATO has many enthusiasts, some of whom sincerely believe in the possibility and desirability of a further Atlantic Union.

There is, furthermore, considerable American disillusionment about Europe in general and the prospects for a Grand Alliance of two pillars in particular. The causes for these feelings are rather contradictory. On the one hand, a Gaullist Europe has refused to become America's federalist homuncule. Thus the sanguine American hopes that the Common Market would turn into a federalist "second pillar" have faded since de Gaulle's veto of Britain in 1963 and his apparent victory over the Commission in the Luxembourg agreements of 1965. It is now increasingly fashionable for Americans to believe that European political union is dead. On the other hand, despite Europe's seeming apostasy from federalism, Americans have increasingly been confronted with the Six acting together as a powerful bloc in a number of highly significant fields. But this phenomenon gives little comfort to the Americans. For when the Europeans do manage to unite, they generally oppose the United States. Thus the Americans sometimes discover that Europe's cohesion is all too effective in questions of world trade and monetary reform. Europeans often seem to find another fruitful area for common agreement in their dislike of American foreign policy outside Europe, which they refuse to support, or in their fear of American technological superiority, which they continually lament.

For a long time it has been common to blame all these developments on General de Gaulle and to assume that after him, Europe would return to its earlier federalist progress and pro-American views. That remains a popular view, but there is growing belief that Gaullist foreign policy draws its strength from rather more durable forces than de Gaulle's personality and may well persist long after him. The apparent attraction for the Germans of their own brand of Gaullism has seemed a further disturbing portent.

These developments have increasingly inhibited America's enthusiasm for building up a strong European bloc as the "second pillar" of the West. Like Doctor Frankenstein, America has been increasingly alarmed about its creation. Tensions have become apparent between American enthusiasm for an independent Europe on one hand, and the continuing desire to maintain a hegemonic military Alliance on the other—an Alliance whose members are meant to concur in America's opposition to nuclear sharing and proliferation, hope for a direct nuclear entente with Russia, and determination to resist Chinese expansion and Communist-inspired revolutions throughout the Third World.

An independent Europe is not likely to favour many of these policies. It seems remarkable that so many Americans seemed to think it would. Nevertheless, it is an understandable reaction for the US to see its former protégé, the revived Europe, as an ungrateful offspring, the troublesome product of idealistic America's inexperienced postwar enthusiasm. These general sentiments appear widespread and strong and are being further enhanced by able people in England and America who have, from the first, wanted Britain oriented primarily towards America rather than towards Europe. But in assessing the probable influence of these anti-continental sentiments on American policy, it would be well to take a longer view of America's whole postwar European strategy. A momentary mutual disillusionment about Europe hardly means that Britain and America's basic perspectives towards Europe are the same. As de Gaulle and Churchill once concluded: "When all is said and done, Great Britain is an island; France, the cape of a continent; America, another world."[2] Furthermore, it is likely that many Americans, having been too hopeful about European unity in the past, are too disillusioned about it in the present. In a number of concrete and significant ways, postwar Europe is evolving into a coherent bloc whose power, in some respects, rivals that of the United States itself. Despite the lamentations of the federalists, a new Europe gradually appears to be taking form. What is America's long-range policy towards it likely to be?

The fundamental assumption of America's postwar European policy has been that a strong Europe, allied to America rather than Russia, is a vital interest for the United States. It has been basic dogma that, as long as Europe and America remain allied, each is safe, but if they each go their independent ways, the world will be exposed to dangerous uncertainties and perilous experiments. Since there is no military balance between Western Europe and Russia, a Europe alienated from America could easily pass under Russian domination with catastrophic results for Europe and for the world-wide balance of power. It was easy enough to maintain the Alliance in Stalin's day. But since Stalin, the growing challenge for the United States has been to find some satisfactory and stable arrangement that will continue to appeal to a Western Europe that feels increasingly strong and secure, and is impatient with the divisive barriers imposed upon it by the Cold War.

As is noted often above, the United States has essentially followed two policies towards organizing its ties with Europe. On the one hand, there has been the "two pillars" or "dumbbell" approach reflected in America's support of the Common Market and in President Kennedy's "Grand Design" of 1961. On the other hand, there has been the hegemonic pattern of NATO by which the vastly superior United States presides directly over a crowd of European allies, without any intervening distinctly European organization to create some semblance of balance between the two sides of the Atlantic.

Each of these two policies has a logic of its own. The first, the twin-pillars design, reflects the economic, financial, and political power of Western Europe. It envisages a Western world composed of two equal partners—a United States of America and a United States of Europe. Americans, bemused by their own history, have generally traced the ills of Europe to its disunity and hence advocated federalism, the essence, after all, of America's own political genius. This is quite a natural view for Americans. America, as a country, is already a sort of European federation, where regional allegiances are almost invariably the refuge of reactionaries. There is a certain inherent tendency to equate European nationalism with American "states-rights", rather than, say, an American disinclination to federate with Mexico. Thus de Gaulle is seen as a kind of European Governor Wallace.[3] Not only would federation be good for Europe, Americans believe, but in guaranteeing the continent's stability and defence, it would remove a major burden from America's shoulders. Thus consolidated, the forces of Western democracy would be more than adequate against any communist challenge; Russia would abandon her hopeless pretensions to world domination, and together the European and American Unions would, along with the new Japan, share the burdens of maintaining peace and economic development among the impoverished countries of the world.

The second, or hegemonic pattern, is based on the logic not of Europe's financial and political strength, but of her military weakness. The American deterrent has all along been the *sine qua non* of any credible European defence against Russian invasion. In today's world, military prowess has seemed to depend primarily on the possession of advanced military technology rather than overall economic strength. Thus Europe's military strength has been far out of line with its economic importance. The centralized American control of NATO has only reflected where the real military power and responsibility lies. But as the Russian threat has apparently receded, Europeans have grown more restive. Nevertheless the United States has seemed uninterested in altering the hegemonic structure of the Alliance.

Above all, Americans have been extremely reluctant to lose their effective nuclear monopoly and have been fertile inventors of military theories emphasizing the advantages of the present centralized control. Proliferation would, it is argued, greatly increase the dangers of war. The division of much of the world into American and Russian blocs provides a certain reassuring simplification of world forces that helps define clearly respective vital interests and encourages the Russians to seek a direct understanding with the United States. According to this view, both superpowers, sobered by their terrible weapons, are inclined to share a common restraint and a common interest in limiting local conflicts whose spread might initiate, by accident, a major confrontation that neither wants. Thus the present concentration of nuclear military technology in two centres greatly enhances the prospects for a long peace in the world. A proliferation of nuclear weapons, on the other hand, would introduce a dangerous complexity and confusion into international affairs that would not be in the real interests of anyone.[4]

Both the two-pillars and hegemonic patterns have a coherent logic of their own. Both offer solutions for major American concerns. Unfortunately, nevertheless, in the long run, the two concepts are not easily compatible with one another.[5] American official policy, however, has held firmly to both and the policy is accurately reflected in the minds of many officials and private observers. Typically, partisans of European Union also insist on NATO partnership, while Atlanticists frequently regret the absence of vigorous and united European partnership to help carry the heavy burdens of world-wide aid and peace-keeping.

The tension between the two patterns of Atlantic relationships has not been unnoticed in the past, as George Kennan's recent memoirs make clear.[6] Today the tension is most apparent in the vexatious question of nuclear proliferation. The United States has been able to maintain the hegemonic military relationships of NATO for so long because the military capabilities of the Europeans have not grown commensurately with their economic or even diplomatic strength. Germany is the most extreme example. In a war with Russia, the Croesus that is today's Western Germany is finally no less dependent on the American deterrent than was the bankrupt and ravaged remnant of 1948. To the small extent that Britain and France are any less dependent militarily, it is not that they are richer than Germany, but that they have, in their own right, nuclear weapons capable of inflicting serious damage on the Russians. Their military power is not a function of their general economic strength—or even of their overall military expenditure, but of their advanced military technology.[7] In short, they have nuclear weapons and some means of delivering them.

There is nothing new in such an anomalous situation. History is full of battles won, not by bigger battalions, but by advanced weapons. Generally, however, countries that desire to retain their independence strive to make up their deficiencies as rapidly as possible. This natural tendency should be all the more pronounced when the superior weapons are, in fact, substantially cheaper to maintain than conventional arms and when their development is thought to have highly beneficial technological side-effects. In short, it is hardly remarkable that first the British, and then the French developed nuclear weapons and that the Germans are reluctant to pledge themselves to permanent nuclear abstinence.

The logic of these tendencies is completely contrary, however, to that of the basic American hegemonic strategy embodied in NATO, and indeed to the whole grand strategy based on limiting nuclear proliferation and arriving at a fundmental Russian-American entente. But many Europeans look with considerable cynicism upon American arguments against the terrible dangers of nuclear proliferation. De Gaulle's words strike a European chord: "In politics and in strategy, as in the economy, monopoly quite naturally appears to the person who holds it to be the best possible system."[8] Nor is the quest for a world order based on a fundamental Russian-American accord altogether pleasing to those Europeans who remember what happened to the continent at Yalta.[9]

The British, however, give much greater official and unofficial support for these American goals than do the continentals. Fear of the bomb, for example, has been a major theme of British politics. As a result, Britain, all along, has been more sympathetic to the NATO hegemonic pattern. But, as has been suggested before, Britain has had some special interests quite different from America's in maintaining the NATO pattern. Indeed, from an American point of view, it could be argued that Britain in her way has done as much to undermine the Alliance as France. It should not be forgotten that Britain was the first of the Western European countries to seek an escape route from American hegemony by acquiring nuclear weapons and that, in spite of Britain's much vaunted concern over the dangers of proliferation, no subsequent British government has yet shown any serious signs of wishing to renounce its Bomb. If Britain with her close ties to America has felt the need for an independent deterrent, it is difficult to understand why the same sentiments should not have been present on the other side of the Channel where the Atlantic identity is less strong to start with and less nourished by a special relationship.

Indeed, a quite respectable case could be made that Britain, in her indirect way, has been as much responsible for the demise of NATO as France. Once Britain acquired nuclear weapons and used them to demand a special military relationship over nuclear

134

matters, a fatal contradiction was introduced into the Alliance that would inevitably destroy it. Once Britain had escaped from America's nuclear hegemony, it was almost certain that France would do the same. America's subsequent unwillingness to extend a similar nuclear special relationship to France has broken up the Alliance. But for America to extend a nuclear partnership to France would have compelled eventually the same treatment for Germany and that was a step that would ruin forever the possibility of the entente with Russia that is the object of the whole NATO pattern. To make this point is not meant in any way to condemn British policy, but merely to reinforce the argument that no major European power is likely to accept willingly a complete and eternal military dependence on the United States. The more Europe revives, the more it is likely to seek to redress its present military weakness and the more the hegemonic NATO pattern will have to give way to the co-operative idea of the "two pillars". Otherwise, there will be no Alliance at all.

Over the years, the United States has tried to escape from the contradictions of its dual pattern with Europe by a number of proposals designed to make the Alliance more co-operative and less hegemonic. In the early fifties, there was a major attempt, the European Defence Community, to give a military dimension to the second pillar. In the early sixties the Multilateral Nuclear Force was a similar kind of essay.[10] Another line of reform has sought not to reorganize the unity of the Alliance around two centres, but to give the Europeans greater participation in decisions taken in Washington.[11] Progress along both lines has been extremely slow. Europe itself rejected the EDC, thus illustrating its own unwillingness to unite into a military "pillar". Any scheme to create an independent "European" nuclear deterrent founders not only on the divisions of the Europeans but on America's unwillingness to connive at proliferation and thus to compromise irrevocably the dream of achieving, through effective arms control, a sort of world nuclear condominium with the Russians.[12] As a result, all American offers of nuclear weapons to Europe, the MLF for example, insist on an American veto over their use. But if the weapons cannot be used except with American permission they therefore do not constitute an independent European deterrent. Thus the American schemes not only fall far short of what Europeans want, but are an insult to their intelligence. Europeans tend to be

135

interested in schemes like the MLF only insofar as they believe they will initiate a process leading ultimately to an independent European deterrent.[13] But it is precisely that possibility that so outrages the Russians and thus conflicts head-on with the fundamental American policy of seeking a concert of the two nuclear superpowers.

In the face of all these difficulties, it is not surprising that many students have concluded that the whole two-pillars approach is inappropriate to the military side of the Alliance and sought instead to find some institutional way to give the Europeans a satisfactory voice in America's own strategic plans and decisions. Many of these proposals have come from the Europeans themselves. In the late fifties, for example, de Gaulle suggested a Triple Directorate of Britain, France and America, to co-ordinate Alliance strategy.[14] Some, indeed, see his whole present policy as the result of his despair of ever being heard in Washington. For several years, British and French military experts have been recommending the development of a more effective consultative machinery.

All proposals have seemingly run into one major obstacle: the unwillingness and possibly the inability of the United States to share control of its significant forces and strategy. Not surprisingly, no American President has been willing to give over to foreigners the decision to begin a conflict that can easily result in the annihilation of most people living in the United States. Nor, in brief moments of supreme danger, has any President shown himself willing to have his freedom to act entangled in the deliberations of some international committee. The result, lack of consultation in moments of supreme crisis, has been unnerving and unsatisfactory even to the most ardent British supporters of NATO, not to mention those on the continent whose enthusiasm for the Alliance and confidence in America are less secure. And many people who are willing to concede that the ultimate decision to use nuclear weapons must be left to a single leader, nevertheless see a wide field for consultation beforehand in weapons-development, general strategy and contingency planning for predictable emergencies.[15] Most allied governments, it is said, would be far more willing to entrust the ultimate decisions to the United States if they were allowed a voice in the complicated discussions that lead to these final decisions. Consultation could somehow compensate for control. But it is extremely difficult, it is also said, to integrate foreign governments into the complicated, hectic and partisan process by which high policy is made in the American government. It is claimed, however, that in the last few years, the NATO Standing Group has finally developed into a reasonably satisfactory consultative forum.[16] But for twenty years of talk, progress along these lines does seem to have been very slow.

Meanwhile the whole structure of the Alliance has been overtaken by events. For the new quarrels between the United States and France are not the result of a lack of consultation, but of a fundamental conflict between Europe's interests, at least as seen by France, and the policies of the American government. The present question is no longer how the Alliance structure might usefully be reformed and according to which of the two patterns. It has rapidly become a question of whether there will be any Atlantic Alliance at all.

The tensions within the Alliance have been brought into sharp focus by the policies and pronouncements of Gaullist France, most dramatically in 1966, when the French withdrew from the military arrangements of NATO, though not, they said, from the Alliance itself. American troops and NATO bases were subsequently ordered off French soil.[17] For years, France has been unhappy with the structure of the Alliance. In the late fifties, as mentioned just above, she began agitating unsuccessfully for some sort of Alliance directorate made up of Britain, France and the United States. In the early sixties, France adamantly opposed the American initiative to create a European Multilateral Nuclear Force while continuing to develop her own national nuclear deterrent. French military experts have promoted a whole strategic doctrine completely at variance with current American nuclear strategy.[18] In 1963, France frustrated President Kennedy's Grand Design by vetoing Britain's entry into the Common Market, which, among other things, greatly reduced the scope of the Trade Expansion Act and hence vitiated the potential of the Kennedy Round.[19] In recent years, France has increasingly criticized American policy throughout the world in general. De Gaulle has been conducting his own exercise in "escalation" as he has gradually moved from describing America's role in Vietnam as "unfortunate" to calling it frankly "detestable".[20] France also went out of her way to take an independent line in the Arab-Israeli conflict in 1967. On the monetary front, by ostentatiously preferring gold for dollars as reserves, France has exacerbated America's balance of payments difficulties while, at the same time, sabotaging American schemes for easing the dollar's problems by reforming the world's monetary system. France's flirting with the communist bloc, including China, has scarcely been reassuring to the Americans. De Gaulle's rude jolt to the Canadians was infuriating and his criticisms of Israel have won him few friends in the United States. In general, his penchant for power politics throughout the world has been regarded as a dangerous unsettling force. Indeed, de Gaulle's France has seemingly gone perversely out of her way to contradict every one of the shibboleths of American policy: European federalism, British entrance into the Common Market, counter-force strategy, the MLF, monetary reform, non-proliferation and containing China.

Most serious of all, not only has France attacked America's policy in the world in general, but she has gradually unfolded a strategy for Europe's future which envisages a sharp reduction in America's European role. Furthermore, the French views have been making considerable progress in altering the perspectives of other Europeans, most notably perhaps in Germany.

How is it possible that France should be able to bid against the United States for the leadership of Western Europe? To begin with, as a territorially self-satisfied country, with a rich and balanced economy, world-wide diplomatic and cultural connections, no seriously debilitating foreign military commitments, and with no vital interests at variance with those of anyone else in Western Europe, France has been in an excellent position to play an independent role in today's world. Directed, as she has been, by a determined and prestigious government, she has been the natural leader of the Six. Thus as the Community has become an increasingly coherent assemblage, France has reaped the greatest political rewards.

While the French have been opposed to supranationalism, as much on practical as ideological grounds, they nevertheless have contributed a great deal to the actual economic integration of Western Europe.[21] Indeed, their pressure for a common market in agriculture has brought about probably the most impressive of the EEC's achievements to date. It might also be argued, and certainly is believed privately by many partisans of federal Europe, that French resistance to Britain in

1958 and 1963 saved the Common Market from being diluted into a politically meaningless free trade area. In any event, on internal matters within the Community, the French generally get their way. This predominance has given France a special position in the international economic issues involving the Six together, the Kennedy Round, for example, or monetary reform. In short, for the moment at least, France has been the chief diplomatic beneficiary of the growing economic and financial strength of the European "pillar". As that bloc has become a great trading and financial power, capable of treating with the United States on something like equal terms, France, with some success, challenged America's economic leadership.

On the military side, on the other hand, as the relation between Europe and America remains ostensibly as unbalanced as ever, France is certainly in no position to replace the US as the military protector. If military power were the determining factor, it would be ludicrous to suppose that Germany, for example, would ever throw over America and turn to France. But military power is not necessarily the determining consideration. There are a number of factors that have seriously reduced the political significance of America's overwhelming military superiority. To begin with, the "balance of terror" by which the two super-powers have effectively neutralized each other's nuclear superiority creates a strange "shadow world" in which the giants are unwilling or unable to make use of their full military strength.[22] Thus the spectacle of the world's military colossus apparently unable to conclude successfully a war with one of the smaller backward states of Asia. Russia's humiliations in the Middle East have been less direct, but not dissimilar.[23]

In addition, the French have further questioned the relevance of America's nuclear superiority by their strategic theory that suggests that a comparatively small national deterrent can protect a country like France from the threat of an actual foreign military invasion. The French have also questioned whether a United States that is increasingly embroiled in the Third World and torn by domestic conflict, can be relied upon in the long-run to go on pledging its cities in Europe's defence. Rather paradoxically, the French have also at other times advanced the argument that the United States can never allow Europe to be overrun by the Russians anyway and that there is no reason to pay too high a price for this inevitable protection.[24] Many Europeans are at least willing to concur that they can do little, one way or another, to affect American policy.

A second major factor undermining America's leadership among the Europeans is the widespread lack of enthusiasm for America's international involvements in such places as the Far East and the Caribbean. Rightly or wrongly, continentals see little danger for themselves in the progress of national communist movements in backward parts of the world. But they do feel keenly the danger of being involved, in spite of themselves, in perilous nuclear confrontations springing from the wayward international adventures of the superpowers.

It can be argued, of course, that these perils are part of the price Europe must expect to pay for American protection against Russia. The United States is committed to stopping communism not just in Europe but throughout the world. This argument was more effective at the time of the Korean War than it is now. Today it is countered by yet another factor working against American leadership in Europe. Europeans now generally see Russia as a far lesser menace to their security than in the early 1950s. De Gaulle has taken this widespread view and elaborated from it a grand strategy calling for the progressive military disengagement of America from Europe. De Gaulle believes that Russia, under pressure from China, will eventually be willing to make a reasonable settlement in Europe that would, at last, repair the ravages of Yalta. But, the Gaullists suggest, Russia would be far more prepared to come to terms with a Western Europe that was disengaged from the world rivalry of the superpowers. Russia could thus ensure for herself a friendly and stable European system that would provide great economic opportunities and pose no military threat. Nothing prevents this development except Russia's forlorn hope of maintaining the present regime in East Germany. But once the German question was settled the relations between the East and the West of Europe would be friendly, intimate and stable. Europe would have no territorial ambitions and thus pose no threat to Russia. What about Russia's threat to Europe?

De Gaulle has seldom been accused of a complacent disregard for national independence. The logic of these ideas would seem to call for a strong independent nuclear deterrent in Western Europe. Europe would presumably have to possess sufficient military force

140

so that her own independence did not depend entirely on Russian good will. This consideration alone suggests a long life for the Atlantic Alliance. De Gaulle himself has said often enough that Europe's security requires a more or less permanent defensive alliance with the American deterrent, perhaps even an indefinite American military presence on European soil. Such a relation, however, cannot continue to be an alliance that in effect gives to America the military control of Europe. With that sort of hegemonic alliance no European settlement with Russia would really be possible. Whereas an independent, self-satisfied Europe cannot be considered a military threat to Russia, immensely powerful America, extended throughout the world, must always be Russia's rival. Thus, according to the French, Europe can never escape from the divisions of Yalta as long as it remains caught up in a military alliance so dominated by America that Europe becomes merely a forward base of American military power.[25] Europe according to the French, has every reason to keep her distance from the United States. For unlike the Americans, Europeans have no more extensive military commitments in the Third World and thus are no longer constrained to fight a depressing and dangerous series of rearguard actions to defend the remnants of Western colonialism. Trimmed of her empires, Europe, in fact, is admirably suited for a future world system organized around indigenous nationalisms rather than ideologies and spheres of influence—both outmoded imperialist concepts, de Gaulle believes, clung to by the superpowers to rationalize their attempts to dominate the rest of the globe.

These Gaullist views, gradually elaborated over the past few years, have a grand sweep and refreshing novelty that makes them extremely seductive for many Europeans. They have made a gradual progress not only in France itself, where they are probably predominant, but in Europe generally. Their most spectacular advance appears to have occurred in Germany with the advent to power of the Kiesinger Coalition Government in 1966. Since that time, de Gaulle's influence over German policy, greatly reduced after the retirement of Adenauer, has had a striking revival. A Franco-German entente has always been, of course, the major precondition for a Western European political bloc. Until recently, at least, the Germans had seemed so preoccupied with the threat of Russian military invasion that they appeared willing to do almost anything to conserve American support. Gaullism is not in high favour with American officials. Why do the Germans now seem to be moving, however cautiously, towards Gaullist views?

To start with, West Germany's traditional policy, after twenty years, has obviously not got anywhere towards reuniting the country. America's overriding interest in a Russian entente is not necessarily a promising sign for Germany's future.[26] Meanwhile, East Germany grows more and more distinctive and the problems and probability of its reintegration more discouraging. In addition, de Gaulle's view of a looser European grouping more open to the East and less tied to the West appeals to a number of elements in Germany. The German Left, for example, has always resisted tying up West Germany in a purely Atlantic grouping that emphasizes her separation not only from her Eastern half, but also from Germany's traditional identity with *Mitteleuropa*.[27] From the early postwar days radical Protestant leaders opposed what they saw as Adenauer's Rhineland Catholic policy of fixing Germany into a tight, anti-Communist Western European Union.[28]

The Vietnam War has not increased American popularity in Germany and de Gaulle's outspoken condemnation of it has gained him considerable admiration, possibly because Germans are weary of the tone of moral superiority and incipient hysteria usually adopted by the Anglo-Saxon press in discussing German politics.

Germans are also increasingly resentful of the high-handed way in which both the United States and Britain try to extract more and more payment for the troops stationed in Germany. The German economy has recently been having its own difficulties.[29] As part of the offset costs, Germans have been strongly pressed to buy American military equipment, to the detriment of Franco-German military and technological co-operation. As resistance to American technological domination becomes a greater concern, so does interest in European rather than American armaments. Rather tactless disregard of long-range German interests in the proposals for a non-proliferation treaty has exacerbated German suspicions that they are coming to be taken too much for granted by their big ally. It is easy, no doubt, to exaggerate the effect of all these forces. Disenchantment with America does not necessarily mean enthusiasm for de Gaulle. Nevertheless, the Kiesinger Government has made it quiet clear that maintaining close and friendly ties with France is a primary German interest, in the same order of importance as maintaining its ties with the United States.[30]

In short, there do seem to be numerous factors pushing the Germans into close collaboration with France and away from the close and rather subservient relation with America that has been the cornerstone of Germany's postwar policy. With the Franco-German entente once again in good health, France, more than ever, assumes a position of leadership challenging America's hegemony within the West. The only development likely to re-establish that hegemony would be a renewal of Russia's military threat, an eventuality neither expected by many in Western Europe today nor hoped for by many in America.

To recapitulate, the economic integration of Europe has created an immense economic power, a development that has not yet been accompanied, as many Americans once hoped, by the creation of a federal state. There is, nevertheless, already a certain tendency for the Six to act together as a European bloc. So far, France has emerged as the leading power within this political concentration. France's pre-eminence arises partly from her natural advantages, partly from the skill of her government in making French policies appear in harmony with the interests of Europe. Increasingly, France has used her base in Europe to challenge the hegemonic structure of the Western military Alliance; and indeed by pulling out of NATO, cultivating Russia, and attacking American policy generally, France had seemed to cast doubts on the continuation of the Atlantic Alliance itself. All this forms the general context of any new American policy towards the Atlantic Alliance.

What should America do about France's challenge? America's first, almost instinctive reaction has been to patch up NATO's bureaucratic structure to carry on without the French.[31] But whether such arrangements will prove durable without major changes is certainly open to question. Should the United States, as advocates of NAFTA suggest, build a smaller but more intense Atlantic military structure, reinforced by an important economic dimension? Or alternatively, should the US seek a new pattern for the Alliance that genuinely fosters and comes to terms with a new independent Europe?

There are strong partisans in America of the first course. Besides the usual partisans of bureaucratic and intellectual self-preservation, there are many who see NATO as the key grouping in a series of interlocking economic and military relationships which offer the

143

best hope for restoring some stable structuring of power to a world thrown into turmoil by the collapse of Europe and its empires. It may well be that this great American vision, discussed in the first section of this chapter, offers mankind's best hope for a civilized future. But like any vast design, it can only succeed if limited resources are governed by realistic priorities. America is doing a great many things at once—fighting a war in Vietnam, upholding NATO, operating a vast aid programme, investing heavily in Europe, running the world's major reserve currency and carrying forward an unprecedented programme of domestic reform.

In due course, it might make more sense for America to accommodate, indeed to encourage, a Europe determined to be independent than to resist it. What would such an accommodation involve? Obviously America must stop insisting on the hegemonic pattern of the NATO military alliance. Bureaucracies, military no less than civil, hate changes and can always be counted on to advance ingenious and solid arguments against them. Nevertheless, there is probably a good deal to be said for scrapping, in due course, much of the whole NATO apparatus. The United States should continue to offer the continent its nuclear guarantee and perhaps a continuing military "presence." A good deal of the initiative for the actual arrangements should be left to the Europeans. After all, it is their security that is at stake and America must escape from the absurd position of begging other people to take her help. In this respect, something might be learned from General de Gaulle's treatment of German demands for the withdrawal of French troops from Germany.[32]

In any event, the new arrangements cannot be such that they assume identical "North Atlantic" policies towards Russia and the Third World. It must be faced that, rightly or wrongly, a great many Europeans do not share America's enthusiasm for intervening to "stop communism" in the Third World. An Alliance based on a common world policy is therefore bound to break down, no matter how much "consultation" takes place.

It may well be, of course, that the U.S., once extricated from the Vietnam War, will come to appreciate more fully Europe's diffidence about getting involved in foreign interventions. It may also be that as the Europeans grow more united and hence stronger and more confident, they may adopt a less complacent and more active stance towards the outside world. Europe and the

United States may meet in a common view, but the necessity for an Atlantic Alliance does not depend upon such unpredictable accidents and vague fluctuations of official and public opinion. It depends instead on the primordial common European and American interest in preventing a world war and in maintaining an independent, prosperous, democratic Western Europe, capable of defending itself against Russian domination. All lesser differences nothwithstanding, this remains the fundamental common interest, and it is best fulfilled by a coherent European bloc, however bizarre its constitution may seem to American federalists and however perverse its independence may seem to American diplomats.

As for the argument that the new Europe will become some sort of Frankenstinian monster, right-wing and unstable inside, aggressive to Russia and the old colonies outside, a force to be feared by America, it is difficult to imagine any objective factors that should make this so. No doubt a strong Europe will have a mind of its own; it will, like America, develop its own special relationship with Russia, and will increasingly compete for trade and influence in the underdeveloped world. It is hard to see the evil in this. It is a return to life in a world whose vitality has been too long frozen by the Cold War. America has little to fear from an open and stable Europe. American businessmen are not unused to competition. American diplomats have no monopoly on solving the world's problems. That Europe, the most vulnerable of all the major world centres to nuclear attack, should ever launch a general war seems the least likely imaginable cause of World War III. In short, the notion of the new European union as a threat to America or to world peace is not likely to gain any deep conviction.

For America to alienate a major part of Western Europe or to attempt to provoke internecine war among the continentals would benefit no one except possibly the Russians. Serious economic or political warfare with the US would inevitably force France and her possible allies to become far more anti-American and far more dependent on Russia than they or anyone else might wish. If the US somehow managed to break up the Six, a divided Western Europe would present the Russians with an almost irresistible opportunity to pursue manoeuvres of the kind that not infrequently lead to war. Furthermore, openly anti-European policies would probably arouse tremendous opposition within the United States and might be the last straw for many Americans already seriously doubtful about the present course of their country's foreign policy. While these considerations may not, in the end, head off angry retaliatory steps by the United States, particularly if the balance of payments does not improve, nevertheless, rational assessment of America's long-range interests may well inhibit radical American initiatives that would run the risk of estranging the United States and Europe. Under the circumstances, it seems questionable that the US will, in a fit of ill-considered pique, saddle itself, as did Britain in 1957, with a free trade area that only fixes and widens the breach with Europe and complicates the tasks of reconciliation.

Upon reflection, it may not seem a wise policy for America to get too involved in Europe's domestic squabbles, particularly on the side that, by any objective view, is not the most dynamic and promising. Britain, in short, may not gain much from America's differences with France; America does not want or need Britain as an anti-French ally in Europe. America's true interest is not to fight France, but to come to terms with her.

Perhaps there is some truth in the English fear of the fifties that European Union was the programme of American isolationists There are not many isolationists in the old sense left in America. But it seems quite likely that a new generation of American leadership, faced with cruel and frightening domestic problems and increasingly serious exchange difficulties, will come to take a very cold look at America's world burdens. Rich Europe is quite capable of taking a much greater share or responsibility for her own defence. It is time she did.

But the US cannot have it both ways. A strong, self-sustaining Europe means an independent, self-determining Europe and the end of American "hegemony". In theory, the American government has always accepted this. But in practice, American bureaucrats, politicians and scholars have been extremely reluctant to acknowledge the possibility of any form of European unity except the rather banal federalist formulas that bemuse the official American imagination. And American diplomacy, in spite of its good intentions, has not been able to resist the time-honoured imperial tactic of sustaining the weak to keep down the strong. Hence, the often pointless quarrel between the US and Gaullist France.

But for an over-strained America, compelled to reduce its commitments to the level of its material and spiritual resources, the real danger is not that de Gaulle's vision will succeed in Europe, but that it will fail, that Europe will remain forever a divided and irresponsible protectorate. While it is doubtless too much to expect the US to foster Gaullist leadership, there is already a certain slight American inclination to see a Gaullist Europe, proud and eager to play a world role, as more compatible with long-range American interests than the docile but sedentary invalid that might superficially seem the better alternative. Upon sober reflection, there are likely to be a great many worse fates for France, Europe and the Atlantic alliance than the grand schemes of General de Gaulle. There is, moreover, no reason to assume that a Europe whose political reconstruction is constantly frustrated by trans-Atlantic and internecine quarrels will retain that domestic tranquillity which has been so comforting a feature in the postwar era. Frustration breeds madness. Both the US and Russia court great dangers in confusing inertia with stability.

What are the prospects for a confederal Europe of States? There can be no certainty, but there is every reason for hope. That Europe has great economic power is already a fact. That there is slowly developing a European point of view, distinct from America's is also true. That this point of view may gradually express itself in a distinctive European political will seems not improbable. That this new grouping will, in the long run, insist on appropriate military capabilities also seems probable, if not inevitable. And such a new Europe is even more certain to reject any subordinate economic and financial position within the institutions of the non-communist world. What all this will amount to is that the Western Alliance, in the broadest sense, will either be a limited partnership of equals or there will be no Alliance at all. And however inconvenient the process of readjusting American ideas and practices may turn out to be, the United States will have to frame its policy accordingly or see itself alienated from a great new force that it has done much to create. In short, the major task of American diplomacy will be reconstituting relations with Europe around economic and military arrangements genuinely acceptable to Europeans.

Doubtless, it would have been convenient for America if Britain had got into Europe, complete with her world-wide views and commitments and special military partnership. But whatever the illusions may once have been, it should now be clear that

147

Britain cannot get into Europe as the Anglo-Saxon "Trojan Horse". To join Europe, Britain must acquire, to a far greater extent, the perspectives of a European power. Washington may not be as reluctant to see this transformation as the British sometimes imagine or the Americans sometimes pretend. Britain should not make too much of America's current involvement in peacekeeping. The tragedy of the Vietnam War has perhaps given a greatly exaggerated view of America's imperial predilections; the experience is not likely to encourage repetition. America too has limited resources and domestic difficulties. Britain, having so gracefully given up her own empire, should not make the mistake of clinging vicariously to America's. Finally, whether Europe is "outward-looking" in the imperial sense is of far less real importance to America than that it should be strong, democratic and stable. A Britain wholeheartedly committed to Europe could do much to ensure its success. A Britain unhappily lurking on the fringes only complicates America's problems.

It is sometimes said that America needs Britain's moral support in her lonely task of watchman on the walls of world freedom. Certainly America will always rejoice in the companionship of Britain, and of Europe generally. No doubt, the Johnson Administration, caught in the toils of a painful dilemma, is grateful for sympathy from anywhere. But, in the long run, America is more likely to profit from conversation with a Europe that is strong, proud and independent, and whose views compel attention. America today is chiefly in danger of that kind of isolation which comes to powerful men who deal with alien lands where people are objects with whom no meaningful conversation is possible. The British should know about these imperial problems. The imperial side of the American character is not one the British will find attractive. A strong Europe may be good for the European soul; it will certainly be beneficial for the American.

Finally, it must be said that while it is all very well for Americans to push Britain into Europe, the decision is Britain's, not America's. No one should underestimate the painful difficulties that joining Europe involves for the British. It is entirely understandable that the difficulties may prove too great. It is possible that if Britain cannot or will not go into Europe, some kind of Atlantic accommodation can be found. But to Americans, it will not seem the ideal solution for Britain's future. The welcome will not be the proverbial joy reserved for the return of prodigal children, but the restrained enthusiasm appropriate to an ageing daughter who cannot find a husband.

5. *Summary: Anglo-Saxon Attitudes*

What, in summary, is to be said of the case for Britain's joining an "Atlantic" free trade area, built around close ties with the US in preference to joining the Common Market? The immediate effect on Britain's balance of trade would probably be marginal. If harmful, it would be less so than joining Europe. British firms and technology, however, would face the full brunt of competition with the American giants, without the opportunities the EEC provides for constructing equivalent European combines in which large British firms might often take the lead. American capital might flow to Britain because of lower costs, but would be more likely to come if Britain were inside Europe. NAFTA might strengthen the useful banking ties and give more dollar support to the pound, but sterling's role as a reserve currency and London's as a financial centre would be increasingly redundant. As the next chapter attempts to show, it seems improbable that the needs of the underdeveloped countries somehow oblige Britain to join NAFTA rather than the EEC. The most convincing argument for Britain's joining the kind of NAFTA envisaged by its proponents is that, since it leaves out agricultural products, Britain can secure freer trade in wider markets without paying the high Common Market food prices. Beyond, for those who fear the loss of sovereignty, NAFTA, like its military counterpart, NATO, offers a tie not likely to grow into a genuine federal association that would gradually merge Britain into a larger nation. If, in this respect, NAFTA poses few political dangers for Britain, it also offers few opportunities. Britain might lead Europe. She will certainly not lead America. Indeed, as the second great power in "Atlantica", she will be increasingly a political anachronism. This may be the price Britain will have to pay for her inability to come to terms with a Gaullist Europe. NAFTA will be the reluctant alternative.

Positive enthusiasm for NAFTA and Atlantica is something else again. It should probably be seen as the last and rather despairing expression of the self-conscious Anglo-Saxonism of the last century.

It is, of course, not the less for that. It is easy to sympathize with the traditions, emotions and values that are, for many people, bound up in the Anglo-Saxon tie across the water. Certainly much that is finest in American life and institutions comes from the conscious and unconscious anglophilia that has informed the great American universities and enriched the culture of the established classes generally.

But Shakespeare was not a Stockbroker Tudor. Both Britain and America have been saved from becoming cultural backwaters by the constant infusion and creative absorption of continental influences. It would be an alarming confession of cultural weakness for Britain and America to allow themselves to become bewildered and frightened by the revival of Europe and to retreat, ignominiously, into a provincial and dated Anglo-Saxonism.

VI.
Commonwealth
Claims

1. *Commonwealth Prospects*

Previous chapters have scarcely discussed what is probably the most singular feature of Britain's world position, the British Commonwealth of Nations. Today the Commonwealth is rather out of favour in England. To many, it appears to offer no real opportunities, only large and tedious burdens.[1] Indeed, the entire notion of a Commonwealth is frequently regarded as nothing more than a grandiose illusion, helpful while Britain gradually reconciled herself to the loss of a world empire. The whole fantastic exercise might have been harmless enough, critics believe, except that it has unfortunately, so totally engaged the British political imagination since the war that there has been very little left for more useful employment elsewhere.

These exaggerated reactions, like the American view that European unity is dead, doubtless come from having naïvely expected too much in the first place. The Commonwealth has often been talked about as if it could be an alternative grouping in which Britain could invest her future—comparable to the EEC or a close Atlantic Union.[2] Measured against this expectation the Commonwealth is inevitably a dismal failure. The day has long since passed, if it ever existed, when the old Empire, or a substantial portion of it, could be translated into a federal world super-state or even a coherent power bloc.[3] But to say that the Commonwealth does not offer in itself a solution for Britain's long-range problems is not to say that the Commonwealth should be destroyed or its needs and opportunities ignored in considering Britain's role and alignments for the future. For the Commonwealth does encompass a real network of communication and interest—a heritage stemming from generations of loyalties, interests, education, friendships and habits—that presents Britain with unique opportunities and obligations. But with the Commonwealth, as with so many other things, an appreciation of its real possibilities demands a firm understanding of its limitations.

On paper, the Commonwealth is still an extremely imposing assemblage of nations richly endowed with population and resources. Indeed, its 755 million people form one quarter the world's population, and its 14 million square miles of territory one quarter the globe's land surface.[4] Why is it impossible to weld all this into an effective world grouping that would provide ample scope for British trade and world leadership? The reasons are obvious to any student of world politics. The most striking feature of the Commonwealth is the extreme diversity of the members. There are, in a sense, several different Commonwealths—each with quite different relations with Britain. There are the old white dominions to whom Britain is still the "Mother Country"—Canada, Australia and New Zealand. There is the Asian Commonwealth, containing two strong and important States, India and Pakistan, and Malaysia and the Chinese outposts of Singapore and Hong Kong. Finally, there is the Black Commonwealth of Africa as well as holdings in the Caribbean, Indian Ocean and Pacific. Beyond there is the schismatic Commonwealth of Rhodesia and South Africa driven out as incompatible with the Afro-Asian members.

Historians are unlikely to spend much time pointing out why such a heterogeneous assemblage could never be transformed from an empire maintained by force into a federal state upheld by consent. It has been an axiom of modern political theory that a democratic state can only exist when there is a political "consensus" among its elements—a shared loyalty and compatibility of interest sufficiently strong to overcome the inevitable centrifugal pulls of separatist interests and allegiances. The Commonwealth obviously is not suited to becoming a unified federal state. Could it become a confederal alliance like NATO or a supranational union like the Common Market? Here again, the same axiom applies. There must be some commonly accepted unifying element that holds the assorted members together. In some alliances unity is provided chiefly because one member is sufficiently powerful or attractive to set policy for the whole. Carried to its extreme, this relationship becomes more of an empire than an alliance. At the other extreme a group of more or less equal powers may persistently act together because they perceive a clear, strong and urgent common interest. If this area of interest widens and co-operation becomes habitual, the alliance may move forward towards some more federal union. NATO is perhaps an example of the first kind of alliance, the Common Market of the second.

For the British Commonwealth neither situation today applies. Britain is no longer a compelling enough centre to hold the outlying elements in their orbits. She is neither powerful enough militarily to dominate and protect the group, not rich enough to serve its economic needs. And with so heterogeneous a membership, spanning all the races and all inhabited continents, there are no sufficiently compelling common interests to replace the bond once provided by British wealth and power.

Not surprisingly, the Commonwealth has developed in a fashion best calculated to disturb as little as possible the inertia of its remaining traditional loyalties. Britain tries to discourage the raising of issues that expose the conflicts of interest inherent in the diverse membership. Hence, the Commonwealth has seldom attempted to act as a bloc on any major issue. Whenever strong feeling has forced discussion of issues important to the members —like the Rhodesia question—the group has come perilously close to breaking up. As a result the Commonwealth's unifying structure has become more and more intangible—indeed so intangible that the institution was recently able to survive a war between two of its principal members, India and Pakistan.

What are these ties at once so durable and yet so indefinite? Institutionally, it is true, there is relatively little on an official level. The Crown has a symbolic role as Head rather than Monarch, since so many of its members have decided to become republics. There is a small Commonwealth secretariat established after much hesitation.[5] There have been annual meetings of Commonwealth Prime Ministers,[6] although the more extensive consultations of ministers once envisaged seem gradually to have been discontinued.[7]

Beyond the inevitably unpromising official level, there are many cultural ties that come from a common language and educational practices and, for many people in important positions, a common

153

university education. These ties are enhanced by a vast private network nourished by numerous foundations and publications. The whole experience of Empire with its confrontations, habits and loyalties is still deeply felt among the former rulers, colonists and subjects. There is indeed an immense *communauté anglophone* that covers all races and continents. These cultural sympathies are different, however, for each part of the Commonwealth and indeed among various social classes in Britain and elsewhere. The ties of "kith and kin" with the old dominions are obviously different, if not necessarily stronger than, say, the relationships formed by generations of Indian students at English universities. Unfortunately, however, many of these Commonwealth loyalties are conflicting. Thus, for example, the conflict between white settlers and the black population in Africa has not only driven a wedge between the black and white members of the Commonwealth, but has gradually polarized Commonwealth sympathies in England into two opposing camps. The Right Wing is worried about the beleaguered whites; the Left about the oppressed blacks. Thus the diverse cultural sympathies between England and her old subjects carry within themselves the inherent conflicts that make a viable union impossible.

Beyond the links of politics and culture, there are the links of money and trade. The economic ties at least might be expected to bring concrete benefits to England. It is true that there is an extensive system of preferential tariffs which give a substantial preferential treatment—roughly an average of 7% before the Kennedy Round and devaluation—to British exports in many Commonwealth countries.[8]

Commonwealth trade has been increasing, although, as we have seen, far more slowly than trade with Europe and the US. As a result, since 1958, the proportion of British exports to the Commonwealth dropped from 32·2% in 1958 to 28·4% in 1965.[9] Nevertheless, Britain still trades more with the Commonwealth than with any other country or bloc. How important is the preferential tariff to that trade? Does it really benefit Britain and the Commonwealth? Common sense naturally suggests that it does, but some economists, concerned about the misallocation of resources caused by distorting effects of preferences, are more dubious and feel the subject has never been adequately studied.[10]

Moreover, there is doubt that the system will long endure in the face of opposition and competition from the US and the EEC.

The sterling area is itself another economic tie between Britain and much, if not all, of the Commonwealth. Whether for England it represents an advantage as well as a tie is, as we have seen, highly doubtful.[11] Likewise, Britain's heavy Commonwealth investment over the years, while obviously beneficial to the recipients, is a similarly ambiguous boon to Britain. As noted earlier, recent studies, though by no means definitive and uncontested, nevertheless do suggest that Britain's high rate of foreign investment has had an adverse net effect on her domestic economy.[12] At any rate, British investment, hampered by the general weakness of the economy, is hardly adequate to meet the needs and opportunities of the Commonwealth countries. Similarly with official economic aid, since Britain's contribution is only 7 or 8% of the world's total effective aid,[13] the Commonwealth is clearly not held together by economic assistance from the British Government. There is nothing, it should be said, that is surprising or shaming in this. The Commonwealth has only 10% of the population of the developed world but 30% of that of the underdeveloped.[14] Obviously, it cannot be a self-sufficient bloc.

In addition to official, cultural and commercial connections, the Commonwealth also involves real if indefinite military obligations for mutual defence. Britain's major effort in recent years has been in Malaysia, first in extirpating the Communist insurgents and then in seeing the new state through its "confrontation" with Indonesia. Both operations were impressively successful. But Britain's precarious balance of payments and faltering domestic economy make it highly unlikely that she will want to continue an important military role throughout the world. The accelerated retreat from Aden clearly seems the likely pattern for the future. Sentiment for withdrawing from "East of Suez" now unites an impressive if heterogeneous coalition of forces in British politics. Since the defence cuts of January, 1968, the withdrawal seems imminent and definitive.[15]

In any event, in those places like the Far East where protection may well be needed in the future, a British alliance alone could offer no security to countries like Australia or India. The real defence of most of the Commonwealth has long ago been taken over by the United States. Acting as a superfluous middleman between Commonwealth countries and the United States is hardly a promising role. As was suggested in the chapter just preceding, Britain's close identification with American military policy in the Third World not only harms Britain in Europe, but may well curtail the influential and useful role she might otherwise be expected to play in the Third World generally.

In summary, although mutual ties of sympathy and culture are still strong, trade remains substantial and Britain's contribution in investment and military support are far from negligible, Britain lacks the resources to build round the historic ties of the Empire a coherent bloc of countries in which she would take the principal role. In the absence of British predominance there is, in so varied an assemblage, no other sufficiently compelling general interest or identity to form an effectively unified association. Under the circumstances, it is not surprising that the Commonwealth structure has remained as ethereal as it has or that no progress has been made towards the dream of many in Britain after the war—a coherent Commonwealth bloc, uniting countries of different races and different stages of economic development and standing for peace and development outside the sterile rivalries of the cold war. This vision was an attractive one, but far too ambitious.

2. *The Commonwealth and Britain's Alternatives*

The situation described above has suggested to some people that the postwar Commonwealth represents a body in search of a head. This view quite naturally leads to the hope that Britain might, by forming a partnership with some other sympathetic advanced country or group, acquire the resources necessary to meet the possibilities and obligations of the Commonwealth ties. France has, in fact, managed to perform such an operation, albeit on a smaller scale, with her ex-colonies, by attaching them to the Common Market.[1] Could Britain, by joining more closely with the United States or Europe, perform a similar feat?[2]

One of the most frequently heard arguments in favour of an Atlantic association like NAFTA is that it would be far better for the interests of the Commonwealth than Britain's joining the EEC. How valid is this position? Do the interests of the Commonwealth impel Britain into an Atlantic rather than the European Association?

This is an argument whose meaning is often not very clear. In the effort to provide something for everybody in NAFTA, a number of unrelated and sometimes contradictory points frequently find themselves restively linked together. On one level, it is argued that membership in a free-trade area—conceived of as a sort of giant EFTA—would, like EFTA, allow Britain to continue with Commonwealth preference arrangements.[3] As there would be no commitment to extensive harmonization of national policies, as in the EEC, Britain in NAFTA would therefore be freer to maintain her old political links with the Commonwealth. The trouble with the first point is that the United Sates is strongly opposed to preferential trading blocs that, like the Commonwealth, are restricted and reciprocal.[4] The US can therefore hardly be expected to look with favour upon a new trading group that allows these preferential arrangements to continue. As for the political links between Britain and the Commonwealth, joining NAFTA in preference to the EEC may not disturb them, but it is unlikely to strengthen them or, more to the point, do much to arrest their steady deterioration. Certainly, it should be clear by now that the US has small need for British introductions in its direct intercourse with the Commonwealth countries.

On another level, it is frequently argued that NAFTA could be an excellent vehicle for organizing a general system of preferences to be granted by the developed countries for the products of the Third World as a whole—a system such as the United States has recommended to UNCTAD II.[5] Perhaps such a role could be annexed to NAFTA, but a free-trade among Britain, Canada and the US will not, in and of itself, be of any particular advantage to the developing countries. Any additional arrangements to stabilize and give preferences to trade from developing countries would be far more effective if they included the EEC, which imports even more from the Third World than does the United States.

But, for those NAFTA enthusiasts who tacitly or openly espouse the anti-Market case, the EEC is an "inward-looking", continental protectionist federation, incapable of joining a free-trade area and selfishly unconcerned with the underdeveloped countries. A NAFTA of Britain, Canada and the US, on the other hand, would be a nucleus of merchant countries, traditionally "outward-looking" and hence more favourable to the trade and welfare of the Third World. This view so neatly corresponds to traditional Anglo-Saxon prejudices that it probably ought to be treated with considerable scepticism. How closely does the view that Europe is comparatively "inward-looking" in its economic relations with the Third World square with the facts?

In the field of government aid to underdeveloped countries, as noted in Chapter II, it does not square at all. While the nominal amount of official American economic aid to the underdeveloped countries is nearly five times that of France, the American GNP is roughly seven times greater. Moreover, when interest and repayment terms are taken into account, effective French aid can be reckoned, in absolute totals, as one-third that of the US. Britain, on the other hand, gives in effect only one quarter as much as France and only one-fifth as much in proportion to her GNP. Britain's aid programme in reality is roughly equivalent to that of the supposedly "inward-looking" Federal Republic of Germany. As for Atlantic "outward-looking" Canada, her aid programme is proportionately only one-eighth the size of France's and only a bit more than half that of Britain and Germany. In short, the relative performance of the EEC countries in giving foreign aid gives no support to the notion that they are less interested in the underdeveloped world than Britain, the United States, or other promising candidates for NAFTA. Indeed, the figures, if anything, lead to the contrary conclusion.[6]

The main case for the "inward-lookingness" of the Common Market must necessarily rest on the EEC's trade policies. These policies, it is said, are bad for the Commonwealth countries and for the Third World in general. If Britain were to join the EEC, what would be the probable effects on the trade of the Commonwealth countries?

The Commonwealth, of course, is made up of a variety of states at different stages of development, each with its own products and interests. Each would therefore be affected differently. One group that presumably would be hurt by Britain's joining the EEC would be the Commonwealth producers of temperate agricultural products—Australia, Canada and New Zealand. If Britain joins the Common Market, these three, New Zealand above all, will face a considerable problem as the Common Market's agricultural programme will end their natural advantages in the British market.

No doubt Britain should consider their interests, sympathetically and make every effort to assist their readjustment. But finally they themselves are rich and advanced countries and must no less than Britain make reasonable adaptations to economic and political facts of life. To do them justice, they have already begun to do so.

The developing countries in the Commonwealth are more dependent. But their agricultural products, generally tropical, seldom compete with the domestic agriculture of the EEC countries. The chief problem for them arises from the Common Market's policy of giving preference to the products of its own Associated Overseas Territories in Africa. But there seems no inherent reason why the interests of the tropical countries in the Commonwealth could not be accommodated within an expanded Common Market Association. Indeed, African Commonwealth countries seem to be increasingly attracted towards the Common Market's African bloc and Nigeria has already negotiated an associate status. The Common Market, for its part, seems willing enough to absorb new African associated members. Indeed it is feared that if Britain does not join the Common Market, she may find herself increasingly discriminated against in several Commonwealth markets.[7]

Exports of manufactures from developing countries constitute another major aspect of trade relations. Britain's preferences are helpful, but her market alone cannot absorb more than a fraction of these exports. Hong Kong, for example, sends only 17% of her exports to Britain. The chief barrier to such exports lies less in tariffs than in the tangle of quotas and other forms of restriction imposed generally by the developed countries to protect their own higher-cost industries. Among the Common Market countries, there is no common policy and, in all countries, there is a wide variety of official and unofficial barriers, varying according to product, and difficult to measure and compare.[8] There would seem only fragmentary evidence for the belief that the Six together are substantially more addicted to these barriers than the US, Britain, or Japan, or any less co-operative in seeking to remove them.

The most sophisticated argument for NAFTA holds that the whole Common Market tendency to build a regional bloc of associated states is contrary to the best interests of the developing countries and world trade in general. The Common Market countries pursue, it is said, a policy of building trade blocs because

159

L

they are naturally "mercantilist" in their economic habits, unlike the "liberal" countries that might be interested in NAFTA. This is an extremely complicated and controversial issue, involving fundamental questions in economic theory as well as complex assessments of actual causes and effects. It is difficult to find reliable research that is relevant. Above all, in examining the issue, it is difficult to make clear separation between reality and ideology.

Is the Common Market really more protectionist? On the whole, as we have seen, its industrial tariffs are substantially lower than those of either Britain or the US.[9] "Liberal" England still promotes the Commonwealth trade system, a protectionist bloc that gives it substantial preferences. The United States, itself runs a protectionist agricultural programme at home and maintains comparatively high tariffs. Nevertheless, in this question of trade with the Third World, there is a genuine issue though it often seems hopelessly entangled with propaganda and sharp practice. What is the issue and does it have any real relevance to Britain's choice between Europe and "Atlantica"?

To begin with, in what respect is the US more "liberal" in its attitudes towards trade with the underdeveloped countries? It is fair to say that, since the war, the trade policy of the United States has been informed by that universalist, non-discriminatory approach to trade expressed in the "most-favoured nation" principle, namely that a reduction granted to one country must automatically be extended to all. Thanks to the US, this basic view is enshrined in the governing principle of the General Agreement on Tariffs and Trade (GATT),[10] which, in turn, has been the constitutional charter for world trade agreements since the war. The principles of GATT are both "liberal" and "multilateral". Although concessions are made for regional free trade areas and customs unions, the general spirit of the Agreement leads towards universal, non-discriminatory free trade.

Carried over to the question of how to organize trade with the Third World, the logic of the GATT approach should presumably lead to the abolition of all impediments on trade among all countries; that is, it should lead to free trade on a "multilateral" or universal scale. Thus the United States, true to the logic expressed in GATT, has always looked with disfavour on the Commonwealth system of preferential tariffs because it was both protectionist and discriminatory. Carried logically to its ultimate conclusion, this whole GATT approach should lead not only to free trade—the abolition of tariffs, quotas, and preferences—but also to the end of subsidies to domestic producers and of all restrictions on the free movement of capital and labour.

Almost everyone believes, however, that these classic liberal principles must be modified in their application to the developing countries. In a world where some countries are more advanced than others, free competition is in itself insufficient to advance the backward regions rapidly enough. Substantial investment and aid must flow to these countries to get them started towards a modern economic system.[11] Otherwise, free trade becomes a formula guaranteeing the perpetual inferiority of the backward nations.

But according to the inherent logic of the GATT system, this aid should be given as far as possible so that it does not interfere with the normal workings of the free market. In short, aid should be given as a direct subsidy to sustain and improve production in infant industries without insulating their goods from competition in an open market. Otherwise the market is excessively "distorted" and resources are wasted.[12] It is also part of the logic of this view that politics should be removed as far as possible from aid-giving. There are thus occasional proposals for channelling all aid through a multilateral agency influenced essentially by economic rather than political considerations.[13]

This whole approach has behind it all the theoretical arguments in favour of free trade generally. The freer the market, the more the principle of comparative advantage directs resources where they are made most productive. The appeal of this view is increased by the notorious amount of economic aid that appears to be wasted, waste dictated by politics rather than economics. Not the least cause of this waste lies in the wrong-headed economic policies of the developing countries themselves, above all their own strong protectionist aversion to submitting their economies to the beneficial discipline of market forces. Among the wasteful distortions must be included not only doubtful economic projects built for political reasons, but the whole general policy of "import substitution". Some liberal economists believe that import substitution often leads to a situation where the underdeveloped countries, in the interests of saving foreign exchange or maintaining economic or military "self-sufficiency", artificially seek to build up

161

industries to produce things they will probably always be able to buy more cheaply elsewhere.[14]

In recent years, this whole classic liberal approach, the informing principle of GATT, has come under increasing attack from the underdeveloped countries themselves. These countries organized and concerted their position in 1964 in the first United Nations Conference on Trade and Development (UNCTAD). The general theme of the conference was "trade not aid". To improve their trade prospects sufficiently to make the slogan a reality, the underdeveloped countries proposed a sweeping reorganization of national and international trade policies. On the one hand, the underdeveloped countries demanded that international markets and national policies be organized in such a way as to guarantee increased and stable incomes for the primary products that constitute the major portion of their exports. And, on the other hand, they demanded a general system giving preferential treatment for their manufactures in the developed countries, without requiring reciprocal concessions in return. Altogether, these demands from the underdeveloped countries called for a world market organized so that their primary products would have special preferences.

The United States, apparently unprepared at the Conference, resolutely opposed this whole movement towards a managed market on a world scale, but found not only that it was opposing the developing countries but also that its position got support neither from the Common Market nor from Britain. Britain, which, after all, runs the Commonwealth preference system, doubtless found it awkward to maintain that such arrangements were, in principle uneconomic.[15]

Since the first UNCTAD Conference, the United States has changed its position and at the second UNCTAD Conference in 1967 advocated a general world-wide series of temporary preferences. At the same time, however, the US has intensified its opposition of any regional preference systems linking together particular groups of developed and underdeveloped countries on the grounds that such groups, by their very nature, distort the world market and make uneconomic discriminations. The US is now opposing, for example, the extension of associational arrangements with the Common Market. Indeed the US would, it appears, hope to see the end of the Common Market's special economic ties with France's old African colonies.[16]

The new US position, in short, abandons its strict construction of GATT principles and acquiesces in the general demand for a world-wide series of temporary preferences and guarantees to foster the trade of the underdeveloped countries. But the US wants these arrangements to be as "liberal" as possible. Unlike the Commonwealth, they are not to be "reverse" preferences that give reciprocal advantages to some developed countries. And unlike Common Market association, these preferences are not to discriminate between particular regions, but to be applied to all underdeveloped countries. Thus it is hoped that these American-style preferences will involve a minimum of "mercantilist" distortion while still fostering the trade of the underdeveloped countries.[17] It remains to be seen to what extent these American schemes can be negotiated and put into practice.

Meanwhile, the Common Market's arrangements suggest a third broad way of organizing the relations between rich developed and poor developing countries. They could be organized not on a world-wide system of preferences, as suggested at UNCTAD and now by the US, but into a number of distinct regional blocs, linking together relatively complementary and compatible advanced and developing countries. For the classic, liberal free trader, of course, this approach is doubly heretical, as it is both protectionist and regional. Therefore, lest Britain be contaminated by this antediluvian continental mercantilism, she should stay out of the Common Market and find more congenial company in a liberal free-trade association.

How valid are these fears of regional "neo-mercantilism"? Arguments for the advantages of free trade are always powerful and seductive. They are always, however, up against the usual political facts of life. There is a logic of politics that often, in the course of events, carries more weight than the chaste logic of economic efficiency. Projects built for prestige, for example, often appear ludicrously wasteful. Yet the main problem in the Third World, economic as well as political, lies in a perpetual instability that makes long-range planning impossible and constantly threatens all foreign and domestic investments. Under the circumstances, the first task of any government is to secure public support against unrest and possible subversion. A government that neglects its immediate prestige for more long-term economic goals may turn out to have been extremely short-sighted. It may be true that, as free traders claim, the policy of "import substitution" is often extremely wasteful. It is not less true that infant industries seldom develop at all without special protection over an extended period. Certainly the protection of infant industries in the developing countries is no less justifiable than the protection of senile industries in the advanced countries. Everyone sympathises with the grievances of the developing countries who confront tariff and quota barriers against their manufactures. Yet political logic in the developed countries dictates that domestic industry must, at the very least, be given a reasonable period to adjust to new competitive conditions. The problem, of course, is determining what is "reasonable".

In any event, in all countries, advanced or backward, politics remain as much a fact of life as economics. Indeed the separation between the two, though useful as a means of analysis, is inherently unrealistic. In a world where governmental action through subsidies, tariffs, regulations, tax discriminations, research and public consumption plays such a commanding role in determining the shape of the economy, it is far from easy to determine exactly what constitutes an "artificial" interference with the natural workings of market forces.[18] When political factors, both domestic and international, so constantly override economic efficiency, it may well be that satisfactory economic relations between less and more developed countries are more likely to be achieved by special negotiated concessions and agreements than by universalist free trade.[19] Furthermore, it seems likely that these protectionist contrivances, involving as they do a great deal of economic prediction, planning and co-ordination, may prove more manageable in a regional rather than a world-wide context. Within a defined bloc there may develop a certain general sympathy and understanding between the developed and underdeveloped partners, an identification that they may make it easier to define a common economic and political interest.

The political logic that dictates that states and alliances can only be formed in limited areas may well apply to economic development as well. In short, given the large political element involved in all trade and aid to the underdeveloped countries, the political logic of regionalism may well indicate a more practical formula than the economic logic of universal free trade. Regional bloc arrangements like those of the Common Market with its associates may be the model of the future.[20] Even in the United States, there is some sentiment for leaving Africa to Europe and building a regional bloc with Latin America.[21]

All this, of course, represents an immensely complicated subject, both in theory and in practice. Here, as in most other great issues, there will be no simple and exclusive alternatives. The world obviously will not go over entirely to one system or another. Liberal criticism of protectionist arrangements will, at the very least, always be a healthy corrective to the grosser forms of resource misallocation. A liberal world system may be the best ideal in the end, but it may well be that a regionalist period is a necessary stage in its development. Only as a country reaches a high level of advancement does it feel strong enough to face the full brunt of competition. That after all has been the evolution of trade policy in the United States, an evolution, it should be added, that is far from complete. In short, there is no clear resolution to the complex quarrel between regional, universal, liberal and mercantilist theories of how to promote world development. In practice, all approaches will be followed.

In any event, one of the earliest blocs, the Commonwealth, must surely grow looser, its members increasingly finding their markets and aid within the world at large. Indeed, many long ago began to do so. The big Asian states seek trade and prefer aid from many sources. The states of Black Africa may continue to develop their already close relations with Europe's economy generally. It does not seem that it matters much to this process whether Britain is in the EEC or an Atlantic grouping. Both sets of countries are sympathetic to the needs of developing countries. Britain's contribution to development will depend ultimately on her own generosity and the strength of her economy. Her influence on the trade policies of others will be no less great in the Common Market than in an Atlantic free trade association.

In summary, is there any reason why Britain's concern for the Commonwealth and the Third World as a whole should lead her to join more closely in an Atlantic association with America? Would the price de Gaulle demands for entering the EEC greatly limit Britain's role in the Third World? Those who answer these questions in the affirmative generally argue that somehow the continentals, being more "inward-looking", are less interested in the welfare of the Third World than is the United States. This is a view that seems difficult to justify by reference to either trade or aid policies. While no one can doubt America's genuine interest in world economic development, there is no valid reason to assume that the Europeans are any less interested, or that Britain in Europe would be any less able to play as useful a role in world economic development than she does at the moment.

A further point should be made. America's concern with economic development is often inextricably bound up with controversial political aims and Cold War rivalries—manifestations of an essentially imperial view of world power. These views, however suited to the interests and responsibilities of the United States, are not perhaps very appropriate for Britain in her present position. Britain's real military contribution to the defence of Commonwealth countries is decreasing rapidly, but her American links mean that she will continue to share the unpopularity that attends America's various military interventions. Thus a close identification with America undermines Britain's extensive connections with the Third World and curtails their usefulness. In short, Britain in a Common Market concerned with development, but renouncing intervention, might make far better use of her old imperial connections than she ever will as America's junior partner around the world.

VII.
Britain
Alone

So far the problems in each of Britain's possible roles seem so formidable that it is difficult not to entertain the thought that none of them will in the end be chosen. It might easily be said, for example, that joining the Common Market's European bloc will require not only economic costs too great to bear, but a reorientation of Britain's world strategy and allegiances too fundamental to be probable. Joining any genuinely significant Atlantic grouping, on the other hand, would seem to involve the unpleasing prospect of increasing submission to American policy without any satisfactory means to influence it. As for the Commonwealth, while it presents opportunities, its extreme heterogeneity and fragility has meant that it never was, in itself, a genuine solution to Britain's search for a new role. If these sceptical conclusions should happen to be true, if the European, Atlantic or Commonwealth alternatives should prove impossible or unacceptable, what then remains for Britain?

There is nothing that prevents her from going on with the traditional postwar policy of trying to balance her interests among Churchill's European, American and Commonwealth circles. Indeed she must do this to some extent anyway, as a more profound commitment to one is unlikely to eliminate altogether the ties with the others. But if Britain continues the balancing act, keeping her options open, what will be the likely result? What is the prospect for Britain alone?

The prospect which many fear is a slow if comfortable decline accompanied by a general withdrawal into insular self-preoccupation. There can be, many feel, no long-range solution to Britain's fundamental economic difficulties without her joining a larger integrated regional market. Meanwhile a sad inexorable logic of events can be expected to push England out of each of the three circles. Europe will become more and more unified without her. Britain's declining strength will erode the special relationship in world politics with America, and Britain's inability to serve the needs of the Commonwealth will lead to its disintegration.

Some who fear these eventualities often believe they see England already sinking into a general defeatist attitude accompanied by a prevailing atmosphere of moral decline and witless frivolity. To some observers the whole society seems immersed in self-indulgence. In the view of some, the working-classes, inherently conservative and better off than ever before, are now increasingly unambitious for themselves and their children, content to enjoy homely pleasures and disinclined to pursue further gains. They have thus become a great conservative dead weight stifling the whole society. The British workman's lack of enterprise seems to find all too warm a response among Britain's notoriously lazy managers. Without some "cold shower bath" of competition, British management and labour can be expected to continue indefinitely their amiable partnership in decline. Those who will not adjust can emigrate. Meanwhile, youth, brought up in a world bereft of challenge and discipline, can naturally be expected to elaborate its own more and more hysterical expression of the self-indulgent national character. Numerous domestic and foreign observers already find the contemporary British scene sufficiently alarming to wonder if much can be expected from the British in the next generation.[1]

Not surprisingly, there is a considerable reaction against these pessimistic views. Defenders of the contemporary rather slack atmosphere in England see it as the sign not of self-indulgence, but civilization. British workmen and managers, having arrived at unparalleled prosperity, are unwilling to worship the sacred cow of economic growth.[2] Having achieved a comfortable living, they sensibly want more leisure rather than more production.[3] For two centuries of empire and war, the British have strained to meet their "responsibilities". Now that the old aggressive role is finished, what need is there for maintaining that competitive Victorian toughness and self-discipline that was both imperialism's social prerequisite and cultural expression? No doubt self-denial has its pleasures, but maladjusted Puritans should enjoy their satisfactions in private and not foist their predilections upon the country as a whole.

Satisfaction with the present state of affairs has become rather less noticeable, however, as it has become increasingly apparent that, without a marked increase in national economic growth, the country's ambitious educational and welfare programme will soon be impossible to maintain without much heavier taxation. The prospects of decline no longer seem quite so comfortable, especially among those advanced people who place a high priority on educational reform and the welfare state.[4]

It is by no means universally conceded, however, that slow decline is the inevitable future for a Britain alone. There are, in fact, a great many people who believe that Britain's economic difficulties can be resolved without either joining a bloc or sacrificing her present role in world politics. All that is required is an intelligent national economic policy. Sir Roy Harrod, the great Oxford economist, the friend and collaborator of Keynes, presents a distinguished example of this view. A cogent and systematic statement of his position was published in mid-1967 as the pamphlet, *Towards a New Economic Policy.* In his pamphlet, Harrod blamed England's difficulties fundamentally on the misguided economic policies of successive postwar Governments. To begin with, Harrod argued that the postwar failings of the British economy have been greatly exaggerated. In the immediate postwar period, Britain was faced with a very great adjustment. The heroic war efforts had forced the liquidation of her huge foreign investments and thus ended the immense income that flowed from them back to England. That income was so sizeable, Harrod noted, that in the four years before the war British merchandise exports had to pay for only 66% of British imports; the balance was covered by "invisible" income, mostly from investments. But in the ten years 1955-1965 merchandise exports were paying for 95% of imports, whereas "invisibles" covered only 3%.[5] In 1938 exports were 10·08% of the National Income; in 1965, they were 16·72%. Meanwhile imports remained nearly stationary at 17·87% of national income in 1938 and 17·89% in 1965.[6] Harrod argued that this represented an extraordinarily impressive achievement. True, other European countries had greatly increased their exports, but it was far more difficult to do what England had had to do, namely to raise exports without raising imports.[7]

Harrod reckoned that Britain's difficulties with her balance of payments would be solved, and her usual military and financial activities could be resumed, if, imports remaining steady, exports rose only 7% higher. Harrod saw this "once-over" jump in exports as the "last lap" of Britain's postwar reconstruction and argued that it is a small task compared with what had already been accomplished. Nevertheless he admitted that the prolonged failure to achieve this relatively small adjustment had led to dangerous and chronic stagnation and was gradually demoralizing the whole economy. This unexpected failure Harrod blamed squarely on successive British governments.

The basic trouble, Harrod argued, stemmed from the premature dropping of import controls after 1954.[8] He was speaking, of course, of controls on finished manufactures competitive with domestic British industry. He noted that whereas the total amount paid for imports as a whole had remained steady after controls were dropped following 1955, the actual composition of the imports had changed spectacularly from food to manufactures. Had import quotas been eliminated gradually, at 10% a year instead of all at once, he believed that Britain, from 1956 through 1965, would probably have enjoyed a comfortable average surplus rather than the deficits she, in fact, had to endure.[9] Harrod blamed Britain's failure to close her small remaining gap not only on the premature liberalization of imports but also on the Free World's inability to arrange for adequate international liquidity.

Harrod's views on the international monetary system have been set forth at some length in an earlier chapter. In several writings he has argued that international reserves are much too small for the present volume of international trade. Other postwar policies, like maintaining full employment and fixed exchange rates, have actually increased the need for reserves, yet in relation to the increased volume of world trade, reserves today are only half what they were in 1938. The general result, he believes, is that countries over-react to relatively insignificant trade deficits. Harrod sees occasional trade deficits as perfectly normal occurrences that should not be allowed to derange national economic planning. In the international system, where it is roughly true that the overall surpluses equal the overall deficits, it is impossible that everyone should simultaneously be in surplus and unlikely that everyone will be exactly in balance. A country temporarily in deficit needs enough reserves so that policies aiming at a return to surplus can be achieved without having to resort to the drastic and self-defeating cure of deflation.[10]

The chief crime of deflation in Harrod's eyes is that it causes quite unnecessarily both waste and hardship. While management of the economy may result in too little demand, there is no such thing, Harrod argues, as too much general production of goods.[11] Thus deflation, which deliberately seeks to restrict production and create unemployment, is a highly undesirable policy, both because it wastes resources and causes real hardship. Nevertheless, the British Government, faced with trade deficits because of its import policy, and lacking adequate reserves for gentler remedies, has had to resort to "Stop-Go" deflation again and again since 1955.

True, deflation restores the balance of payments temporarily, but the cure is self-defeating. Harrod, like so many other economists, believes that it has been these periodic bouts of demoralizing deflation that have been chiefly responsible for the failure to close the trade gap. A stagnant industry cannot improve its productivity and absorb the usual wage increases. Hence British prices go up faster than those of countries that are growing. Thus British exports become less competitive. They lose their appeal not only in the foreign market but increasingly in the domestic market as well.[12]

The whole deflationary policy, according to Harrod, has been not only ruinous but absurd. The actual deficits in the balance of payments, after all, have represented only a small proportion of Britain's total outpayments and a miniscule proportion of the national income. From 1961-1965, for example, the deficits averaged 3% of outpayments and only 0·8% of national income. Harrod observes:

> It is surely very irrational indeed to tolerate "stop" measures, lasting two years or more, causing a loss of output of perhaps 3% of national income in the first year and 6% in the second year, merely to correct a deficit amounting to 0·85% of the national income.[13]

In short, Harrod's fundamental axiom: under no circumstances should the Government resort to deflation. On the contrary, full

171

economic growth must be the abiding national policy. It is the only real cure for the trade gap. But how can Britain gain enough respite from immediate exchange difficulties to expand production sufficiently to complete her postwar trade adjustment?

In his pamphlet Harrod advocated two fundamental reforms: a major increase in international liquidity and a domestic incomes policy. Monetary reform, he argued, is necessary if all countries are to be able to finance their deficits until sound non-deflationary but relatively slow-working policies can eliminate them. An incomes policy is necessary to keep wages and prices from rising faster than productivity.

Harrod admitted that the probable success of either policy was doubtful. Monetary reform would require a degree of international co-operation that was unlikely in the near future.[14] An incomes policy would require the co-operation of labour and management and might not, for one reason or another, work well enough to cure, by itself, the British trade deficit. But in the event that either or both reforms could not be achieved, he advocated two additional weapons: first, direct intervention in trade through import quotas and export incentives, and, second, regular currency devaluation.[15]

Harrod admitted that his remedies might cause intense annoyance to other countries, but argued that such steps would be perfectly allowable within the present rules of GATT and the IMF. GATT, he said, permits non-discriminatory import quotas when a country is in trade deficit, and revaluation is allowed by the IMF.[16] Harrod's "moveable peg" policy of occasional revaluation would, he admitted, lead to large precautionary movements in and out of sterling. To head them off, the pound would occasionally need massive support from the reserves of foreign central bankers. The central bankers would doubtless be annoyed by Britain's policy which would offend their cult of hard money and fixed exchange rates. But if they refused their co-operation, Harrod believed Britain should go over to floating rates. He admitted that floating rates might be had for international business and he admitted as well that his other remedy, import quotas, would represent a retrograde violation of the sound logic of free trade. Nevertheless, he argued both expedients would be more than justified by the world's perverse unwillingness to agree on an international monetary system that provided enough liquidity.

172

Under no circumstances, Harrod argued, should British domestic prosperity be sacrificed further to the ignorant prejudices of central bankers. For the collaborator of Keynes, the benefits of free trade, of further international specialization at the margin, however great, are minor compared with the blessings of full domestic growth. It is the obstinate stupidity of the world's bankers and politicians that had put growth in conflict with free trade.[17]

Needless to say, these views have led Harrod to oppose Britain's joining the Common Market or any other trade association whose regulations would commit the British Government to fixed exchange rates or free trade, and thus prevent the kind of remedies he believes essential for Britain to complete her postwar readjustment. In common with many other British economists, not to mention General de Gaulle, Harrod has argued that it would be a tragedy for Britain to go into the Common Market at any time before her present basic trade imbalance was thoroughly cured. But his powerful economic objections to entry appear, like de Gaulle's, temporary rather than permanent in nature.

In devaluing at the end of 1967, the Government has at least followed part of Harrod's prescription for a return to economic health. But by doing so, of course, it has not immediately achieved a balance of payments surplus, nor is one generally expected until 1969.[18] More fundamentally, it remains to be seen whether or not the Government's devaluation "package", including several measures that are sharply deflationary, will result not only in a return to balance, but in that resumption of growth that is Harrod's fundamental concern. There are many conflicting views on the probable efficacy of devaluation and much will naturally depend on the subsequent course of domestic and international events in the next year. In any event, following Harrod's logic, and indeed de Gaulle's, it should be some time before Britain's economy is sufficiently strengthened to hazard the shocks of joining the Common Market. Nevertheless, if devaluation ultimately rights the trade balance and restores conditions for growth, then Harrod's economic objections to joining should vanish.

Harrod, however, would probably never favour Britain's joining Europe if it required the political commitments de Gaulle now demands. For Harrod has continued to believe not only that Britain ought to go on with her world-wide role, but that, with

173

sound economic management, she can perfectly well afford to do so. In this sense Harrod's policies are fundamentally conservative: they recommend neither profound internal changes in the economy's structure, nor any recasting of Britain's world role. These views separate him not only from those who see Britain's future in Europe but also from those left-wing critics who have opposed deflation and joining the Common Market, but also advocated radical changes in the relatively conservative foreign and domestic policies of Wilson's Labour Government.

A coherent and powerful expression of this left-wing point of view can be found in *Though Cowards Flinch*, another book that appeared a few months before devaluation. The author, a young Cambridge economist and ardent socialist, Richard Pryke, worked briefly as an assistant to the Prime Minister's close economic adviser, Dr Balogh, but resigned in July, 1966, as the Government retreated from the National Plan and went over to a frankly deflationary policy. Pryke's book reflects the disaffection of a left-wing socialist with the Government's conservative pre-devaluation policy.

In his book, Pryke accused Wilson not only of having failed lamentably to solve the country's economic problems, but, what is more, of having betrayed fundamental socialist principles. When Labour took office in October, 1964, its inherited difficulties, Pryke admitted, were formidable. An all too accurate Treasury estimate had predicted a deficit in the balance of payments of £800 million —the biggest in history.[19] At that time, the government, eschewing deflation, could either have devalued or taken effective direct action to cut back imports and defence expenditures. Pryke argued that the Government should have done both but in fact had done neither.[20] Devaluation had been dismissed, and the particular form of direct action chosen, the import surcharge of 15%, had been less effective than straight import quotas would have been. Meanwhile, despite vague good intentions, the Government had made no genuine progress in cutting back overseas military expenditures.[21] All the while, the Government had gone confidently ahead with its expansionist National Plan. But by the time the crash came in July, 1966, the Government still had taken no effective measures to solve the exchange problem.

The new crisis had made it clear to everyone that Britain's balance of payments was suffering from a fundamental disequilibrium. Speculators were in full cry, two years of dallying had sapped confidence, and it had been apparent that drastic action could no longer be delayed. Once again, the Government had refused to devalue. Instead the National Plan had been abandoned and the Government had turned ignominiously back to the old Tory remedy of "Stop-Go". For Pryke, this obstinate failure to devalue represented the Wilson Government's unprincipled and thoroughly unjustified retreat from socialism. Deflation had meant that the annual growth rate of 3½%, sustained from 1960 to 1964, had been condemned to drop to 1% or less.[22] Each percentage point lost had cost the country £300 million in output. Thus £750 million to £1000 million, annually, had been sacrificed. The National Plan with its heavy investment of confidence had been scrapped. The book marshalled the usual arguments to prove that deflation is not only costly but short-sighted. Furthermore, Pryke maintained that the deflationary policy had seriously compromised the Government's highly necessary attempt to develop a sound incomes policy. Unless wage restraint is coupled with rising productivity, the sacrifices of workers are wasted and the whole idea of an incomes policy becomes associated with stagnation and unemployment. The Labour Party had thus invested the workers' goodwill and loyalty, built up for over two-thirds of a century, in an economic policy bound to lead to disillusion.

Pryke saw devaluation as the lost key in 1964 and especially in 1966. The usual arguments against it impressed him not at all. Internationally, he found it hard to believe that the world's central bankers would have acted so foolishly as to bring down the dollar with the pound. Domestically, he granted that all sorts of additional measures would have been necessary to keep down domestic costs and stimulate exports. But devaluation, he believed, would have provided the essential breathing-space during which other measures could have improved productivity and export competitiveness. Devaluation, in itself, would have greatly helped exports. Price, Pryke argued, is an important factor in determining sales. So are profit margins for exporters. British prices have been too high and profit margins too low because British firms, with their low productivity, have had such relatively high costs.[23]

In addition to devaluation, Pryke argued for greatly accelerating the cuts in overseas defence expenditures and believed this

M

could probably have saved the balance of payments £200 million a year. Finally, he proposed an elaborate scheme of export promotion. Unlike Harrod, Pryke saw little reason for confidence in the capacity of British business to rise to an occasion. It was Pryke who observed that "British industry always performs far worse than it is reasonable to expect."[24] Export performance had, he maintained, been exceptionally dismal, unfavourable conditions notwithstanding. He suggested an "Export Performance Act" by which the Government would be empowered to fine or even nationalize firms that persistently failed to keep up with the norms set for their industry.[25]

Pryke believed that these measures, presumably combined with an incomes policy, could have eliminated the deficit in the balance of payments for several years. A proper Socialist government should then have had the opportunity to shape the British economy into a far stronger structural pattern. The basic problem, Pryke argued, was that British industry has lagged further and further behind the continent in productivity. This he blamed primarily on a constitutional lethargy of British management. Although he admitted that "Stop-Go" had created a discouraging climate, he pointed out that American firms generally had done far better in England than comparable English companies while British subsidiaries abroad generally had done far worse than their native competitors. What British industry needed, Pryke concluded, was not widespread nationalization but what he described as "New Public Enterprise". By this he meant that the government should participate competitively in industry by buying or starting individual firms in selected fields. Such a policy could increase capacity in a number of industries, like steel, whose undercapacity meant that in times of general industrial expansion there were serious bottlenecks and an excessive rise in imports. In addition, his New Public Enterprise could greatly aid regional planning and development by establishing a nucleus of industries that would inevitably attract others. Finally, by creating competition, it could be used in place of the "blunderbuss" of nationalization as a "rapier" to prod backward and monopolistic industries.

Pryke admitted that it would be difficult to create the machinery to run such ambitious state enterprises out of the conservative and cautious civil service. He suggested the formation of a giant State Holding Company—something along the lines of the big public corporations that have been such dynamic forces in the postwar Italian economy. By such an overall strategy, which he saw as a pragmatic socialist combination of private and public enterprise, Pryke believed that the British economy would ultimately have been put on a strong and stable basis. Britain would then have been able to find the means to continue in the democratic renovation of her society.[26]

But Pryke also argued that before any such effective domestic economic policy could be established, Britain would have to find a more appropriate role for herself in the world. He maintained that the record of the Wilson Government clearly demonstrated that many of Britain's domestic failings in policy were dictated by the exigencies of her international role. Thus mistaken domestic policies were continually reinforced by mistaken foreign policies. Neither set could be changed, he believed, without changing the other. The Wilson Government provided him with his illustrations.

It had become clear, Pryke said, that Wilson's priorities had been to avoid devaluation, maintain the special relationship with the United States, and maintain Britain's "world role". These three policies all depended on one another. The Americans feared British devaluation because of its possible effects on the dollar and also wanted Britain to continue in her world role in order to avoid having to take on even more commitments themselves. Thus a special relationship with the US depended on Britain's continuing to avoid devaluation, which, in turn, depended on special American financial support for the pound. This support depended on Britain's maintaining those foreign bases that were to a considerable extent responsible for the payments deficit. Thus all the Wilson priorities were interlocking. According to Pryke, the chief loser, always, was the domestic British economy. It was time, Pryke argued, to knock down the whole house of cards. Britain was now so weak that the US no longer counted on the special relationship for serious help. A weak Britain had no noticeable influence on American policy and hence gained nothing but the satisfactions of vicarious participation. Thus, for Pryke: "The special relationship has degenerated into a desperate effort to retain, through an influential friend, an importance and prestige which are no longer properly ours..."[27]

Not only did Pryke urge cutting the Atlantic strings, but he was equally opposed to seeing Britain joining with Europe. He gave the usual arguments about the disastrous short-term effects on the balance of payments and doubted, as might have been expected, that British industry would be up to the competitive challenge. He went on to argue that the Community's nation states had by then lost much of the power to control their own economic affairs but without having transferred any comparable power to Community institutions. As a result, Pryke believed there would soon be neither national nor Community planning in Europe. He elaborated the interesting point that the Common Market, because of its structure, was developing a serious deflationary bias that would eventually lead to a decline in its growth rate. The increase of trade and the free flow of capital among the Six made large oscillations in their respective payments positions increasingly likely. Since governments had given up devaluation and all trade and exchange controls, when they were in difficulty deflation was the only recourse remaining to them. Logically, countries in surplus should be willing to inflate, but given the biases and fears of bankers and governments, such a balanced policy was unlikely. Thus, since every country would deflate when in balance of payments deficit and no country would be willing to inflate when in surplus, the Community could well develop a fixed deflationary bias and growth would gradually slow down as a result.[28]

The creation of a genuine federal power was, Pryke argued, the only solution in the long run. It was just possible, Pryke believed, that the Six might accomplish it, but the presence of Britain and the EFTA countries would ruin whatever slim opportunity there might otherwise have been: "It is just conceivable that Six may be company, but quite certain that ten or eleven is a crowd."[29] Anyway the programme of British Labour, as a democratic socialist movement, had been to use the power of the state to bring about the right changes in society. The Common Market, which had annihilated the planning power of the national state without replacing it with anything else, was no alternative for a socialist England. Britain's role in the world, Pryke maintained, was to provide a "working model of democratic socialism in action." The tragedy, in Pryke's view, was that the Labour Government had forgotten why it was in power. It was a Party, in Cromwell's words, that no longer "knows what it fights for and loves what it knows."[30] Pryke's ultimate goals, of course, did not incite universal enthusiasm but his critique of the Wilson Government was a forceful statement of what a great many economists, in and out of the Government, had been saying for some time.

There were, of course, many who defended the Government's deflationary policy to the very end. The basic argument for it was that, with luck, it would achieve a surplus, pay off debts, and build up the reserves. Several thin years would be a powerful incentive to competition, the rationalization of production and the mobility of labour. Meanwhile the incomes policy would have the opportunity to sink tenacious roots and other measures, like the Selective Employment Tax, would work beneficial changes on the whole economic structure. Leaner and fitter, as the Chancellor used to say, Britain would emerge in far better shape for the opportunities of the 1970s.[31]

Callaghan's was not a popular policy, but, before devaluation intervened, the Tories had not yet got round to offering any alternative to Stop-Go. Heath and Maudling, at least, gave no comfort to those who looked to devaluation as a remedy. The Tories in general seemed to be stressing the need for structural reforms that would allow the normal incentives of a free market a greater chance to do their work. They would have liked, it appears, to have simplified the tangled tax legislation and allowed those whose economic activities earned them high returns to keep much more after taxes. They talked of curbing the restrictive power of the unions, perhaps by making them responsible for maverick work stoppages that violate official contracts. In general, the Tories seemed inspired by the prospects for a more liberal economy with fewer restrictions on initiative and greater rewards for the winners.[32] Economic fashions, of course, change rapidly. It is hazardous to predict what the Tories may be advocating by the next scheduled General Election in 1971.

Labour's devaluation at the end of 1967, a move caused perhaps by bad luck as much as anything else,[33] represents a spectacular reversal of policy. Some of Pryke's original prescription has thus been adopted. But the question remains whether devaluation will lead to that resumption of growth and improvement in productivity that was the fundamental objective for Pryke and for Harrod as well. Pryke saw devaluation not a cure in itself, but only a device to gain breathing-space for fundamental industrial reforms—his "New Public Enterprise." It remains to be seen whether the Government will move towards the kind of policies Pryke

179

suggested and whether devaluation, with or without them, will succeed in promoting growth and productivity.

If this devaluation fails, the Government will doubtless try something else. And as their time of opportunity draws near, the Tories may develop some comprehensive strategy for avoiding Stop-Go. Finally, somebody's policy ought, sooner or later, to cure the economy's short-range troubles, allow the country to accumulate some reserves and resume growth. What then?

To return to the original question: What prospect is there for Britain alone—whether as Harrod's traditional world power or Pryke's advanced socialist commonwealth? To begin with, it ought to be said that Britain may very well be alone in the short run whether she likes it or not. Given General de Gaulle's attitude and the necessarily precarious state of the economy for at least some months more, Britain's immediate prospects for joining the Common Market are not brilliant, particularly if the Government continues to reject out of hand all proposals for a lengthy transitional association as a preliminary to full membership. The possibility that the United States will, in the near future, propose an Atlantic Free Trade Area, is, to say the least, uncertain, even if the British Government were to show any real enthusiasm for the scheme. The special relationship with the United States is, in general, not likely to grow any more intense. America's leadership remains controversial as the Vietnam War continues. Britain may well lose her stomach for "peace keeping." In any event, the continuing fundamental weakness of the British balance of payments suggests an inexorable withdrawal from Britain's overseas bases. The Government is moving in this direction,[34] urged on not only by its own left wing eager to save domestic welfare programmes, also by many ardent Europeans in both parties.[35] Meanwhile in the Commonwealth, the self-evident logic of dispersion continues its progress. In short, Britain seems to be losing her old ties without acquiring any new ones.

Above all, it seems increasingly apparent that a complete rejuvenation of the economy is the fundamental task before Britain. This is a task that, in the end, only Britain herself can perform. Merely leaping into Europe or the Atlantic is no solution. Until the fundamental balance of payments disequilibrium is really cured, Britain is not a very promising partner for any collective enterprise. As we have seen, Labour's bid to enter Europe may well turn out to have been premature. Britain's only European alternative may be a lengthy residence in a sort of Common Market Purgatory, associated with Heaven but not admitted until her economic sins are thoroughly expiated. Thus the Labour Government, driven by force of circumstances, may have no choice but to give domestic economic rejuvenation a first priority to which everything also must defer.

Could the necessary interval of British self-preoccupation be extended into a basic policy? In the light of all the difficulties attending the alternatives, could Britain alone be a viable long-range alternative? Could Britain find a satisfactory role as a major but not "super" power or would it be happy as Pryke's model socialist Commonwealth?

Pryke and Harrod are probably right in believing that with an intelligent Government policy, the national economy could be made viable without joining some larger European or Atlantic association. Britain, after all, remains a rich country endowed with a splendid profusion of talents. Nothing prevents her from carrying on a large and profitable trade with the rest of the world. The reasonable success of the Kennedy Round has reduced tariffs with the Common Market and the United States. It should not be impossible to reduce them still further. EFTA has been a great commercial success,[36] and it should not be impossible to organize further special arrangements for limited commercial purposes, perhaps even a trade agreement between the Six and the Seven. But if a purely national Britain would be a viable economic proposition, it seems far less likely that it could continue for long many of the cultural and institutional attributes of the great past. In the new world, Britain would be left alone on the sidelines. She would doubtless continue to enjoy the world, but not have much to say about running it.

Britain might, to be sure, hope to aspire to some version of the independent world role de Gaulle has laid out for France. But de Gaulle has prepared France for the leadership of those who reject the rival hegemonies by jettisoning the connections, both colonial and Atlantic, that contradict such a role. And above all, France, by cultivating a continental bloc and by putting herself in a position to be its intellectual and political leader, has acquired a base far greater than her own national resources. Without such a base, Britain's future as a world power is likely to be rather constrained, either as an independent force or as the continuing special relation of the United States.

What of Pryke's socialist Commonwealth? Would his little England be a happy place? Would he himself, with an obviously keen interest in the great affairs of the world, be content in a Scandinavian socialist paradise, cut off from the mainstream of history? Perhaps his is the wisdom of a truly civilized and un-aggressive people who have evolved beyond the need for grandeur. But if somehow Europe does become a great power without her, it may be somewhat painful for future generations of Englishmen when they look across the Channel.

VIII.
Leadership and
Political Imagination
in Today's Britain

Ever since the war, Britain, in common with many other countries, has been trying to reform her society after the various socialist and technocratic ideals current in modern times. But absorbing as these tasks have been, Britain has never abandoned her old concern with the outside world nor abated her efforts to keep an important role in its affairs. In a world of superpowers and blocs, Britain has been faced with the task of finding some suitable connection that would maintain for her an influential position in the future.

Two broad and complementary themes emerge from the study of this postwar search. The first is complexity, the second is indecision. Leaving aside isolationist musings and the diversions of the Commonwealth, Britain has essentially been faced with the choice of whether to invest her future and her loyalties primarily with America or primarily with Europe. The preceding chapters are not likely to convince anyone that Britain's choice is either clear or easy. Europe offers the opportunity to become a principal part in an exciting new nation. As for an Atlantic union, though there is some shadowy prospect for a kind of Atlantic Anglo-Saxon League or for Britain as the "fifty-first" state, the attractions have more to do with the opportunities and obligations of helping the United States create a stable world order. It is Europe, whose members need each other, that might someday become a federal state; the Atlantic, dominated by its colossus, will probably always be an empire.

Both ideals, the American military empire and the European

political union have behind them distinct visions of the future world order. Both have strong appeal to Britain. Who more than the British can understand the imperial ideal of world law maintained by the altruism of nations upon whom history forces such thankless and vital tasks? What country is better situated to appreciate the dangers of nuclear war? Thus many feel that even if Great Britain is no longer the modern Rome, her place, nevertheless, is beside those new Romans who are sprung from her stock and now carry so many familiar burdens. Britain's role, as Macmillan used to say, and as de Gaulle still suspects, is to act the part of Greece to America's Rome.

But imperialism is not the only political tradition in Britain. In the last century, England had not only Europe's greatest world empire, but also her first successfully democratic nation-state. The tension between a bureaucratic empire ruled by law and a national political community governed by consent—both pre-eminently—British—bedevilled much of the country's political life in the nineteenth century.[1] In a sense, it still does. This tension explains much of Britain's indecision before the competing attractions of Europe and America.

Thus Britain today stands frozen between the austere imperial ideal of international order and the heady excitement of building a new nation in Europe. Under the best of circumstances it would be difficult to reconcile the two enthusiasms. The ideal of the nation, applied internationally, leads not to orderly empires or a world rule of law but to a squirming, untidy, plural world of independent national states, in short, to de Gaulle's world. For Bergson's military disciple, the tensions and abrasions of nationalism's pluralist world are the inevitable concomitants of humanity's life force.[2] The peace of empire is the peace of death. Thus de Gaulle has insisted that America's imperial task is not shared by Europe and indeed is now the chief obstacle to Europe's own independence. De Gaulle's logic has frustrated Britain's whole effort to be both imperial and European at the same time. It may be that de Gaulle, prescient and hasty, has forced the issue prematurely and thus harmed Europe's cause as well as Britain's. But the conflict between the goal of a resurgent Europe and that of American world government was bound to come sooner or later. It was already foreshadowed in America's own ambivalent postwar policy towards Europe.

In any event, Britain, unable to reconcile European and Atlantic goals, has been unable to decide on either. This is the second main theme, the indecisiveness of British postwar policy. It is an indecisiveness easy to sympathise with. All through this period of the "three circles", the British sense of duty has been haunted by the fear of letting someone down—the Commonwealth, Europe, or America. Yet in a way, Britain, by not choosing one path or the other, has been gradually forced to let down all three. In the fifties, it was Europe, struggling to lay the supranational foundations of a new community, that felt itself cruelly deceived. Britain has never been forgiven for the contrast between her rhetoric and her policy. In the sixties, it has been the turn of the Commonwealth. The inevitable facts of life have changed what began as a sincere sense of duty toward the old Empire into something perilously close to humbug. With bases closing around the world, and Britain looking back to Europe, it is obviously now America's turn. It is scarcely a new observation that the best intentions, weakly applied, often lead to precisely the opposite of what is wanted. Ironically, an excess of unrealistic idealism leads to an unenviable reputation for hypocrisy. But whatever the real or imagined grievances of others, the British themselves have been the chief victims of their own indecisiveness. The continual overstraining of military, diplomatic and economic resources has today reduced the country to a position that is not only painful but faintly ridiculous.

Much of this book has been concerned with showing how natural it has been for Britain to have hesitated as she has and how difficult it would have been for her to have acted otherwise. Nevertheless, when all is said and done, the postwar era in Britain is unlikely to be praised for its qualities of vision and statesmanship.

To many observers, the ambiguous choices and ambivalent loyalties inherent in Britain's postwar international situation seem reflected, all too faithfully, in the quality of contemporary British thought and administration. It is almost impossible to pick up a serious study of any aspect of contemporary British economic and political activity that does not complain bitterly of a fundamental inability to plan and administer effectively. Not that there is a shortage of planning as such. But example after example shows the same failure to set out alternatives clearly, decide on the goals to be achieved, and frame a coherent policy to achieve them.[3] Indeed, one of the most distinguished students of contemporary British economic and political institutions, Andrew Shonfield, holds this incapacity for planning, in any fundamental sense, a characteristic of British administration in general:

> ... there is, even among reformers, an established penchant for the piecemeal ... It is as if the British political genius were entirely devoted to the business of make-do and mend.[4]

The inability to organize a more successful response to a changed world makes the postwar British appear relatively ineffectual in comparison with their great European neighbours, the Germans and the French. Certainly no countries could have been more miserable than those two after the war. As noted earlier, Germany's truncated economy is now similar to Britain's in several basic features. Both Germany and Britain need massive imports to live; both are compelled to export. Yet Germany has been continually in surplus and enjoyed a much higher rate of growth. As for the neighbour across the Channel, whatever may be thought of de Gaulle's grander visions, he has performed a miracle for France. He has reconciled French pride to the losses that were inevitable, brought the economy and society into the modern world, and dramatically opened the way to a new international order not devoid of excitement and idealism. For all his talk of grandeur, he has kept France's actions well within the bounds of her resources. It is not the French whose economy is overstrained, currency weak, or armies fighting in far-away places. The gods may bring him to an ignominious end, but it takes a very mean and short-sighted view to deny the extent to which his rule has brought France to terms with her situation and given her a role for the future. Indeed, France today is probably better adapted to the world and fundamentally stronger and more confident than she has been for a very long time.

Does England need a leader as she needed a Churchill in 1940 —someone to formulate a vision and set the country off towards it? Or is England, like France after Napoleon, heading for a long period of drift and decline? Britain, of course, does not take easily to leaders like Churchill or de Gaulle. Neither for that matter did parliamentary France. Parliaments never call such figures until the last moment of urgent crisis when the bankrupt regime stands exposed before a despairing nation. Once the situation is restored, parliamentary government returns as soon as possible to its old routines. This pattern is sensible enough when the situation of a country is sufficiently favourable so that tolerable results can be expected from routine reactions and the ordinary workings of private self-interest. But in the absence of drama, the country's position can deteriorate indefinitely. Britain since the war has never had a single moment, like Algeria in 1958, when the national difficulties suddenly focused sufficiently for the whole people to demand the sort of leadership that might make fundamental decisions. Do the unhappy careers in the thirties of Lloyd-George, Churchill, and Macmillan suggest that the situation in Britain is always just a shade too comfortable for timely radicalism?

In any event, if Britain's problems today lack drama, they are real enough. In the world of continental superpowers, the tide of events is running against Britain, as indeed it is running against Europe. Both Britain and Europe, of course, can relax in their golden chains and take their chances with the gentle hegemony of America. The lot of Greece was not a bad one, particularly when discussed from the point of view of the Romans. But if Europe wants a different fate, it is unlikely to come about without a great deal of effort. Even against an unfavourable tide, great ideas and great leaders can perhaps make history something to be shaped as well as endured. These exercises in commanding history require a high degree of what might be called "political imagination", something for which the British were once famous. That faculty, however, seems in a very flaccid state in contemporary England. Why?

Such a question, of course, is immense and indefinable. Its answer has to do with the whole complex of Britain's culture and institutions, and lies far beyond the scope of this book. While it may be interesting to raise what may seem relevant questions, I make no pretence, however, at answering them.

The British civil service is a frequent target for critics of the contemporary British intellectual climate. Shonfield complains of a certain smug and arrogant lack of intellectual rigour among civil servants, a cast of mind that greatly reduces their capacity for sustained confrontation with great problems. He also complains of the traditions of secrecy that absolve civil servants from the need to explain their decisions and protects them from that "need for exposition" that can "wonderfully stimulate the capacity for systematic thought."[5] Schonfield contrasts the present climate with the tough-minded combative rationalism of the great Victorian reformers—men like Jeremy Bentham, Edwin Chadwick or John Stuart Mill.

These criticisms suggest that the atmosphere in the civil service may be part of something more general in contemporary English culture. A not unconvincing argument could be made that the hardiest stock of political imagination would find it difficult to prosper in the current cultural climate broadly typical of a great deal of contemporary British history, philosophy and university study generally. That there is much that is genuinely excellent in all these fields scarcely needs to be said. That there exists infinite variety in England's intellectual life is equally true. Nevertheless, many observers find a certain prevailing negative tone that seems uncongenial to planning and vision. The country seemingly abounds in books showing that muddle is and always has been the fundamental law of history. There almost seems a certain tendency to cut history and biography down to the size of common-room conversation—the small point sharply made rather than the grand theory hopeless for conversation. Perhaps the political imagination cannot thrive under the tyranny of these small points. Whatever can be said for the intellectual finesse of the philosophical pragmatism reigning in some leading universities, it is not generally thought to lend positive encouragement to grand plans or large-minded views of the past or future. Once again, some observers profess to see a certain spirit of smug "littleness" hovering over the contemporary scene.

It could be argued that considerable damage to contemporary British political culture has come from the much-exploited discovery that, in the history of thought, there is a certain plausible link between philosophical idealism and totalitarianism—between Hegel and Hitler. This, like Burke's connection between liberal idealism and the French Revolution, is perhaps one of those insights which, even if true, is nevertheless fatal. It sometimes almost seems that a whole generation of British undergraduates has been brought up with the impression that their country's political structure is based on a solid "English" pragmatism, a completely different and wholly superior foundation from that of the miserable continentals, steeped as they are in rationalistic system-mongering and the dangerous delusions of philosophical idealism. Quite apart from a rather distorted picture of Britain's own cultural past, this complacent praise of "pragmatism" reinforces a side of the English character that perhaps does not need such powerful encouragement.

The sceptical temper is a mixed blessing. For the vigorous creative mind, it can be a powerful tool for cutting away preliminary rubbish. But for the complacent and second-rate, there is perhaps no greater friend to routine unimaginative laziness than scepticism, no trait more likely to lead to self-indulgent emotionalism. Making successful visions is rather hard work. "Pragmatism" is an essential ingredient of planning, but when pragmatism destroys vision it becomes impractical.

Shonfield points out the danger of seeing the theoretical opposed to the practical. Theories, he notes, are the only efficient guides to practice. British aversion to theory all too frequently masks "a profound reluctance to engage in the tedious business of sorting and analysing a mass of empirical data."[6] Are the British, as Shonfield suggests, anti-empirical? One of the great dangers of the excessively "practical" mind is its tendency to take leaps in the dark. The sharp distinction between theory and practice often means that theories and ideals are not very practical. Any nation that imagined and sustained for so many years the intangible ties of the British Commonwealth of Nations should perhaps be more sceptical of its scepticism.

It is interesting to speculate on the relationship between philosophical climates and political creativity. I have tried to argue elsewhere that the Romantic Idealism of Burke and Coleridge was the most creative force in British politics during the nineteenth century.[7] The movement reached its fullest expression in the British Idealist School before World War I. Then partly because in those days it seems Hegel had led to the Kaiser, the Idealist tradition suddenly lost its force in England. At the same time it was just gathering its strength on the other side of the Channel—in the days when the young Charles de Gaulle was soaking himself in Bergson. Can it be that scepticism and "pragmatism" are basically conservative, that the climate of philosophical idealism is far more conducive to a creative era in politics? No doubt, this all seems a rather abstruse way to explain Britain's difficulties over the balance of payments. But anyone who has read his Coleridge, a good British Idealist by the way, knows better than to ignore the philosophy dons and their predilections.

Cultural explanations of this sort are always hazardous. British intellectual life is too rich to decide easily on any prevailing tone. And the best philosophers, critics and historians are always too complex to fit into simple categories. Still the general atmosphere often owes more to the second-rate, and Shonfield is certainly not unique in believing contemporary Britain obsessed by impractical pragmatism.

Critics of the actual institutions of the British political system suggest another line of explanation for the country's failure to frame successful long-range policies. British parliamentary government, even if badly understood, was once the model for most of the democratic world. American political scientists, for example, used to dream of how their awkward system might be made to imitate the excellences of the British. But in recent years the British model has been abandoned for systems that are more "presidential", not only by most of the Third World, but by both France and, to some extent, Germany. Is there some lesson in this shift? Is the British system ill-adapted to the contemporary world? Many people seem to think so. Still, it is difficult to extricate the virtues of a system from its vices and Britain, with so many civilized habits worth preserving, has some cause to be conservative. In any event, an adequate discussion of this subject would soon lead to a new book before this one is finished.

My task here has been to show that Britain's choices would have been painful and complex whatever the evolution of her institutions. No one can doubt that a successful resolution will require leadership of a high order. In the past, the system has generally managed to throw up leaders when they were needed. Those who love Britain can only hope that the old genius for adaptation will not fail, that the springs of imagination have not dried up, that a race that has given so much to the world will somehow make itself heard in the future.

Notes

I. BRITAIN IN SEARCH OF A ROLE

1. The classic statement of this view, which caused much resentment in Britain at the time, was by ex-Secretary of State Dean G. Acheson at West Point, December 5, 1962.
2. See Calleo, *Europe's Future,* Chapter 6.
3. Speech at Conservative Party Conference, Llandudno, October 9, 1948.
4. At Labour Party Conference, Brighton, October, 1962.
5. In 1700 England and Wales had a population of between 5.5 and 6 million; by 1750 it had risen to about 6.5 million. See B. R. Mitchell and P. Deane, *Abstract of British Historical Statistics,* Cambridge, 1962, p. 5. The population of France in 1700 appears to have been about 21 million. In 1800 and 1900 the populations of the principal European countries were approximately as follows:

| | (millions) | |
	1800	1900
Europe	188	401
France	27	39
Germany	25	56
Italy	18	33
United Kingdom	16	42

See Joseph J. Spengler, *France Faces Depopulation,* Duke University Press, 1938, pp. 18, 23.

6. Britain became a regular and substantial net importer of foodstuffs in the 1830s—a trend which was strongly reinforced by the repeal of the Corn Laws. See Mitchell, p. 291.
7. The present Commonwealth Preference system dates from the Ottawa agreements of 1932 which exempted Commonwealth

trade from the increased tariffs put on during the depression to match the protectionist measures of other countries. See H. G. Johnson, "The Commonwealth Preferences", p. 363. The idea of a preferential system, however, had been a major issue in British politics since the end of the nineteenth century. Joseph Chamberlain was the protagonist of the idea that trade would be the bond to keep the diffuse Empire together: "I say that it is the business of British statesmen to do everything they can, even at some present sacrifice, to keep the trade of the colonies with Great Britain ... even if in doing so we lessen somewhat the trade with our foreign competitors." Joseph Chamberlain, *Imperial Union and Tariff Reform*, London, 1903, p. 8. Lord Beaverbrook made Commonwealth preference his abiding political cause.

II. THE ECONOMIC BASE

1. *Trade and Growth*

1. For one discussion of the persisting difficulties of the British economy in historical perspective, see Alfred E. Kahn, *Great Britain in the World Economy*, Columbia University Press, New York, 1946. For some of the results of Britain's loss during World War II of her investments abroad, see Sir Roy Harrod, *Towards a New Economic Policy*, p. 21 ff. Harrod notes that in the four years before World War II, merchandise exports paid for only 66% of merchandise imports (f.o.b.) and the rest was met by net invisible exports. From 1955-65, by contrast, merchandise exports were meeting 95% of imports and invisibles not always quite making up the difference. Balance, however, did not mean growth. See note 7.

2. The EEC countries in 1965 accounted for 26% of world exports and 28% of world imports. The comparable figures for EFTA were 14% and 19%. Europe as a whole, therefore, accounts for about three times much trade as the US.

3. France's record improved dramatically after the devaluation of January, 1959. In the early fifties her balance of trade was seriously and chronically adverse. For the five years ending in 1958 her deficit averaged $545 million p.a. Source: *IMF International Financial Statistics*, December, 1962.

4. Such self-sufficiency, as the French example before 1959 and in 1964 shows, does not guarantee a favourable trade balance. But it makes trade less important relative to GNP than in less self-sufficient countries, and means that corrective policy measures are not frustrated by a hard core of inelastic demand for food and basic raw material imports.

5. Since 1958, only in the second and third quarter of 1965 has

the German trade balance moved into deficit—and even then the return to surplus was rapid.

6. These percentages are based on valuation of both exports and imports f.o.b., i.e., excluding the cost of carriage insurance and freight (c.i.f.). Table E, however, gives data based on exports f.o.b. and imports c.i.f.: hence the value of imports is overstated, compared with exports. For the purpose of general comparison between countries and between years such data are not seriously misleading. On an imports f.o.b. basis the average British balance of trade deficit was $456 million from 1958-1961, $708 million from 1962-1965. These figures differ absolutely from the average given in the text, based on Table E, but reveal the same trend. See *UK Balance of Payments*, HMSO, 1966.

7. No country with more than 1% of world exports in 1965 shows a smaller percentage increase in exports since 1958. Only New Zealand and South Africa (each with less than 1%) have worse records among nations of any size.

8. See Harrod, *Towards a New Economic Policy*, p. 24. For some of the reasons—superior design, performance and price—why foreign goods are now preferred, see *Imported Manufactures: An Enquiry into Competitiveness* (NEDC, 1963). About half the machinery purchased by manufacturing industry now comes from abroad. See *The Times*, October 14, 1966.

9. In assessing even this small consolation it should not be forgotten that the national income per head in the US remains twice that of Britain.

10. In recent years the Japanese GNP has been growing at between 9% and 12% annually. See *OECD Economic Outlook*, December, 1967, p. 83.

11. See Maddison, *Economic Growth in the West*, p. 53. America's low level of return presumably results not from under-investment relative to Europe but from a much greater accumulated investment, now suffering relatively from the law of diminishing returns.

12. See Maddison, p. 53.

13. See Maddison, p. 40. Figures for 1960.

14. See Maddison, p. 37.

15. Table K as presented in Maxwell Stamp Associates, *The Free Trade Area Option*, The Atlantic Trade Study, London, 1967, p. 50.

16. It is not, of course, true that Britain's economy is the worse off for having to import more. In economic terms she is obviously wise to concentrate on what she does best, though her lack of self-sufficiency does make her more vulnerable militarily and perhaps politically.

17. The level of public expenditure in Britain has been a favourite target of City and right-wing critics of the management of the British economy. See, for example, Pryke's account of Lord Cromer's speeches, *Though Cowards Flinch*, p. 19. The

level of welfare expenditure has come in for similar attacks. For a refutation of the proposition that Government expenditure in Britain is higher than in comparable countries, see Peter Jay, *The Times*, May 18, 1967.

18. See, for example, the contributions to the July, 1963, issue of *Encounter*, reprinted as *Suicide of a Nation*, ed. Arthur Koestler.

19. It has been claimed, for example, that Britain lost 155 scientists and 507 engineers to America in 1966 (Lord Bowden, *The Times*, March 11, 1967, p. 3). Among these, 146 were aeronautical engineers (*Financial Times*, March 31, 1967, p. 13).

20. Anthony Sampson in his *Anatomy of Britain* concluded with the observation that "the long-term prospects of Britain lie not with an immediate shake-up, or with tinkering with institutions, but with the drastic reform of the educational system which has helped to fix so many of our antiquated traditions." See *Anatomy of Britain Today*, London, 1965, p. 679.

21. See Pryke, p. 67.

22. See Pryke, p. 96, for a summary of the results of a number of recent studies comparing output per man hour for key industries in the UK and in the main EEC countries. In nearly every case British productivity is inferior to all, or all but one, of her continental competitors. On average German productivity is, for the industries covered, about 30% superior and French about 45%.

23. See J. H. Dunning "Does Foreign Investment Pay?" (*Moorgate and Wall Street*, autumn, 1964), and "US Subsidiaries in Britain and their UK competitors" (*Business Ratios*, autumn 1966). American firms in Britain earned 12·5% on net assets, compared with 7·8% for all firms operating in Britain. By contrast, British firms in the US earned profits below the US average (6·6% compared with 9·1%). Comparison with Common Market firms reveals similar results.

24. Two recent examples have been the swing-wing aircraft, invented by the British designer Barnes Wallis and exploited by General Dynamics in the USA, and the Hovercraft, invented by Christopher Cockerell. Cockerell resigned from the board of the company which was developing Hovercraft on the grounds that the government-sponsored National Research Development Council had been forced to sell manufacturing rights in the Hovercraft to potential foreign competitors in order to raise money for further British development. This, he maintained, was a result of the parsimonious attitude of the British Government to the NRDC, the budget of which did not allow it to give the Hovercraft the support it deserved. Meanwhile in the US up to £30 million of research expenditure was proposed. See *The Times*, February 28, 1966.

25. Between 1958 and 1965 wages went up by 63% in France, by 85% in Germany, but by 56% in Britain. See *ILO Year Book of Labour Statistics* 1966, Table 19. In the same period export prices

rose 2% in France, 9% in Germany and 9% in Britain. See *IMF International Financial Statistics*, March, 1967, p. 30. Between 1954 and 1964 net profit before tax as a percentage of total assets fell in Britain from 12·2% to 9·7%. See Robert Appleby, *Profitability and Productivity in the UK*, British Institute of Management, London, 1967, p. 20.

26. Complaints of this kind have been particularly frequent in the aircraft industry, which has been increasingly dependent on the Civil Service as its dependence on Government contracts has increased. See Stephen Hastings, *The Murder of TSR2*.

27. See G.S.A. Wheatcroft, "A Study in Surtax" (*The Banker*, March, 1967).

28. See Sir Edward Beddington-Behrens, *The Times*, February 2, 1967, p. 13. Sweden, he says, is the only important European country whose tax on higher income brackets approaches that in Britain—a fact which Sir Edward thinks may help to account for the slower rate of Swedish industrial growth. Yet the cost in Britain of allowing people to retain 25% of their earned income would amount to a quarter of one per cent of the estimated total tax revenue of 1966-7.

Two articles in *The Times* of February 17 and 18, 1966, compared the salaries of executives of comparable ability and responsibility in various industrial countries. The study was based on the salaries paid by one large international company to executives of the same standing in the various countries. The company attempted to make its salaries competitive in each country with those offered by other companies there. The data covered jobs which in the UK got salaries of between £5,000 and £12,500 p.a. gross: thus all except the highest paid executives were included. The results show that British executives at these levels were paid less before tax than in any other of the countries examined, and less after tax than in any except the Netherlands and perhaps Sweden.

29. The Richardson Report on Turnover Taxation gives a full and clear survey of the arguments. The report rejects the European value-added tax (TVA) version of turnover taxation primarily because prices would rise if it were introduced and the expected increase in investment would not be forthcoming. British businessmen, it is argued, would look on TVA as an additional cost to be passed on to the consumer. Their investment decisions are made on the basis of expected before-tax returns and are not therefore affected by tax changes. Many critics now believe, or hope, that the Richardson assessment of businessmen's attitudes was exaggerated, or that businessmen have become more sophisticated since 1963. Sir Robert Shone sets forth some of the disadvantages of the British tax structure in a published paper he read to the Royal Society of Arts, "Economic Developmpent of the UK Steel Industry", March 22, 1961. For a more recent advocacy, see

Reginald Maudling's article on current UK economic problems in *The Times*, June 15, 1967.

30. Furthermore, TVA can, under the rules of GATT, be refunded on exports and would provide an export incentive far greater than the derisory amounts available under the export rebate scheme which operated prior to devaluation.

31. For an examination of social security contributions in Britain, the US, and the EEC countries, see Peter Jay, "Britain's Tax Dilemma" in *The Times*, May 19, 1967.

32. Nicholas Kaldor, *Causes of the Slow Rate of Economic Growth of the United Kingdom*.

33. For a convenient tabulation of the major acts of policy by British Governments between 1946 and 1960, see Dow, *The Management of the British Economy, 1945-60*, p. 113. There has been a fairly regular cycle of balance of payments crises since the war. In 1949 there was devaluation; in 1951 the Korean crisis; in 1957, after two years' difficulties, Bank Rate went up to 7% for the first time in decades; in 1961 there was Selwyn Lloyd's freeze; and in 1964 the crisis which led to devaluation began. See also Dow, p. 388.

34. Economists and politicians who believe that exports are stimulated by domestic deflation argue that a fall in home demand leads firms to seek business abroad, or provides spare capacity to fill otherwise unsatisfied export demand. Businessmen, by contrast, make much of the effect of reduced turnover on unit costs, when high fixed overheads have to be spread over a lower volume of production. Only recently has there been any detailed empirical work on the connection between the state of home demand and the level of exports. See R. J. Ball, J. R. Eaton and M. D. Steuer, "The Relation between United Kingdom Export Performance in Manufactures and the Internal Pressure of Demand", *Economic Journal*, September, 1966.

35. For a survey of the amplitudes of economic fluctuations and the associated rates of growth in a number of countries since the war see Professor Thomas Wilson, "Instability and the Rate of Growth", *Lloyds Bank Review*, July, 1966.

36. See Maddison, p. 180; Pryke, *passim;* and Harrod, *Towards a New Economic Policy*, Part I.

37. For a hostile account of the City's role in the 1964-66 sterling crises see Pryke, p. 18 ff.

2. *Financial Problems and Remedies*

1. See Clarke, *The City in the World Economy*, p. 143 ff.
2. See Maxwell Stamp, "Sterling and the Common Market", *The Banker*, December, 1966.
3. See Clarke, p. 137.
4. See Pryke, p. 32 ff.

5. Among those who in 1965 advocated an incomes policy in preference to exchange depreciation was Sir Roy Harrod. See *Reforming the World's Money*, Chapter 2. He has also been a strong advocate of import controls. By 1967, in *Towards a New Economic Policy*, p. 67 ff, he had concluded that the evolving situation might well require devaluation. See Chapter 7 below.

6. See Clarke, p. 203 ff. The success of British dealers in developing and dominating the Euro-Dollar market—a post 1957 phenomenon—shows both the adaptability of the City and its independence of sterling.

7. See Harrod, *Towards a New Economic Policy*, p. 21.

8. See Reddaway, p. 130. Reddaway concludes that investment overseas is, typically, profitable in the long run, but that the deflation which is necessary to cure the payments deficits caused by capital outflows loses Britain more in national income than investments can ever earn.

9. For successive trade balances in other countries of Europe see Table E.

10. The sterling area now includes the British Commonwealth (except Canada and Rhodesia), the Irish Republic, Iceland, Jordan, Kuwait, Libya, South Africa, SW Africa, W Samoa, and British Trust Territories and Protectorates. See *Bank of England Quarterly Bulletin*, September, 1967, p. 246.

11. See "Financing the World's Trade", *The Economist*, June 18, 1966, and Stamp, *The Banker*, December, 1966.

12. *Bank of England Quarterly Bulletin*, March, 1968.

13. See Harrod, *District Bank Review*, December, 1966.

14. "Leads and lags" arise when traders, British or foreign bring forward their purchases and delay their sales of foreign exchange, because they anticipate a change in the price of sterling, which will give them a speculative profit. Such behaviour is distinguished from pure speculation by the characteristic that the exchange transactions take place as a result of trade: it is only their timing which is affected by speculative considerations. The Radcliffe Committee believed leads and lags to be substantial. See *Committee on the Workings of the Monetary System (Cmd. 827)* §639. For a less alarmed view of their size, see *Bank of England Quarterly Bulletin*, May, 1961.

15. The reserves at the end of June, 1967, were £1,012 million. The Chancellor in his April budget speech had promised the repayment of the 1964 IMF drawing (£357 million) by December 2. Of this, £170 million was repaid or drawn in sterling by other IMF members before the end of June, 1967, leaving a debt of £187 million. See *Bank of England Quarterly Bulletin*, September, 1967.

16. The decrease in US gold and foreign exchange reserves has been as follows ($ billion):

1958	1959	1960	1961	1962	1963	1964	1965	1966	1967
1.93	1.03	2.15	0.61	1.53	0.38	0.17	1.22	0.57	0.05

This represents an outflow of $9·64 billion in ten years. Source: *IMF International Financial Statistics,* February, 1968.

17. At the end of 1966 Germany had $8·028 billion reserves, France $6·733 billion and Italy $4·566 billion. None had any substantial short term liabilities. *See IMF International Financial Statistics,* March, 1967.

18. See the summary of Rueff's proposals in the *Financial Times* of December 13, 1966. They include a revaluation of gold to release gold hoards, the paying off by the US and the UK from their own gains of all the dollar and part of the sterling balances, and the use of windfall gains by other countries, in part, to make a loan to Britain to pay off as much of the rest of the sterling balances as she wishes, in part to assist underdeveloped countries. See, for Britain's net gold reserve position, Ch. V. 3, note 26.

19. See Chapter V. 3, *passim* and pp. 127 ff, especially.

20. "What I deprecate strongly are attempts to chop and change our policy at very short intervals and before the effects of a given policy have had time to work themselves out"—Callaghan in the Commons, July 24, 1967.

21. Optimistic early forecasts saw, by 1969, an improvement in the trade balance of £500 million, which they reckon would lead to a surplus of £300 million. See *The Economist,* November 25, 1967, p. 872; or the *National Institute Economic Review,* 42, November, 1967, p. 3.

22. The British devaluation of 14·3% on November 18, 1967, was followed shortly by devaluations in Denmark (7·9%), Ireland (14·3%), Spain (16·7%), Iceland (24·6%); also in Israel, Kuwait, Hong Kong and Ceylon.

23. The increase from $2·40 to $2·80 is a rise of 16·7%, whereas the decrease from $2·80 to $2·40 is a fall of 14·3%.

Other Burdens

1. See *The Military Balance,* p. 46. The absolute figures are Britain $5937 million, France $4215 million, Germany $4607 million. The French figure is believed not to include some elements of the nuclear programme (*The Military Balance,* p. 18).

2. For the deployment and exchange costs of British troops abroad, see Hugh Hanning, "Britain East of Suez" and Christopher Mayhew, *Britain's Role Tomorrow.*

3. *UK Balance of Payments,* HMSO, 1966, p. 11.

4. Germany has a foreign exchange cost to meet in the form of amounts paid under offset costs agreements to the US and the UK. Under the Gilpatrick Agreement Germany paid the US DM 15·4 billion between July, 1965, and July, 1967. The

British have had, or will receive, DM 0·6 billion p.a. during the same period. The total cost to Germany is therefore about DM 8·3 billion p.a.—excluding weapons purchases. Source: Air Attaché at the German Embassy, London.

5. On January 16, 1968, Prime Minister Wilson announced to the Commons an extensive series of cuts in defence. British forces were to be withdrawn entirely from Malaysia, Singapore and the Persian Gulf by the end of 1971. An order for fifty F111 American aircraft was cancelled; defence research and naval construction were cut; the aircraft carrier force was to be phased out and man-power cuts were planned for all the services. Savings in the 1968-69 and 1969-70 Budgets were estimated at £110 million. By 1972-73, further savings of £210-260 million were expected. See *The Times*, January 17, 1968, p. 7.

6. In 1964 British direct investment and other private capital flows to less-developed countries totalled $283 million. The equivalent figure for France was $388 million, Germany $117 million and the United States $1146 million. See OECD *Geographical Distribution of Financial Flows to Less Developed Countries*, Paris 1966, p. 178.

7. See Chapter VI. 2, note 6.

8. For a clear statement and discussion of the various arguments that have been used to reduce the significance of the high French aid figure, see Teresa Hayter, *French Aid*, ODI, London 1966, p. 48 ff. She rightly argues that critics of tying typically fail to distinguish between the balance of payments cost of aid and its real cost in resources foregone. There is no doubt that the French system helps to reduce the first, but the burden of the second is unaffected.

III. BRITAIN IN TRANSIT:
THE POSTWAR MUDDLE

1. See Chapter I, note 3.

2. Churchill's speech at Zürich, September 19, 1946.

3. Churchill made this statement on May 11, 1953, referring to the powers attempting to build a European Defence Community. See Northedge, p. 159.

4. Charles de Gaulle, *Salvation*, p. 58.

5. *Salvation*, p. 59.

6. Charles de Gaulle, *Unity*, p. 253.

7. *Salvation*, p. 59.

8. *Salvation*, p. 57. It was chiefly thanks to Churchill, however, that France was readmitted to the great powers in the occupation of Germany and the founding of the UN. see Northedge, p. 17; and Hansard, 403 HC. Deb 5s. Col. 495 (September 28, 1944). For

Churchill's analysis of his policy towards de Gaulle near the end of the war, see W. S. Churchill, *The Second World War*, vol. 6, *Triumph and Tragedy*. London: Cassell & Co., 1954, Chapter 16 and also p. 353.

9. Seventh Press Conference held by de Gaulle in Paris at the Élysée Palace, January 14, 1963. See Major Addresses, p. 213.

10. The Assembly of the Council of Europe had, according to Spaak, only 60 members out of 135 who believed in the need to create Europe. See Brugmans, *L'Idée Européenne*, 1918-1965, Bruges, 1965, p. 123. Since the Council had been created to satisfy Britain, its lack of enthusiasm was taken to reflect Britain's luke-warm attitude to European unity.

11. See A. Nutting, *Europe Will Not Wait*, London, 1960, and J. H. Huizinga, *Confessions of a European in England*, London: Heinemann, 1958. There is also Lord Boothby's extraordinary speech in the House of Lords on June 30, 1960. Also, Sir David Maxwell-Fyfe, *Political Adventure: Memoirs of the Earl of Kilmuir*. London: Weidenfeld & Nicolson, 1964.

12. For more than twenty years before the Macmillan application to join the EEC there had been a substantial body of opinion favouring a federal solution to the problems of Europe. The 1947 formation of Churchill's United Europe was a crucial stage in the development of what was later to become pro-Common Market opinion. The members included Robert Boothby, L. S. Amery and Sir David Maxwell-Fyfe. The group soon became divided on the extent and nature of the federation to be advocated: Its importance during the fifties was not as great as the distinction of its sponsors suggests. The 1958 Britain in Europe group, formed under the chairmanship of Gladwyn Jebb, was explicitly in favour of British entry into the Common Market and, despite a reluctance to define its position too closely, appears to have been federalist in its declared opposition to de Gaulle's Europe of States. By 1961, therefore, there were in Britain a considerable number of eminent and well-informed men who had helped to move public opinion towards acceptance of the EEC, and were able to help maintain the impetus of the new initiative once negotiations had started.

13. Northedge, p. 46. Northedge provides an excellent account of this whole period.

14. Northedge, p. 140. See Hansard, 450 HC Deb 5s Col 111o, May 4, 1948.

15. For a knowledgeable discussion of the events and policies referred to, see Nicholas, especially p. 50 ff.

16. For an American view see Moore, pp. 21-22. Britain, as the leading member of the OEEC, saw her interests in the revival of world, rather than solely intra-European trade.

17. See Calleo, *Europe's Future*, p. 84. At this early date, de Gaulle offered a counter-proposal for a confederation — an early

version of the Fouchet Plan—including a referendum among the peoples of Europe.

18. Northedge, pp. 138-40. It should not be forgotten that Roosevelt, at Yalta, had announced that American troops would be out of Europe two years after VE Day. Northedge, p. 17.

19. Northedge, p. 135 ff. Also Henry Pelling, *A Short History of the Labour Party*, London: Macmillan, 1961, p. 99 ff, and Eugene J. Meehan, *The British Left Wing and Foreign Policy*, Rutgers University Press, 1960, p. 152.

20. Northedge, p. 150 ff.

21. Harold Macmillan, Council of Europe, Consultative Assembly, second session, seventh sitting, August 14, 1950, pp. 436-8.

22. A European army united command had been proposed by Winston Churchill at Strasbourg in 1950. Northedge, p. 153.

23. Calleo, *Europe's Future*, pp. 49-51. See also Raymond Aron and Daniel Lerner, *France Defeats EDC*, New York: Praeger, 1957; Henri Brugmans, *L'Idée Européenne, 1918-1965*, Bruges, 1965.

24. Charles de Gaulle, speech at Sainte-Mandé, November 4, 1951. *Speeches, Statements and Press Conferences*, 1946-1958, R.P.F. files, on microfilm, Bibliothèque de Fondation Nationale des Sciences Politiques.

25. Calleo, *Europe's Future*, pp. 87-88. De Gaulle, Press Conference, November 14, 1949, and interview with M. Bradford as representative of the United Press at Colombey-les-deux-Églises, July 10, 1950.

26. One of the crucial arguments put forward by French Socialist opponents of EDC in the National Assembly was that British participation, not merely promises to maintain forces on the Continent, would be necessary if France were not again to find herself faced in Europe by a German-Italian alliance. See Aron and Lerner, Chapter 1, in particular pp. 7 and 15; and Northedge, p. 152 ff.

27. Paul-Henri Spaak was President of the Consultative Assembly of Europe when Britain announced that she would not join the EDC. Spaak, who is a distinguished Belgian politician and lawyer, had by 1950 been several times Prime Minister and Foreign Minister of his own country and chairman of numerous international and European organizations. He resigned in frustration on hearing the news. He had told Nutting that the British federalists "had waited too long for Britain to get aboard the European bus . . . the Eden plan was a neat halfway house arrangement which might suit Great Britain, but halfway houses were not enough for Europe." Nutting, p. 44-5. See also note 10.

28. See Camps, p. 25 ff. Camps provides a thoroughly detailed and well-documented study.

29. For EFTA, its origins and achievements, see Chapter VII, note 36.

30. "A European Free Trade Area, UK Memorandum to the OEEC," Cmnd. 72, HMSO, February, 1957.

31. Hansard, House of Commons, November 26, 1956. See also Harold Wilson's reply. For a short account see Camps, p. 106 ff.

32. For a discussion of the relative virtues of customs unions and of free trade, see James E. Meade, *The Theory of Customs Unions*, Amsterdam: North-Holland Publishing Co., 1966, esp. Chapters V and VI.

33. An attack on the "stupidity" of harmonization was made by R. F. Kahn in his contribution to *The Free Trade Proposals*, ed. G. D. N. Worswick, Oxford: Basil Blackwell, 1960, p. 62. The whole book is an interesting collection of reactions from professional British economists, mostly with a free trade background.

34. See p. 139 of "The Common Market: the Economists' Reactions," in *The Free Trade Proposals*, p. 135-42. Johnson is speaking here specifically of the contributors to this symposium.

35. See Nicholas, *Britain and the United States*, Chapter 10.

36. For a brief discussion of the events leading up to the 1960 Summit Meeting and Macmillan's role, see Northedge, p. 272-6. For a discussion of Macmillan's relations with Eisenhower and Kennedy, see Sampson, Chapter 9 and 15.

37. British postwar growth, although disappointing by comparison with other countries, has been excellent if a longer perspective is taken. Between 1913 and 1950, for example, the annual rate of growth was 1·7%; between 1950 and 1960, 2·6%. See Maddison, p. 28.

38. See Dow, *Management of the British Economy*, p. 111.

39. See Lord Windlesham, *Communication and Political Power*, London: Jonathan Cape, 1966, Chapter VI, "Public Opinion on the Common Market."

40. See David E. Butler and Anthony King, *The British General Election of 1964*, Macmillan, 1965, Chapter II, for a discussion of the prevailing social malaise at the time of the first British application.

41. Gallup Polls between July, 1960, and January, 1963, reveal that at no time was more than 80% of the public decided; in July, 1961, as many as 42% answered, "Don't know" to Gallup's curious question: "If the British Government were to decide that Britain's interest would best be served by joining the European Common Market, would you approve or disapprove?" To the more straightforward: "On the facts as you know them at present, are you for or against Britain joining the Common Market?" in December, 1962, 36% were for, 26% against, and 38% didn't know: see *Journal of Common Market Studies*, September, 1966, p. 49 ff.

It is, of course, obvious that all the top political élite were not for joining the Common Market, e.g., Hugh Gaitskell and Harold

Wilson. Nor were all company directors, university teachers or lawyers, e.g., John Paul, Sir Roy Harrod and Sir Derek Walker-Smith. But it seems incontestably true that the great majority of those in the higher ranks of British business and professional life favoured entry. In August, 1966, Gallup poled 411 people selected from "Who's Who" and found 90% approving, and 6% disapproving, with 4% answering, "Don't know". (*Daily Telegraph, October 24, 1966*). It is also generally believed among students of public opinion that the Common Market has been much more popular among the young.

42. The Chairman and driving force of the Anti-Common Market League was Mr John Paul, then a company director in the oil business and once Chairman of the South Kensington Conservative Association. Eventually, the Earl of Sandwich, formerly Lord Hinchingbrooke, MP, and now Mr Victor Montagu, became President of the League. For a general study of the group, see Windlesham, *op. cit.* Typical views of various prominent anti-Marketeers can be found in the pamphlet, *Britain not Europe*, ed. R. Hugh Corbett, London: The Anti-Common Market League, 1962.

43. For a defence of popular judgment in foreign policy, see R. H. S. Crossman, "Democracy and Foreign Policy", in *Planning for Freedom*, London: Hamish Hamilton, 1965. Mr Crossman, Lord President of the Council in the present Labour Government, has been an opponent of Britain's entering the Common Market.

44. For a discussion of Macmillan's views of the advantage of entry as well as those of Sir Frank Lee's committee of top civil servants that reinforced him, see Camps, Chapters 9 and 10. Also for an excellent summary of the pro-Market case at the time, see U. W. Kitzinger, *The Challenge of the Common Market.*

45. See A. Lamfalussy, "Europe's Progress: due to Common Market?" *Lloyd's Bank Review*, October, 1961.

46. Sir Donald MacDougall, *Britain and the Common Market*, p. 15. Those who have been opposed to entry, or who have voiced strong reservations on economic grounds, include Thomas Balogh, Sir Roy Harrod and Professor Nicholas Kaldor.

47. For a comprehensive and powerful summary of the political arguments against joining see William Pickles, *Not With Europe*,

48. Denis Healey, for example, said during the 1962 debate that he feared the Common Market was becoming a "rich man's club" and for this reason alone the Commonwealth was preferable.

49. See Camps, chapters 14 and 15 for a detailed account and analysis of the final stages of negotiations. For some important interpretations of the state of the negotiations at their breakdown, see Charles de Gaulle, Press Conference, January 14, 1963, in "Major Addresses", 211-16; Mr Heath's speech at the break up of the negotiations in Agence Internationale d'Information pour la

Press, Luxembourg, EUROPE, Documents No. 186/187, February 5, 1963; also European Economic Community, Commission, Report to the European Parliament on the State of Negotiations with the United Kingdom, Brussels, February 26, 1963.

50. For a discussion of the implications of the common agricultural policy, see Calleo, *Europe's Future*, pp 62-3.

51. Hugh Gaitskell, the Leader of the Opposition, had put forward five conditions which would have to be fulfilled if the Labour Party were to support entry. They amounted to a refusal to join:
1. Safeguards for the Commonwealth.
2. Safeguards for EFTA.
3. Suitable arrangements for British agriculture.
4. Freedom to pursue an independent foreign policy.
5. Freedom to formulate and carry out national economic planning.

52. Charles de Gaulle, Press Conference, January 14, 1963, in *Major Addresses*, p. 215-16.

53. Between 1961 and 1965 exports to the Commonwealth from the UK increased by 18%; to the EEC by 37%. Source: Annual Abstract of Statistics 1966 p. 223.

54. Chapter IV. 4, note 3.

IV. BRITAIN IN EUROPE:
THE ELUSIVE ALTERNATIVE

2. *Britain's Case for the Common Market*

1. For an account of Britain's fears about the stability of Europe in 1961, and their grounds, see Camps, p. 281. An early believer in Britain's ability to counteract this tendency by joining European supranational bodies was Duncan Sandys. See his speech at the time of the UK-ECSC agreement in 1955. Camps, p. 46: Hansard HC 21 February, 1955, cols. 881-7.

2. Some of these ideas can be found spread through the comments of a large number of political and intellectual figures published in the *Encounter* symposium *Going into Europe*, December, 1962—March, 1963. A. J. P. Taylor, for example, writes: "I don't like the people who are running the Europe of the Common Market...I prefer Nehru to Adenauer or even to de Gaulle. Who doesn't?" December, 1962, p. 62.

3. See HMSO Annual Abstract of Statistics 1966, p. 223 for an analysis of the value of exports by destination 1958-1965.

4. Between 1958 and 1965 Britain's trade with industrialized countries grew substantially faster than with non-industrialized countries, as is suggested by the figures for EEC and the Commonwealth given in the text: the rate of increase for trade with EFTA (89·2%), US (64·6%) and the rest of the world (19·4%) confirm this conclusion. See Annual Abstract of Statistics 1966, p. 223.

Wells estimates that the balance-of-trade cost to Britain of the present EEC/EFTA split in Europe is about £20 milion (net). See Wells, p. 46.

5. UK/Commonwealth trade, although growing slowly in absolute terms, has, as has been shown, become steadily less important for both sides as a proportion of total trade. Surprisingly, the degree of preference granted to Britain seems to have been relatively stable: the successive GATT tariff reductions have not eroded preferences, because the pattern of British trade has moved towards those Commonwealth countries which offer wider preference margins, and towards products which carry high tariffs. But the Commonwealth is unlikely in the long run to be willing to continue special privileges (even if reciprocated) for one among an increasing number of equally important trade partners. See Wells, p. 24 ff; and, for the current level of Commonwealth preferences, p. 129.

6. At the Conservative Party Conference in October, 1961, Macmillan described entry into Europe as "a bracing cold shower ... not a Turkish Bath." Quoted in Sampson, *Macmillan*, p. 215.

7. See Chapter II, pp. 27-28.

8. For a discussion on the argument that entry into the EEC would involve devaluation, see William Davis in *The Guardian*, November 17, 1966.

9. See Chapter V, p. 104 ff.

10. R and D costs for Concorde, the Anglo-French supersonic passenger aircraft, are expected to run to at least £528 million, divided between the two countries. The Ministry of Technology estimates that the number of planes which will be sold will only allow recovery of about a third of the development costs. See *The Times*, August 2, 1967.

11. See for example, on the computer and aircraft industries Layton, *Transatlantic Investments*, p. 99.

12. In 1962, estimated gross expenditure on research and development in Europe was as follows:

	$ million	% of GNP
Belgium	133	1.0
France	1,108	1.5
Germany	1,105	1.3
Netherlands	239	1.8
United Kingdom	1,775	2.2

See C. Freeman and A. Young, *The Research and Development Effort in Western Europe, North America and the Soviet Union*. OECD, Paris, 1965, p. 71.

13. Layton proposes further European co-operation as a solution to Europe's difficulties in this field. There should be a European policy administered by a General Staff to rationalize research

and development and allocate projects among the participants. Governments should agree to buy the products of such national projects, thus guaranteeing a substantial market. See Layton, p. 101 ff. The experience of the British and French in developing the Concorde and swing-wing aircraft suggests that even between two countries, let alone between six or more, such co-operation can lead to serious conflicts. The fundamental precondition for success is that all the participants in a project should have the same requirements. It is rare that such circumstances arise.

14. Susan Strange, p. 28 ff, p. 51 ff.

15. For a discussion of European capital markets, see Layton, Chapter VI, and the references given in Chapter V. 3, Note 50. The Segré Report has attempted to show how a genuinely European capital market could be created out of existing national markets. See *Le Developpement d'un Marche Européen des Capitaux* (Brussels, 1966).

3. *The British Case Against the Common Market*

1. See Chapter III, Note 46.

2. In 1962 the Council of Ministers agreed on a general outline for the transition period, the system of levies and the institution of the European Agricultural Guidance and Guarantee Fund. The 1965 crisis, which led to the French abandoning their part in the negotiations for a time, centred on the proposal of the Commission that the European Parliament should have powers to amend the budget which disposed of the agriculture revenues; and that their amendments could only be reversed by the votes of five or in some cases four of the states on the Council of Ministers. This measure, if accepted, would have represented a substantial increase in the powers of the supranational organs of the EEC, and thus was unacceptable to de Gaulle. The crisis was resolved in May, 1966, after what amounted to a French veto, and agreement was reached on a programme for the period to 1969. See, for the Commission's proposals, Calleo, *Europe's Future*, pp. 63, 71.

3. Speech by Fred Peart, Minister of Agriculture, November 25, 1966, as reported in *The Guardian*, December 5, 1966. Joseph Godber, the Opposition's spokesman on agriculture, after noting that with a transition period of six years the rise in food prices would be roughly 2% per annum, observed: "The first two years of the present Government have seen a rise of over 6½% in the cost of food to the housewife, over 50% more rapid than would have to be faced by entry into the Common Market." Quoted in *The Financial Times*, November 25, 1966, p. 2. Recent studies of the effects on Britain and her farmers are T. Kempinski, *Entry into the Common Market and British Agricultural Income*, Uni-

versity of Manchester, 1966; and the National Farmers' Union pamphlet, *British Agriculture and the Common Market*, 1966. A succinct summary of the EEC's agricultural support system and its effects on Britain is "Massive Leap Forward in EEC Farm Policy", in *The Financial Times Survey: Towards One Europe*, December 5, 1966. See also *The Financial Times* of November 22, 1966 and *The Times* of November 21, 1966.

4. See Harold Wilson in the Commons, May 8, 1967.

5. On joining the EEC, Britain would gain by getting inside the tariff wall of the Common External Tariff, but would lose the preferences she enjoys with EFTA and the Commonwealth. Calculations of the precise effect of such changes in trading circumstances are notoriously difficult: but some indication of the consequences can be taken from Wells' detailed study. He considers a situation different in several important respects from the alternatives which are considered in this chapter. He compares the situation of Britain as she is today with her position in a Free Trade Area including the US, Canada, EFTA, Japan and the EEC. In these circumstances, the balance of trade between Britain and the EEC would move £29 million against Britain: her overall position would deteriorate by £13 million. Wells also suggests that, without the EEC, the effect on Britain would be negligible. No firm conclusion can be drawn from these results for the present purpose: but there is little here to suggest that there will be a large improvement in Britain's balance of trade in industrial goods to compensate for the loss on agriculture. See Wells, in particular Chapter 5 and Table 7, p. 131.

6. The same article cited a noted economist, Wilfred Beckerman author of *The British Economy in 1975* as having arrived at a figure of £800 million.

7. Hansard HC 8 May, 1967, cols. 1061-1097.

8. Between 1958 and 1965 the cost of living rose 21% in Britain—an average annual rate of just under 3%. Source—International Labour Office, Yearbook of Labour Statistics, 1966, p. 630.

9. Not by any means all economists agree that the VAT would raise prices. See C. D. Foster's contribution to *Economic Growth in Britain*, Weidenfeld & Nicolson, 1966, p. 189.

10. Others have argued that if it is so easy to increase exports by £500 million over five years (without any accompanying increase in imports) it is difficult to understand why Britain has not put her trade difficulties right before. Moreover, it has been Britain's repeated experience that a 3% growth rate soon leads to a crisis in the balance of payments.

11. *The Times*, May 1, 1967.

12. See General de Gaulle's Press Conference, May 16, 1967, quoted p. 78.

13. It is by no means accepted that the rapid growth of the GNP in the Common Market countries—4·1% per capita from

O

1955 to 1965 as opposed to 2·4% for Britain—has stemmed from the Market itself. In the same period Belgium grew at only 2·5% per annum. See on this point A. Lamfalussy, *Lloyds Bank Review,* October, 1961.

14. See Professor Kaldor's ideas, Chapter II, p. 28.

15. See Chapter II, note 58.

4. *The French Case Against Britain*

1. The British have attempted to reassure the French on the question of sterling by undertaking not to invoke mutual assistance under Article 108 of the Rome Treaty in support of sterling's international role. See Callaghan's speech in the Commons, May 10, 1967. The French, on the other hand, appear to be working on a final solution, as yet secret, to the problem of sterling's reserve role and overseas balances. See *The Times,* June 26, 1967, p. 17.

2. Charles de Gaulle, Press Conference, May 16, 1967.

3. One of the few new arguments brought into the 1966-67 Common Market debate was the notion of a European Technological Community. The "Technology gap" controversy (e.g. see the series of articles in the Paris edition of the *New York Herald Tribune,* February 8-12, 1967) kept the subject alive after the Prime Minister initiated the idea of such a community at a speech at the Guildhall in November, 1966. See *The Times,* November 15, 1966.

4. Valery Giscard d'Estaing, Speech before the Federal Trust for Education and Research, and Britain in Europe, May 3, 1967. "Can one seriously envisage a technological community," he asked, "so long as pressures are exerted on certain European nations to compel them to buy their armaments on the other side of the Atlantic?" Selected documents from the conference, p. 7.

5. Heath suggested that the French and British deterrents should be controlled by "some sort of committee—the MacNamara Committee or something of the sort—in which members of the enlarged community can deal with these matters... We would hold the deterrent in trust for these European countries." See House of Commons debate May 9, 1967.

6. The appointment of Lord Chalfont as chief negotiator for Britain in the Common Market negotiations added to these doubts. Chalfont had joined the Government in 1964 as Minister for Disarmament, and had therefore been at the head of the British delegation to the non-proliferation discussions. He was neither a Cabinet Minister nor a significant political figure in his own right. Moreover, he replaced Fred Mulley, a noted pro-European. See *The Observer,* May 28, 1967, for an account of the criticism aroused by his appointment.

7. Giscard d'Estaing, p. 7: "... the relations among Atlantic

nations are poisoned by monetary problems and, for years, the defence of the pound has led this country, not only faithfully to adopt American points of view, but also stand in opposition to the nations whose partner she would like to become. Is it possible to speak of competition on terms of equality when the unsettled conditions of the gold exchange standard enable the United States to obtain unlimited credits?"

8. De Gaulle saw Yalta as a sign that the US and Russia felt that only they could and ought to determine the future of Europe. *Salvation*, p. 86. In a radio and TV speech on April 27, 1965, he revived the issue. See Calleo, *Europe's Future*, p. 121.

9. See Earl of Avon, *Full Circle*. London: Cassell, 1960, p. 36.

5. *Britain's Prospects in Europe*

1. For a distinguished version, see Lord Gladwyn, *The European Idea*, Weidenfeld, 1966, Chapter 6.

2. Charles de Gaulle, Press Conference, May 16, 1967.

3. Bela Balassa, in *Quarterly Journal of Economics*, November, 1965, pp. 545, 566, 550; as quoted in Pryke, *Though Cowards Flinch*, p. 141.

4. Even this is an overstatement of the amount of British reserves. Britain's net reserves are negative if the high level of short-term liabilities is taken into account.

5. See William Pickles, *Not With Europe*, p. 8. Pickles, who opposed joining, anticipated many of Britain's subsequent difficulties.

V. BRITAIN IN ATLANTICA:
THE RELUCTANT ALTERNATIVE

1. *Imperial Relations*

1. The idea has recurred in various forms since the war. In 1952, *The Economist* advocated an Atlantic Union as part of a solution to the dollar problem; and at about the same time, Professor Meade advocated closer integration for a more sensible sharing of the Western defence effort. Britain hinted at free trade with Canada in the early days of the EEC (See Chapter III p. 53).

Harold Wilson was an early advocate of NAFTA: "I feel that a Common Market on an Atlantic basis—provided that the Commonwealth were part of it—would have many advantages to this country which we could not hope to receive on the basis of the Common Market in Europe." (Speech at regional party conference, Leeds, November 5, 1961.)

Christian A. Herter, American Secretary of State at the end of the Eisenhower Administration, in an article entitled "Atlantica" (*Foreign Affairs*, June 1963) proposed an association comprising those nations of North America and Europe willing to accept "close political ties". Such a bloc was intended as a counterpoise to an integrated Europe, though political unity was not to be its primary objective. In general, the precise nature of the political consequences of the association remains obscure; indeed, one of the attractions of the North Atlantic solution is that, even in its rather extreme forms, it seems to involve no substantial or specific surrender of national sovereignty.

2. These proposals arose primarily as a result of Canadian-American talks on future economic relations. The Canadians were unenthusiastic about free trade but felt that they might not be swamped if other countries were included, for example Britain, the EFTA countries and Japan. In November, 1964, Berthold Ohlin, the Swedish Opposition Leader, reported to the Netherland Benelux Committee that private talks for a free trade area of EFTA and North America were taking place. For a discussion of more recent proposals and reactions, see pp. 100 ff.

3. See Chapter III, p. 43 ff.

4. Harry Johnson has studied the necessity for sacrifices of national sovereignty in a free trade area in *The Implications of Free Trade*. He maintains that "by contrast (with the EEC), a free trade area entails no positive commitment to the harmonization either of tariffs on trade with third parties, or to the harmonization of other policies than commercial policies in the interests of economic integration". Ibid p. 2.

5. See, for example, Herbert Nicholas, *Britain and the USA*.

6. Thus Macmillan, for example, felt—wrongly as it turned out —that he could not maintain so close a relationship with Kennedy as with Eisenhower who had been a wartime colleague. See Sampson, p. 225.

7. Nicholas, p. 65.

8. See Beaton and Maddox, *The Spread of Nuclear Weapons*, p. 83 ff.

9. See Nicholas, Chapters 6-8, for Anglo-American relations in the Near and Far East.

10. See Nicholas, p. 85.

11. The suddenness with which the British abandoned their Suez partners is remarked on by Anthony Nutting, *No End of a Lesson, London*, Constable, 1967, pp. 133-35. See also Sir Anthony Eden, *Full Circle, London*, Cassell, 1960; and Nicholas, pp. 122-25, 146, 178. For some Frenchmen, this served to confirm their suspicion that, for France, Britain is generally a most

unreliable ally. It brought to mind the old Vichy propaganda about Britain's defection from the Battle of France and, more credibly, seemed to confirm the old charges that, but for her excessive deference to British reluctance in the 1930s, France would have acted forcefully enough against Hitler in time to stop him. For that argument, see Georges Bonnet, *Quai d'Orsay,* Isle of Man: Anthony Gibbs and Phillips, 1965, pp. 102-3; also 76, 182, 186. Whatever French diplomats may believe about the past, there is a certain predisposition among many of them to distrust a close relationship with Britain. Suez did not lessen that bias.

12. See Sampson, p. 127 ff.

13. Although Macmillan made it clear at Nassau that, if the Americans withdrew Skybolt, rather than lose face and lose power, Britain would go ahead with an independent deterrent, de Gaulle took the incident as an indication of Britain's true loyalties. See Arthur Schlesinger, Jr. *A Thousand Days,* London, Deutsch, 1965, p. 790. Macmillan insisted after the veto, however, that de Gaulle had known his intentions all along—that he had told the General at Rambouillet of Britain's determination to seek an alternative to Skybolt. He was sure that de Gaulle "fully understood our position". See Steel, *The End of Alliance,* p. 92; and Camps, p. 487.

14. For the economic theory of the take-off point see W. W. Rostow. *The Stages of Economic Growth,* New York, 1952. Rostow, who was appointed a Special Assistant to the President in early 1967, outlined the political and military policies associated with this idea in the 1967 Montague Burton Lecture at the University of Leeds—reported in *The Times,* February 24, 1967.

15. See, for example, Walter Lippman's article, "The Great Powers Dethroned", on the meaning of the Arab-Israeli War, *New York Herald Tribune,* July 8/9, 1967. See also Senator James William Fulbright, *The Arrogance of Power,* Random House, New York, 1966. A recent book that has evolved widespread debate is Ronald Steel, *Pax Americana,* Viking Press, New York, 1967. For an earlier expression of the American anti-imperial tradition that emphasizes the relationship between imperialism and American culture, see the writings of Irving Babbitt, e.g. *Democracy and Leadership,* Boston, 1924.

16. Both Prime Minister Wilson and George Brown, while Foreign Secretary, made much of the part Britain could play in bringing the Vietnam War to an end—partly, it is clear, to appease anti-American pressures from the left wing of the Labour Party. 1965 saw a number of attempts to play such a part—the fact-finding mission of Mr. Gordon-Walker, the ex-Foreign Secretary, to South-east Asia, ending in a refusal by Hanoi to receive him; the attempt to send a Commonwealth mission to North Vietnam, and the despatch of Mr. Harold Davies, Parliamentary Secretary

to the Ministry of Pensions and National Insurance, to Hanoi in July. Nothing came of these initiatives.

17. See Chapter II, note 65.

18. It appears that General de Gaulle's much-criticized pro-Arab policy during the June, 1967 Arab-Israeli conflict may achieve by political means what French oil companies have never gained by orthodox commercial methods—the hope of oil concessions from Arab countries comparable with those held by US and British interests.

2. *Atlantic Prospects for Trade and Industrial Growth*

1. For a brief history of these proposals in the whole postwar period, see Maxwell Stamp Associates, *The Free Trade Area Option: Opportunity for Britain,* The Atlantic Trade Study, London, 1967, Chapters 1 and 3.

2. See Javits' speech before the US Senate on August 12, 1965, *Congressional Record,* Vol. III, No. 148; also his remarks at the Savoy Hotel, London, November 8, 1965 (reported in *The Times,* November 9).

3. In addition to considerations of future British, Canadian and American relations, two more universal ideas have been behind the recent resurgence of interest in NAFTA. First, there has been concern to find some new basis for the liberalization of trade after the Kennedy Round. Second, it has been hoped that NAFTA would do more for the economic and political developments of underdeveloped countries than the "inward-looking" Common Market. A crucial moment came in May, 1966, with the recommendation of NAFTA by the US Mutual Planning Association's Canadian-American Committee (See *A New Trade Strategy for Canada and the United States,* Canadian-American Committee, Washington, D.C., and Montreal, May, 1966). In November, 1966, the result of the Committee's detailed research was discussed at an International Conference on Canada and the Atlantic Economic Community, Montebello, Canada. It appears that Whitehall began its investigation at about the same time (see *The Times,* February 22, 1967). Among economists who have worked on NAFTA are Professors John Kenneth Galbraith, Randall Hinshaw, Harry G. Johnson and, of course, Maxwell Stamp.

In addition to the Stamp study mentioned above, The Atlantic Trade Study is producing several further pamphlets exploring the possibilities for NAFTA. See also Randall Hinshaw, *The European Community and American Trade,* Council on Foreign Relations, Praeger, New York, 1964; former Senator Paul H. Douglas, *America in the Market Place,* Holt Rinehart and

Winston, New York, 1966; an article by Ralph I. Straus, "A Proposal for New Institutions in US Foreign Trade Policy", *Orbis*, University of Pennsylvania, Philadelphia, 1967; and Theodore Geiger and Sperry Lea, "The Free Trade Area Concept as Applied to the United States, submitted to the Subcommittee on Foreign Economic Policy, Joint Economic Committee, US Congress, Washington, DC, July 28, 1967.

A recent and fervent defence of an Atlantic political grouping is Lionel Gelber's *The Alliance of Necessity*, New York, Stein and Day, 1966. These views have not been without support among politicians. For example, a letter signed by a number of US governors, senators, congressmen and university chancellors and presidents, at the instigation of Senator Javits of New York, appeared in *The Times* of February 21, 1967, advocating "mutually beneficial trade and fiscal reforms for saving and strengthening the historic relationship between the US and Britain". This provoked a prompt letter of support from leading opponents of the Common Market headed by Sir Derek Walker-Smith (*The Times*, February 23, 1967).

4. "I do not discount the possibility of this [a wider economic grouping] if the present application were to fail or plough into the sands." Harold Wilson in the Commons debate, May 8, 1967.

5. See Geiger and Lea, "The Free Trade Area Concept as Applied to the United States", *op. cit.* The Kennedy Round, in the end, was much more successful than had been expected for some time. Its achievements were nevertheless disappointing compared with the hopes entertained when the Trade Expansion Act was signed in 1962. Then it was expected that Britain would be in the Common Market when negotiations began. Had this been the case, the "dominant supplier" authority, which under the Act allowed the US to offer 100% cuts in tariffs in commodities in which the US and the EEC accounted for more than 80% of free world trade, would have been operative. See Johnson, *World Economy at the Crossroads*, p. 56 ff. But this disappointment apart, the results achieved—cuts averaging 35% in tariffs covering industrial goods—are extremely important. It may be, however, that as trade liberalization must increasingly deal with non-tariff barriers, the GATT framework will be less effective. See Maxwell Stamp Associates, *The Free Trade Area Option*, p. 27.

6. Stamp Associates, *Free Trade Area Option* p. 8. notes that EFTA proves that free trade need not be accompanied by federalist harmonization of domestic policies and practices.

7. Stamp Associates, p. 40.

8. For further discussion of Wells' study, see Chapter IV 3, note 5. In the case of trade with the USA, Wells saw the deterioration for Britain arising not from differences in tariff levels, which are small, but from lack of spare capacity which would make it hard

for her to expand production without raising prices. The inclusion of Japan—a high tariff country—in NAFTA would, he thought, be much to Britain's advantage. See Wells, Ch. 5.

9. Stamp Associates, p. 42. Reflection on the hazards in such a projection reveals how perilous is the profession of economic forecasting. First of all, such a projection must assume some constant and predictable relationship between price and demand for all exported manufactures—a notion highly controversial in theory and extremely elusive in practice. Moreover, when considering trade diversion, there are imponderable questions about the relative quality and allure and hence substitutability of products. Then there are all the problems connected with supply. In an economy near full employment, how much can production be increased without raising the price and thus reducing the new demand presumably called forth by the tariff cut? There is, in addition, the question of what year to use as the base for the projection. The Stamp Study used 1965. The swings from one year to another, however, can be very large. In the period 1963-1966, for example, Britain's annual net balance of trade with the US ranged from −$207 million to −$622 million. Similarly her net balance with the EEC ranged from +$346 million to −$171 million. There is, moreover, the factor of possible trade diversion working against Britain's exports to the EEC as the Six achieve internal free-trade and harmonization. As the EEC market has been much larger for British exports than the American (see text), it is not surprising if British businessmen remain more concerned about the dangers of being shut out of the EEC than the advantages of building NAFTA. (Figures from *Overall Trade by Countries*, OECD, January, 1967, and *Overseas Trade Accounts of the United Kingdom*, HMSO, December, 1966).

10. Stamp, p. 43

11. Stamp, p. 45. With Japan a member, the trade creation for British exports would be $317 million and the trade diversion $304 million.

12. Sources: *Overall Trade by Countries*, OECD, January, 1967. Figures for 1966 suggest a certain shift in British trade towards the US. British exports to the US rose to $1810 million and the deficit dropped to $207 million. Exports to the EEC rose to $2920 million, but the deficit rose as well—to $171 million. See *Overseas Trade Accounts of the United Kingdom*, HMSO, December, 1966.

13. Stamp, p. 43.

14. Stamp, p. 45.

15. Stamp, p. 43.

16. Wells, pp. 39-42, 44-5. Wells argued that Britain's supply elasticity was much closer to that of Western Europe than to the US and Canada. Hence, increased trade with the EEC would be less likely to lead to a relative rise in UK prices, p. 40.

17. Wells, p. 48.

18. The Confederation of British Industry, itself strongly pro-EEC membership for Britain (see *Britain in Europe*, Vol. 1, p. 2, London: CBI, 1966), conducted a survey of 1700 British companies; just over half replied (865); of these, 90% felt there would be a "clear and progressive" advantage in gaining membership and felt that the Community's arrangements were acceptable, provided there was a reasonable transition period. *The Times*, March 8, 1967, p. 17.

19. In general, statements on NAFTA by British industrialists have been rare. One exception is Sir Paul Chambers, then Chairman of ICI, in *The Times*, June 20, 1967: "What may be called partnership may in reality be absorption, and that Britain may become a satellite where there could be manufacture but no determination of policy." Maxwell Stamp Associates ran a much smaller survey (41 participants) than the CBI, which it nevertheless regarded as a significant indicator of business receptivity. Fifty per cent felt there would be an advantage to their firms from NAFTA. For the interesting details, see Stamp, Chapter 5. Stamp concluded that British management is not, in general, fearful of American takeovers.

20. Of the 200 largest companies outside the US in 1966, 56 were British, 26 German and 22 French. *Fortune* magazine, September, 1967.

21. The high rate of American productivity and the relatively low rate of investment in Britain in recent years means that there is a large technological gap which could be filled by the import of American capital and "know-how". See Maddison, p. 60 ff, for the growth opportunities which this gap offers to Europe and Britain.

22. See John H. Dunning, "US Subsidiaries in Britain and their UK Competitors", *Business Ratios*, autumn 1966.

23. See *First National Bank of Chicago Business and Economic Review*, February, 1967, p. 7.

24. See Dunning, p. 8. The Standard Research Institute, in a survey of 200 US firms in Europe, found that these firms undertook only 4% of their research activities in Europe, compared with 10% of their investment. See Layton, p. 93.

25. See Layton, p. 90 ff, for the existing dependence of European firms on US "know-how".

26. The aerospace industry in the UK has already suffered seriously from US competition in advanced areas of technological development. For an angry account of recent setbacks see Stephen Hastings, *The Murder of TSR2*, London, MacDonald, 1966.

27. Figures on the brain-drain are unreliable and tend to concentrate on the outflow of talent, ignoring those who return. The professions most affected appear to be doctors, teachers and scientists. In the year to June 30, 1966, 3,593 "professional, tech-

nical or kindred workers" emigrated to the US from the UK. See *The Financial Times,* March 31, 1967.

28. See Nicholas, p. 64-5.

29. IBM was prevented by the US government from providing a large computer for the French nuclear programme in autumn 1963. For an account of the French response, see Layton, p. 39. The attempts of the American government to regulate the activities of the foreign subsidiaries of American companies can be expected to be a continuing source of international friction. For an interesting discussion of such problems of international corporations, see Raymond Vernon, "Multinational Enterprise and National Sovereignty", *Harvard Business Review,* Vol. 45, no. 2, March-April, 1967, p. 156 ff. The author notes: "Most generally, the US government would probably feel most uncomfortable with the idea that a system of enterprises controlled by a US parent did not necessarily owe total and unambiguous loyalty to the United States." p. 168.

30. Hastings, p. 108 ff, gives recent examples of allegedly superior British aircraft being rejected in favour of US alternatives as a result of skilled Pentagon salesmanship.

31. A McGraw Hill survey in 1960 discovered that in 16% of US decisions to invest abroad the existence of trade restrictions was the principal consideration. See Layton, p. 22.

32. The US Government's new measures to restrain American foreign investments were issued by an Executive Order and became effective on January 2, 1968. They were aimed at "direct investors", i.e. those owning or acquiring as much as 10% of a foreign business (sum exceeding $100,000 per annum). Such direct investors were required to repatriate the same percentage of their foreign earnings as, on average, during 1964-66 and to reduce and hold their foreign liquid assets to 1965-66 levels. Foreign countries were divided into three categories: 1. Developing countries, where new investment could be up to 110% of the investor's average direct investment in 1965-66; 2. Developed countries requiring a large inflow of American capital for growth and stability, i.e. Canada, UK, Australia, New Zealand, Japan and the oil producing countries, up to 65% of average for 1965-66; 3. Other developed countries, a moratorium.

33. In 1965, US exports to the EEC came to $4906 million, 18·2% of total US exports; imports were $3317 million—resulting in an American surplus with the EEC of $1589 million. By contrast, in the same year, the US sent 9·8% of its exports to all the EFTA countries, and they earned a net trade surplus of $273 million. Source: *Basic Statistics of the Community,* 1966.

3. Sterling, the dollar and international liquidity

1. For an account of the help given to sterling under swap

credit arrangements during the 1966 crisis, see Charles A. Coombs in *The Bulletin of the Federal Reserve Bank of New York*, March, 1967. The Federal Reserve System continued to be the pound's main ally up to and after devaluation. At the gold crisis meeting in Washington in March, 1968, the total of the Bank of England's swap facilities with the Federal Reserve was increased from £625 million (of which some £438 million had been drawn) to £833 million: taking into account previous drawings: the Federal Reserve therefore contributed about £400 million of the £1040 million unused swap facilities then available to the UK. Given the United States' own reserve position, such further help is dependent on the co-operation of the European central banks. See *National Institute Economic Review*, May 1968, p. 17; *Economist*, March 23, 1968, p. 70.

2. A noted American study considers a union of the two currencies. See Walter S. Salant *et al*, *The United States Balance of Payments in 1968*.

3. The Federal Reserve had in March 1968 a total of $9355 million credit lines with foreign banks. See *The Economist*, March 23, 1968, p. 70.

4. Reserves are defined here as gold, Foreign Exchange and the IMF gold tranche. In the same period the US credit tranche position with the IMF improved from $2·75 billion to $4·12 billion; but because of the conditions attached to the use of these credits they cannot be counted as true reserves. See Harrod, *Reforming the World's Money*, p. 13. The long-term US position is better; nearly all her liabilities are short-term, but she had $4·52 billion long-term claims on foreigners. If all external claims and liabilities are taken into account, therefore, the US had in 1965 net liabilities of nearly $13 billion compared with reserves of $15·45 billion. For details see IMF International Financial Statistics, March, 1967. If private assets and liabilities abroad are included, the US becomes a considerable net creditor, because of her huge overseas investment. The UK is in a similar position: see the statement of UK assets and liabilities in the *Bank of England Quarterly Bulletin*, September, 1967. Thus the difficulties of both countries arise in part from the traditional bankers' practice of borrowing short and lending long.

5. *New York Times*, February 1, 1968, p. 54. The whole of the US gold reserves is now available against foreign held short-term liabilities. The statutory 25% gold cover for the American currency was abolished in March 1968. See *The Economist*, March 16, 1968, p. 47.

6. "In the nineteenth century the development of natural resources in the 'regions of recent settlement' as they are frequently called—North and South America, Australia, New Zealand and South Africa—was complementary to British economic growth but laid the foundations for subsequent industrial growth in these

regions. Britain's central position in the world economy as leading manufacturer, exporter of manufacturers, and importer of foodstuffs and materials, and supplier of capital for the finance of the world's trade and development investment, also meant that the international monetary system, though increasingly a gold standard system in form, was essentially a sterling standard system, controlled by the Bank of England." H. G. Johnson, *The World Economy at the Crossroads*, p. 15.

7. In 1948, externally held sterling balances (other than those held by international institutions) were 712% of the 1938 figure. By 1965 they had risen only to 729%. See Harrod, "The Role of Sterling", *District Bank Review*, December, 1966.

8. These arrangements, which include the willingness of the central banks to hold dollars in excess of normal requirements for an indefinite period, have been designated "systematic ad-hoccery" by Robert V. Roosa, the former US Under-Secretary of the Treasury for Monetary Affairs. They are discussed by Sir Roy Harrod in *Reforming the Word's Money*, Chapter 4. The support given to sterling since the war has been on a smaller scale, and subject to prompt repayment, whereas the dollar has benefited from arrangements maintained over a number of years, without any time-limit.

9. For a discussion of sterling's role if Britain should join the EEC see Susan Strange, *The Sterling Problem and the Six*.

10. For US trade balance see Table E. The surplus has tended to decline in recent years. There was a deterioration of nearly $2000 million in 1965 and of over $1000 million in 1966. See M. F. W. Hemming, *The Banker's Magazine*, May 1967. In 1967 the trade balance was practically unchanged. See *The Times*, February 16, 1968, p. 19. March 1968 saw the first monthly trade deficit for five years: and the cumulative position over the first four months of the year showed a marked deterioration on 1967. See *The Times*, May 28, 1968.

11. For an economist who agrees that the US should not be blamed for failing to correct her trade deficit, see Harrod, *Towards a New Economic Policy*, p. 32. Before the 1967-8 crisis, Henry Fowler, the US Secretary of the Treasury, was satisfied that the US had rectified the position suitably. See his comments on the 1966 payments figures in *The Financial Times*, February 17, 1967. Some British politicians agreed: see Maudling, *The Maudling Plan and After* in *International Monetary Problems*.

12. This attitude recurs in General de Gaulle's public utterances. See, for example, his Eleventh Press Conference on February 4, 1965, and his references at his Press Conference of May 16, 1967 to "... la pression exercée par les Americains et par les Britanniques pour amener l'Europe à accepter, à ses frais et au profit des balances déficitaires anglo-saxonnes la création de moyens monétaires artificiels qualifiés de liquidités."

13. See Harrod, *Reforming the World's Money*, p. 6. For elaboration of this theme into a world history, see Brooks Adams, *Law of Civilization and Decay*, Macmillan, New York, 1895.
14. See Harrod, *Reforming the World's Money*, p. 18.
15. *Ibid.*, Harrod, p. 12.
16. See Jacques Rueff, "The Gold Standard", in *International Monetary Problems*, p. 40.
17. See Harrod, *Reforming the World's Money*, p. 12.
18. From 1958 to 1964, dollars formed 51% of all new gross reserves, sterling 5%, claims on the IMF 9%, and gold 31%. See *International Monetary Problems*, p. 43.
19. See Robert Triffin, "The International Monetary System", in *International Monetary Problems*, p. 2.
20. See Harrod, *Reforming the World's Money*, Chapter 3.
21. See General de Gaulle's Press conference, February 4, 1965, for a Rueffian eulogy on the immutable value of gold:

> Nous tenons donc pour nécessaire que les échanges internationaux s'établissent, comme c'était le cas avant les grands malheurs du monde, sur une base monétaire indiscutable et qui ne porte la marque d'aucun pays en particulier.
>
> Quelle base? En vérité, on ne voit pas qu'à cet égard il puisse y avoir de critére, d'étalon autre que l'or. Eh! Oui, l'or, qui ne change pas de nature, qui se met, indifferémment en barres, en lingots ou en piéces, qui n'a pas de nationalité, qui est tenu, eternellement et universellement, comme la valeur inaltérable et fiduciaire par excellence.

22. See Rueff, *International Monetary Problems*, p. 39.
23. For a comprehensive attack on the Rueff solution see Triffin, *International Monetary Problems*, p. 5.
24. The UK has, as a result of the repeated crises since 1964, incurred considerable debts to the IMF, the Bank for International Settlements, and foreign central banks. For a summary of these, see the *National Institute Economic Review*, May 1968, p. 17. In addition to the undisclosed (but certainly considerable) amounts due under swap arrangements with central banks, there are known repayments due in the next few years which amount to about $1·8 billion—predominantly to the IMF. Britain's gold holdings at the end of 1967 were about $1·3 billion.
25. See E. M. Bernstein in *Quarterly Review and Investment Survey*, Model, Roland and Co., 4th quarter, 1963; Harrod, *Reforming the World's Money*, Chapter 5, in particular p. 135 ff.
26. For an authoritative account of Keynes' influence in the negotiations leading to the founding of the IMF, see Sir Roy Harrod, *The Life of John Maynard Keynes*. London: Macmillan, 1951, Chapters XIII ff.
27. This power has, however, only a short time to live. The Stockholm meeting of April 1968 agreed that in future the IMF rules

should give the EEC countries a blocking vote on major IMF issues.

28. According to the French Finance Minister there are two prerequisites to the creation of additional liquidity—the disappearance of the reserve countries' deficits and collective recognition of a shortage of international liquidity. Neither of these is at present fulfilled. See Interview with Michel Debré, *Le Monde*, January 9, 1967. The August, 1967, agreement on international liquidity recommended the creation of a new reserve asset—the "special drawing right" or SDR—to be administered by the IMF. These assets would be made available to all members, not only those in balance of payments difficulties, without investigation by the IMF, and could be used freely in international settlements provided the net average use by any country did not exceed 70% over five years. SDRs are therefore very near to the IMF-created money advocated by Harrod and others. The arrangements are governed by an 85% vote in the IMF—which gives the EEC countries collectively a veto. For details, see *The Economist*, September 2, 1967, 799. Even if their five EEC partners override the French and permit SDRs to be created regularly, it would be surprising if the annual distributions were large enough to finance American deficits at their 1966 levels, let alone at the 1967. In the financial crisis following the pound's devaluation, European misgivings over the dollar were appeased by frequent promises to bring the American deficit under control in 1968. Should these pledges be unfulfilled, Europeans may, of course, come to accept large American deficits as a fact of life and, recognizing their benefits or at least their inevitability, agree to finance them indefinitely. This "imperial" monetary system, as the French call it, is a possible but not necessarily attractive or stable resolution to the free world's monetary problems.

29. Johnson writes: "When freedom of international competition becomes subservient to the maintenance of a particular set of exchange rates, as it has increasingly done in recent years, means have changed places with ends." *The World Economy at the Crossroads*, p. 35. See also Johnson in *Review of Economics and Statistics*, 1964.

30. A third alternative to fixed and floating exchange rates is the adjustable peg, which is the system visualized at Bretton Woods when the IMF rules were formulated. The IMF Articles of Agreement provide that exchange rates can be adjusted in the face of balance of payments difficulties which are those of fundamental disequilibrium (Article IV, Section 5). The country concerned undertakes to maintain its currency at the new parity, and not to let it float except within narrow limits. Since the war, however, there has been a growing tendency to regard exchange rates as immutable.

31. Johnson, *Review of Economics and Statistics*, 1964, p. 32.
32. *Ibid.*, p. 31.

33. See the meeting of the Joint Economic Committee of Congress on January 7, 1967. Relevant extracts are reprinted in *The Banker*, March, 1967.

34. Because the US is committed to considerable expenditures abroad on military and aid programmes which are fixed in terms of foreign exchange, she is in a position similar to that of a trading nation which has a low elasticity of demand for imports. It may require a very large adjustment in exchange rates to reach equilibrium; and the process of adjustment may be seriously disrupting.

35. See Harrod, *Reforming the World's Money*, Chapter 2, and *Towards a New Economic Policy*, p. 36 ff.

36. Harrod concedes that if a system of flexible exchange rates had worked very smoothly with official intervention for a considerable period, say for two decades, official intervention might gradually be needed less and less, so the ideal of those who want absolutely freely floating rates could be realized. *Reforming the World's Money*, p. 51 ff.

37. See *Towards a New Economic Policy*, p. 64.

38. See Salant, p. 259 ff.

39. See Harrod, *World's Money*, p. 89; also Salant, p. 259 ff.

40. See H. G. Johnson, *A Decade Ahead*, p. 6.

41. Johnson, *Ibid*, p. 10.

42. Johnson, *Ibid*, p. 9-11.

43. Johnson, *Ibid*, p. 12.

44. See Chapter II, p. 18 Table D.

45. The extent to which exchange rate adjustment has been renounced as a means of balance of payments adjustment in the EEC is exemplified by General de Gaulle's statement that "the fact that the organization of the Six is bringing down all trade barriers between them necessarily means that their currencies must have a constant relative value and that if one of these were to be shaken, the Community would put it right." (Press Conference, May 16, 1967.) Most important, the rules of the agricultural Common Market mean that devaluation would have far less effect within the EEC than elsewhere. For further discussion of this point see Calleo, *Europe's Future*, p. 62.

46. This is the assumption made by Salant, p. 259.

47. In September, 1965, for example, the Basel Club arranged a $1 billion credit for Britain.

48. For the slow development of the European capital market compared with the progress in other areas of economic union, and proposals for its reform, see *Le Development d'un Marché Européen Des Capitaux*, Brussels, 1966, (the Segré Report). An account of the Euro bond market and its importance in providing funds for investment in Europe is given by Robert L. Genillard in *The European Capital Market*, Federal Trust For Education and Research, London, 1967. As Segré says in his contribution to the same conference, there is general agreement that there is no

Net domestic issues of medium and long term securities
(Annual average, 1960–1965)

	Equities ($ million)	Fixed interest ($ million)	All securities as % of gross domestic capital formation
Germany	653	2,474	12.7
France	803	1,744	15.5
Italy	815	1,992	31.6
United Kingdom	724	1,093	12.0
United States	1,016	32,369	32.8

See the Segré Report, Statistical Annex, Table 7.

such thing as a European capital market. But the performance of national markets compared with the US and UK is impressive. See, for example, the rather extraordinary relative performance of the European stock exchanges as providers of new capital.

49. Finance Minister Michel Debré, instituted reforms in November, 1966. French banks were to be allowed to lend abroad more freely, and offer interest on foreign deposits; foreigners could raise capital on the Paris market, and most other exchange control regulations were to be dropped. For a discussion of the main proposals see Michael Green, "Restoring Paris as a Financial Centre," *The Banker*, December, 1966.

4. *America's Perspectives*

1. In 1966, US exports and imports combined came to a total that was 7·7% of the GNP. In Britain, by contrast, they were 28%. OECD, *Economic Outlook*, December, 1967.

2. Charles de Gaulle, *The Call to Honour*, p. 104.

3. George Wallace, former Governor of Alabama (1962-66), succeeded as Governor by his wife in 1966, strong advocate of states' rights and opponent of racial integration in the schools, has announced his intention to stand as a third-party Presidential candidate in 1968.

4. A classic statement of this view is to be found, surprisingly, in Walter Lippmann, *Western Unity and the Common Market*, London: H. Hamilton, 1962. For example: "We are at odds with him [de Gaulle] because in fact his ambition to take the leadership of Europe is irreconcilable with our vital need to retain the ultimate power in nuclear affairs. We must have that power because we have the ultimate responsibility," p. 30.

5. For a prescient assessment of the inherent contradictions in America's early dual policy, see Moore, Chapter 2. He remarks: "In the consideration of the North Atlantic Treaty there was no

real debate over the two alternative ways of organizing the new commitment to come to the defence of Europe, or over the fundamental elements underlying this decision. Although Congress was increasingly insistent that the European recovery programme be used to promote European economic and even political unity, there was no similar pressure to apply American military commitments and aid to promote European defence integration."

That pressure came later with American efforts to organize a European Defence Community along federalist lines, an arrangement strongly resisted by General de Gaulle on the grounds that it would only be a continuing cover for American hegemony. See Chapter III, p. 49.

6. George Kennan, *Memoirs: 1925-1950*, New York: Little, Brown and Co., 1967. See especially Chapters 17 and 19. Recalling widespread European confusion as to the ends and means of the Atlantic effort beyond the scope of military defence, Kennan decries the failure of American policy in the late forties "to explain to them just what we had in mind" (p. 450). Indeed, he was virtually alone in believing that, "we were not fitted, either institutionally or temperamentally, to be an imperial power in the grand manner, and particularly not one holding the great peoples of Western Europe indefinitely in some sort of paternal tutelage. Some day, it appeared to me, this divided Europe, dominated by the military presences of ourselves and the Russians, would have to yield to something more natural—something that did more justice to the true strength and interests of the intermediate European peoples themselves. What was important was that our plans for the future should be laid in such a way as to permit that "something" to come into being when the time for it was ripe— not in such a way as to constitute an impediment to it," (p. 464).

7. Until the intensification of the war in Vietnam, US military expenditures were not much higher proportionally than those of Britain, France or Germany.

Defence Expenditure as % of GNP

	1958	1962	1963	1964
United States	10.9	10.1	9.6	8.8
Britain	7.8	7.1	6.9	6.9
France	7.9	7.3	6.8	6.7
West Germany	3.4	5.6	6.1	5.5

Source: *The Military Balance 1966–1967*, London: The Institute for Strategic Studies, p. 45.

8. Charles de Gaulle's Press Conference, January 14, 1963, in *Major Addresses*, p. 217.

9. See, for example, de Gaulle's speech on radio and television, April 27, 1965, discussed in *Europe's Future*, p. 121. See also p. 82.

P

10. For a discussion of the MLF see Robert E. Osgood, *The Case for the MLF: a Critical Evaluation*, The Washington Centre of Foreign Policy Research, 1964. See also my *Europe's Future*, Chapter 5.

11. For this view, see Alastair Buchan, *NATO in the 1960's: the Implications of Interdependence*, London, Chatto and Windus, 1963.

12. For example, the United States, enthusiastically supported by Britain, has been seeking for the past several years to reach a Non-Proliferation Agreement with Russia and then with as much of the rest of the world as possible. The progress of these negotiations has amply illustrated the tensions within American policy. The chief obstacle to the Agreement has not been the Russians, but America's continental and Asiatic allies who are reluctant to acquiesce in what seems like a permanent nuclear subordination to the two super-powers. In the face of European resistance, the United States has decided to reaffirm its support for the right of Europe ultimately to organize its own nuclear deterrent. A great deal of diplomatic ingenuity has been expended in the search for language that can compromise the aim of Soviet-American nuclear condominium with the aspirations of Western European Union.

13. For example, intimations to this effect were contained in a speech by Presidential Assistant McGeorge Bundy on September 27, 1962, when he spoke of a "multilateral", "unified" and "integrated" European force ("Building the Atlantic Partnership: Some Lessons from the Past," Department of State Bulletin, October 22, 1962). For a discussion of its implications, see Henry Kissinger, *The Troubled Partnership*, New York, McGraw-Hill, 1965, p. 130 f.

14. For a discussion of the de Gaulle-Eisenhower-Kennedy correspondence on this matter, see David Schoenbrun, *The Three Lives of Charles de Gaulle*, New York, Atheneum, 1966. See also James Reston's summary in *The New York Times*, May 1, 1964, p. 34, and May 3, 1964, IV, p. 10; and the editorial May 6, 1964, p. 46. In addition there is Drew Middleton's summary of the State Department's statement on the subject, *The New York Times*, August 14, 1966, p. 5, and his own analysis the next day, p. 13. For a more detailed analysis, see Werner Imhoof in the *Neue Zürcher Zeitung*, May 8, 1964 p. 1 (Morgenausgabe).

15. See Buchan, *NATO in the 1960's*.

16. The Permanent Nuclear Planning Group of Seven, established on December 14, 1966, represented an important step in the campaign to achieve genuine effective consultation on nuclear strategy within NATO. That effort has seemed all the more urgent since the withdrawal of France from the military arrangements of the Alliance. See *The New York Times*, December 15, 1966, p. 1.

17. For the text of the note to the US and the other 13 Allies on moves France would take to regain exclusive control over its

forces and territory, see *The New York Times*, March 13, 1966, p. 14.

18. For representative arguments by Gaullist generals, see Pierre Gallois, "Réflexions sur l'Evolution des Doctrines Americaines", *Revue de Défense Nationale*, July, 1964; General Charles Ailleret, "Opinion sur la Théorie Stratégique de la 'Flexible Response'," *Revue de Défense Nationale*, August-September, 1964.

19. See Chapter V. 2, note 5.

20. "... the bombing of a small people by a very great one and the loss of men suffered on both sides seems to us absurd and detestable." De Gaulle, Press Conference, October 28, 1966.

21. A good detailed analysis of the workings of the Common Market institutions is Leon Lindberg, *The Political Dynamics of European Integration*, London, Oxford University Press, 1963. His case studies reveal the extent to which governmental initiatives, particularly from the French, are often crucial.

22. For a stimulating discussion of the implications of the nuclear situation, see George Liska, *Europe Ascendant*, Baltimore, Johns Hopkins Press, 1964.

23. See Walter Lippmann's article on the Arab-Israeli War, *New York Herald Tribune*, July 8/9, 1967.

24. De Gaulle believed this even during the darkest days of Stalinism. See de Gaulle, Press Conference, November 14, 1949, and interview with Mr. Bradford as representative of UPI at Colombey les-deux-Eglises, July 10, 1950, microfilm.

25. For a general survey of Gaullist policy as of 1965 and its underlying principles, see Calleo, *Europe's Future*, Chapter 4. A solid intellectual and political biography of de Gaulle is Paul-Marie de la Gorce, *De Gaulle entre deux Mondes*, Paris, Payard, 1964.

26. For an outspoken statement of tension between German and American aims, see Ronald Steel, *The End of Alliance*, New York, Viking Press, 1964. For a German argument along similar lines, see Hans-Georg von Studnitz, *Bismarck in Bonn*, Stuttgart, Seewald Verlag, 1963.

27. The SPD Leader, Dr Schumacher, crystallized this attitude in his references to Dr Adenauer as "Chancellor of the Allies" in the Bundestag debate of November 24-25, 1949, on the Petersburg Agreement. See Konrad Adenauer, *Memoirs 1945-53*, London: Weidenfeld and Nicolson, 1966, p. 277, and for the whole debate, p. 222 f. These views are not necessarily limited to the Left. Franz Josef Strauss, more than a decade ago, said, "In all negotiations about reunification, risks and chances must be weighed against one another. The risks will diminish, the chances will improve, the more Germany herself has to throw on the scales. Although there exists a preference [among the Allies]for a reunited Germany to belong to a military alliance with the West, the hard political requirements of the German people might cause them to make

a decision according to the Austrian pattern." Quoted by Steel from *The New York Times*, February 20, 1957. Strauss' views of course have undergone considerable alteration from time to time.

28. This opposition was led by Pastor Niemoller and Dr Gustav Heinemann. Heinemann was Minister of the Interior in the Cabinet of September, 1949, but resigned on the issue of the German contribution to a European army in 1950. See Adenauer, *Memoirs*, p. 291-301.

29. For the account of these payments see Chapter 2, note 64; for balance of trade difficulties see Chapter 2, note 5.

30. See, for example, Dr. Kiesinger's interview with *Der Spiegel*, March 20, 1967. For an analysis of the trend in mid-1967, see the dispatches of David Hotham in *The Times*, July 12 *et seq.*,

31. For the official American view of the effects of French withdrawal from NATO, see the speech by Secretary of State Rusk, Department of State Bulletin, December 5, 1967. The speech is otherwise notable for its indication of a new American flexibility towards European unification and trans-Atlantic arrangements.

32. See General de Gaulle's Press Conference of October 29, 1966: ". . . we have not reconsidered our decision to forget our grievances, or to practice cordial relations with Federal Germany. And even, whilst keeping, there as elsewhere, our forces fully under our control, we have agreed to maintain for the moment on its territory an important military force, which is quite clearly contributing to its security, which we should withdraw the moment the Federal Republic asked us to, and for which, unlike its other allies, we ask no financial compensation."

VI. COMMONWEALTH CLAIMS

1. *Commonwealth Prospects*

1. A turning point in British attitudes to the Commonwealth and her role in the postwar world, was the appearance in 1964 of a series of articles signed "A Conservative" which described the Commonwealth as "a gigantic farce" and claimed that Britain's world-wide commitments "combine the maximum chance of involvement, embarrassment, expense and humiliation with the minimum effect on the course of events." See *The Times*, April 1-3, 1964.

2. Among the most notable proponents of closer ties with the Commonwealth has been Patrick Gordon-Walker, briefly Foreign Secretary and later Minister of Education in the Wilson Government. See his *The Commonwealth*, London, Secker and Warburg,

1962, Part 5, especially Chapter XXIV. See also William Pickles, *Not with Europe*, Fabian Tract 336, 1962, pp. 33-35.

3. Many of today's beliefs in the viability of the Commonwealth as a political bloc seem echoes of the ideas current at the turn of the century. The Imperial Federation League was founded in 1886 with the theme that "the relations between Great Britain and her colonies must inevitably lead to federation or disintegration." Joseph Chamberlain encouraged the creation of an Imperial Customs Union and of a mutual system of imperial defence. This approach—which was based on the idea of a white Commonwealth—was unattractive to both Canada and South Africa which had to create unity between two peoples and could not afford to allow the British to be given a higher status. Since then circumstances have become even more unfavourable to the federation idea. See Gordon-Walker, p. 89 ff.

4. For a convenient summary of the main features of the Commonwealth see *Whitaker's Almanack*, London, 1967, p. 693ff.

5. The Secretariat, which was established in June, 1965, was the result of the 1964 Prime Ministers' Conference. See K. Robinson, "The Intergovernmental Machinery of Commonwealth Consultation and Co-operation" in *A Decade of the Commonwealth, 1955-1964*, ed. W. B. Hamilton, K. Robinson, C. D. W. Goodwin, Duke University Press, Durham, 1966, pp. 89-123.

6. In 1955-66, meetings were held every year except 1958, 1959 and 1963. See Robinson, p. 112. No meeting was held in 1967.

7. In the first decade after the war, meetings of foreign, defence, supply and finance ministers took place. Since 1954, only the finance ministers have met. Robinson, p. 119.

8. See H. G. Johnson, "Commonwealth Preferences", p. 365.

9. Changes in United Kingdom Trade, 1958-65:

	% of Total	
Exports to	1958	1965
Commonwealth	32.2	28.4
EEC	13.8	19.1
EFTA	10.8	14.1
United States	9.2	10.5
Others	34.0	27.9

Source: *Annual Abstract of Statistics*, 1966, p. 223.

10. See Johnson, "Commonwealth Preferences", p. 337.

11. See Chapter II, p. 31ff.

12. See Chapter II, note 45. At the end of 1962, the net asset value of UK companies' direct investment in the Sterling Area was about £2,100 million. See *Bank of England Quarterly Bulletin*, March, 1964.

13. See note 6 to Chapter VI.2 below.

14. See Gorell Barnes, *Europe and the Developing World*, p. 42.

15. See Prime Minister Wilson's speech in the Commons, *The Times*, January 17, 1968, p. 7.

2. *The Commonwealth and Britain's Alternatives*

1. See Gorell Barnes, p. 16ff.
2. A main theme for Lionel Gelber, *Alliance of Necessity*.
3. See Maxwell Stamp Associates, *FTA Option*, p. 27.
4. For an admirable presentation of the US position, see Anthony M. Solomon, US Assistant Secretary of State for Economic Affairs, *Statement before the sub-committee on Foreign Economic Policy of the Joint Economic Committee of the Congress*, Wednesday, July 12, 1967.
5. See the speech at UNCTAD II by US Under Secretary of State for Political Affairs, Eugene V. Rostow, Department of State Bulletin, February 5, 1968. The proposal that NAFTA could be the instrument for such a system of tariff preferences is floated in David Wall, *The Third World Challenge*, The Atlantic Trade Study, London, 1968.
6. Aid Commitments at Discounted Present Value, 1962 ($US million)

Country	Nominal	Loans discounted at own discount rate	GNP	Aid as % of GNP
Canada	73.1	58.8	37,000	0.16
France	1,034.6	908.4	68,580	1.32
Germany	497.4	231.4	84,275	0.27
Italy	137.1	27.7	38,400	0.07
Japan	295.6	128.7	52,000	0.24
Netherlands	63.5	35.4	13,100	0.27
Portugal	60.2	6.2	2,800	0.22
United Kingdom	570.4	210.8	79,115	0.27
United States	4,975.0	3,069.0	553,600	0.55

Source: Johnson, *Economic Policy*, p. 122, as derived by him from cols 1, 2, 4, and 5; Tables 4 and 5: from Pincus, *Review of Economics and Statistics 45*, November 1963, p. 364.

7. Gorell Barnes discusses this problem in relation to Nigerian association with the EEC, p. 39 ff.
8. Gorell Barnes, p. 45, discusses the problem of Commonwealth manufactures and suggests that real progress lies not in more preferences but in fewer restrictions. Johnson, *Economic Policies*, p. 104 ff., takes up the question of non-tariff barriers to manufactures and the difficulty of measuring their effects. See also Mark S. Massel, "Non-Tariff Barriers as an Obstacle to World Trade," *The Expansion of World Trade; legal Problems and Techniques*, Dennis Thomson ed., The British Institute of Inter-

national and Comparative Law, 1965 (Brookings Institute Reprint 97).

9. For simple arithmetical averages of the US, EEC and UK tariffs, see Chapter, IV p. 101. Johnson argues (*The World Economy*, p. 84) that the protective effects of a tariff schedule should be measured by the effective rate of protection on value added in manufacturing processes. In *Economic Policies*, p. 98, he gives the effective rates of protection, calculated on this basis, by the US, Britain, the EEC and others, on a wide range of manufactured goods. The effective rates of duty were, in 1962, for Britain 27·8%, the USA 20·0%, the EEC 18·6%.

10. GATT succeeded the abortive scheme for an International Trade Organization and aimed to create a free-trade background to world trade in opposition to the protectionist policies of the thirties. For further details of its evolution and progress since the war, see Johnson, *The World Economy*, p. 48ff.

11. See W. W. Rostow, *The Process of Economic Growth*, London, Cambridge University Press, 1960.

12. This point is powerfully argued by Professor Johnson in his criticism of the 1964 UNCTAD Final Act. See *The World Economy*, p. 95 ff.

13. The creation of a Special UN Fund for Economic Development (SUNFED) has been the most frequently suggested means for the multilateral distribution of aid. It was advocated in particular by the underdeveloped countries in the fifties. For a discussion of its main features, see I. M. D. Little and J. M. Clifford, *International Aid*, London, George Allen and Unwin, Ltd., 1965, pp. 46-7.

14. Professor Johnson is the leading proponent of this attitude. Dr. Raúl Prebisch, the Secretary General of UNCTAD, in *Towards a New Trade Policy for Development*, argues that in the past, developing nations have concentrated too much on "inward-looking" industrialization and recommends a future policy of developing exports to advanced countries. See Johnson, *The World Economy*, pp. 83, 96 ff.

15. Johnson suggests that there is a *prima facie* case against the Commonwealth preference system, which should be studied in detail to assess its overall efficiency. "The Commonwealth Preferences", p. 377.

16. The Yaoundé Convention of 1962, which is the cornerstone of the Common Market's association arrangements in Africa, provides for the establishment of a Free Trade Area, to include the EEC and eighteen African states, without a common external tariff. GATT allows such free trade areas; but the scale of this agreement constitutes a considerable breach of the non-discriminatory principle. See Teresa Hayter, *French Aid*, London, ODI, 1966, p. 77ff.

17. See note 4. For a statement of the alternatives as he believes the US should see them, see Professor Johnson, *Economic Policies*, p. 240.

18. Recent developments in welfare economics suggest that if all the conditions necessary for a welfare optimum do not exist it may be harmful to attempt to create a few of them. See J. E. Meade, *Trade and Welfare*, Oxford University Press, 1955, Chapter VII.

19. Johnson suggests the need for further empirical studies of the proposition that the practice of tying aid results in a greater real volume of aid than would otherwise be available. See *Economic Policies*, p. 246.

20. For Sir Oswald Mosley's ardent advocacy of Europe-Africa as a co-ordinated economic and political system, see his *Europe: Faith and Plan*, Euphorion Books, 1958, p. 29 and Chapter 2, *passim*.

21. See Gorell Barnes, p. 41. For an excellent discussion of this whole issue indicating a possible greater American tolerance of regional arrangements, see the testimony of George W. Ball, former US Under Secretary of State, in "The Future of US Foreign Trade Policy", *Hearings Before the Subcommittee on Foreign Economic Policy of the Joint Economic Committee, Congress of the US, July 20, 1967*, US Government Printing Office, Washington, DC, pp. 274-77. For a lucid statement of the alternatives as Professor Johnson believes the US should see them, see his *Economic Policies*, p. 240.

VII. BRITAIN ALONE

1. For a substantial collection of these views, see Arthur Koestler, ed., *Suicide of a Nation*, London, Hutchinson, 1967.

2. The most recent attack on growth as an overriding objective of national policy comes from E. J. Mishan, a distinguished welfare economist. He objects to the failure of conventional measure of GNP to take account of such important contributions to human happiness as leisure, quiet, and amenity. See *The Costs of Economic Growth*, London, Staples, 1967.

3. See, for an early example of this attitude, the conversation of Sir Roy Harrod with a group of Americans in 1943 reported by him in *Towards a New Economic Policy*, p. 67.

4. If the Labour Government had continued its 1967 policies for the social services, it has been reckoned that even a 3% growth rate would have meant a rise in personal consumption for 1965-75 of only 2·5% p.a., as compared with 2·9% for the previous decade. See Peter Jay, "Social Services: a 70s Crisis?" in *The Times*, May 31, 1967. Substantial cuts in the social services were announced

along with the defence cuts of January 16, 1968. See the *Times,* January 17, 1968, p. 7.

5. Harrod, *Towards a New Economic Policy,* p. 21.

6. *Ibid.,* p. 24.

7. Only Holland has achieved a similar rise in exports without a corresponding increase in imports. *Ibid.,* p. 21.

8. *Ibid.,* p. 26.

9. *Ibid.,* p. 27.

10. *Ibid.* p. 34.

11. Harrod, although a strong advocate of growth as an aim of policy, is concerned that the advantage of leisure should be recognized as opposed merely to producing more goods. *Ibid,* p. 50.

12. For the effect of Stop-Go, on industrial prices, *ibid,* p. 13, Table III. See also Chapter II, note 8.

13. *Ibid,* p. 30.

14. Effective monetary reform, in Harrod's view, requires at least a doubling of world reserves. *Reforming the World's Money,* p. 69ff.

15. He goes on to list a further series of policies for various other contingencies. If there is a successful incomes policy but not monetary reform, then trade controls will be necessary during periods of deficit. If the incomes policy fails, but the monetary reform is achieved, adjusting the exchange rate will probably correct the trade deficit. But if both the incomes policy and monetary reform fail, Britain will need to use both trade controls and devaluation.

16. Article IV Section 5 of the IMF Articles of Agreement allows changes in the par value of a currency provided that the member's balance of payments difficulties are those of "fundamental disequilibrium". GATT allows import quotas, but no tariff increases nor export incentives, as remedies for trade difficulties.

17. Harrod, *Towards a New Economic Policy,* p. 61.

18. For an authoritative forecast of Britain's balance of payments in 1968 and 1969, see *National Institute Economic Review,* May, 1968.

19. The outgoing Tory Chancellor of the Exchequer, Reginald Maudling, has since defended the 1964 deficit on the grounds that half of it arose from long-term capital outflows. Since these represented the acquisition of earning assets abroad, they should not be regarded as a loss or expense. Only the remainder was a true deficit; but this was the result of the increase in imports which, for Britain, must necessarily precede an increase in exports. The Labour Government should have kept calm and financed the deficit by using reserves and IMF drawings until the expected increase in exports arrived.

20. Pryke, *Though Cowards Flinch,* p. 16.

21. *Ibid,* pp. 7-28.

22. The growth rate for 1965 was 2·7%, for 1966 1·6%, and for 1967 1%. See *National Institute Economic Review*, May 1968, p. 58.

23. Pryke, p. 53ff.

24. Pryke, p. 67.

25. *Ibid*, pp. 73-79.

26. *Ibid*, pp. 92-123. The Industrial Reorganization Corporation (IRC), which began operations in January, 1967, and the Industrial Expansion Bill tabled in January, 1968, provided for Government intervention in industry somewhat along the lines which Pryke advocated. The IRC is authorized to encourage the concentration of British industry into units large enough to take advantage of economies of scale and to compete with international companies. It has already been responsible for two important amalgamations—of English Electric with Elliott Automation, and of GEC with AEI. The Industrial Expansion Bill provides for certain ministries to provide finance—via loan, or equity—for industrial projects beneficial to the national economy. But the IRC is to sell any shareholdings which it may acquire in providing finance for amalgamation as soon as the reason for this intervention is passed; and its resources amount to only £150 million. It cannot therefore play a role anything like that played by IRI in Italy, and falls far short of what Pryke would want. For the functions of the IRC and the Government's purpose in setting it up, see *Industrial Reorganization Corporation* (HMSO 1966; Cmnd 2889).

27. Pryke, p. 130.

28. *Ibid*, p. 139.

29. *Ibid*, p. 145.

30. *Ibid*, p. 147.

31. See F. W. Paish, *Studies in an Inflationary Economy*, London, 1962, Chapter 17, for the theory that appears to have influenced the Government's predevaluation policy. Paish advocates a permanently higher level of unemployment than has been normal in Britain since the war to encourage labour mobility, damp down wage demands, and thus right the balance of payments. Mr. Callaghan, the former Chancellor of the Exchequer, appeared to believe in at least a long period of deflation, if not in the permanently lowered pressure of demand which Paish advocates. See *The Times*, June 17, 1967.

32. See Maudling, "Breaking out of the Stop-Go Cycle", *The Times*, June 15, 1967; his article in *The Sunday Times* of September 3, 1967; and Heath's speech at Carshalton, reported in *The Times*, July 10, 1967.

33. It is generally felt that the failure of Labour's deflationary policy was ensured by a combination of unfortunate, unexpected and more or less uncontrollable events—among them the Arab-Israeli conflict of June, 1967, which resulted in the prolonged closure of the Suez Canal; the continuing German recession; and

the British dock strikes. The ultimate success of the policy based on devaluation, of course, will remain no less vulnerable to external events, in particular on the general effects of American efforts to bring their balance of payments deficit under control.

34. See the Defence White Paper (Cmd. 3357) of July, 1967, which announced the intention to withdraw from the bases in Singapore and Malaysia by the mid 1970s. The defence cuts of January, 1968, advanced the timetable to 1971. See Prime Minister Wilson's speech to the Commons, *The Times*, January 16, 1968, p. 7.

35. Among the earliest cabinet opponents of Britain's remaining East of Suez was R. H. S. Crossman; see his 1962 address, "Western Defence in the Sixties", reprinted in *Planning for Freedom*, London, Hamish Hamilton, 1965, p. 242. Another, Christopher Mayhew, resigned in 1966 as Minister of Defence for the Navy on this issue. See his *Britain's Role Tomorrow*. Enoch Powell, the Shadow Minister of Defence, was another early advocate of Britain's military withdrawal to Europe.

36. EFTA rose from the break-down of the Maudling Committee negotiations to establish free trade between all the countries of the OEEC. During the talks there had been a group of countries—Austria, Britain, Denmark, Norway, Sweden, and Switzerland—all of whom were in favour of a free trade area without a common external tariff and without "harmonization". Their main common factor was a reluctance to allow any political interference from other countries or supranational institutions, in the case of Austria, Sweden and Switzerland because of concern for maintaining their neutrality. The Stockholm Convention of January, 1960, signed also by Portugal, provided for progressive elimination of quotas and tariffs on manufactured goods in parallel with the Six. Along with the Convention, the Seven adopted a resolution which stated that the Association was to be regarded as "a step towards an agreement between all member countries and the EEC." The British, in particular, looked on EFTA as a second best and were obviously anxious that it should be abridged to a later accommodation with the Six. See the debate in the House of Commons, December 14, 1959. The fundamental differences between the aims of EFTA and of the EEC are revealed by the exclusion of agriculture, which would have had to be included had full economic integration been intended; the provision for withdrawal by any member after 12 months' notice, which shows the impermanence of the association; and, subsequently, by the failure of the EFTA Council to grow because there was no real integration for it to administer.

By December, 1966, complete free trade on most industrial products had been achieved—ahead of EFTA's own schedule and of the Six. In seven years intra-EFTA trade has increase by an average of 11% p.a., EFTA members' trade with the EEC has increased by 9%, and with the rest of the world by 5%. Progress in agricultural trade has been by the way of bilateral agreements and therefore less dramatic. Finland has joined as an associate member; and the association has survived the rude shock of the imposition of the import surcharge by Britain in 1964.

EFTA has therefore, as a trade area, fully lived up to expectations, modest though they were. There have, however, been no concerted attempts to reach agreement with the EEC. Each individual country, except Switzerland and Portugal, has at some time made application for full or associate membership. But for Britain, at least, chances of success have been reduced by the train of adherents she brings with her to the negotiations. See General de Gaulle's Press conference, May, 1967. For an account of the creation of EFTA, see Miriam Camps, *Britain and the European Community*, London, 1964, Chapter VII; and for a survey of EFTA's achievements to date, *The Financial Times*, December 29, 1966.

VIII. LEADERSHIP AND POLITICAL IMAGINATION IN TODAY'S BRITAIN

1. For a further discussion on this point, see Hannah Arendt, *Origins of Totalitarianism*, New York, The World Publishing Company, 1958, Part 2, particularly Chapters 5 and 7.

2. For further discussion, see Calleo, *Europe's Future*, Chapter 4.

3. Perhaps the most impressive evidence for this failure comes from the reports of official bodies and commissions on various aspects of British administration. See, for example, the reports of *The Select Committee on Nationalised Industries*, in particular on *British Railways* (House of Commons Paper 254, 1960); of *The Committee of Public Accounts*, in particular the *Fifth Report* (House of Commons Paper 647, 1967); of *The Committee of Enquiry into the Aircraft Industry* (The Plowden Report) (Cmnd. 2853, 1965). Further support comes from many of the studies cited in other chapters, eg. Hastings, *The Murder of TSR2;* Mayhew, *Britain's Role Tomorrow*.

4. Andrew Shonfield, "The Pragmatic Illusion", *Encounter*, June, 1967, pp. 10-11. Shonfield also cites a number of legal scholars who complain of a similar lack of vigour and clarity in British legal thought.

5. *Ibid*, p. 11.

6. *Ibid*, p. 12.

7. Calleo, *Coleridge and the Idea of the Modern State*.

Bibliography

This Bibliography includes only those works which have been of particular influence in writing the book, or in frequent use as works of reference. In the case of statistical publications, the latest edition available at the time of writing has in most cases been used. Works included here have been referred to in the footnotes only in enough detail to allow them to be identified with certainty in the bibliography.

Annual Abstract of Statistics. London, HMSO, published annually.
Bank of England Quarterly Bulletin.
Basic Statistics of the Community. Brussels, Statistical Office of the European Communities, annually.
Beaton, Leonard, and Maddox, John, *The Spread of Nuclear Weapons*. London, Chatto and Windus, 1962.
Buchan, Alastair, and Windsor, Philip, *Arms and Stability in Europe*. London, Chatto and Windus, 1963.
Calleo, David P. *Europe's Future*. London, Hodder and Stoughton, 1967.
Camps, Miriam, *Britain and the European Community 1955-1963*. Princeton University Press, 1964.
Churchill, Sir Winston S., *The Second World War*, vol. 6, *Triumph and Tragedy*, London, Cassell & Co., 1954.
Clarke, W. M., *The City in the World Economy*. London, Institute of Economic Affairs, 1965.
Dow, J. C. R., *The Management of the British Economy 1945-60* Cambridge University Press, 1965.
Dunning, J. H., "Does Foreign Investment Pay?" *Moorgate and Wall Street*, autumn 1964.
U.S. Subsidiaries in Britain and their UK Competitors. Business Ratios, autumn 1966.
de Gaulle, Charles, *Major Addresses, Statements and Press Conferences of General Charles de Gaulle, 19.5.1958 - 31.1.1964*

New York, French Embassy Press and Information Division, 1964. Also subsequent releases.

Speeches, statements and press conferences 1946-1958. RPF files on microfilm, Bibliothéque de Fondation Nationale des Sciences Politiques.

Unity, 1942-1944. London, Weidenfeld and Nicolson, 1959.

Salvation, 1944-1946. London, Weidenfeld and Nicolson, 1960.

Gorell Barnes, W., *Europe and the Developing World.* London, PEP, 1967.

Hanning, Hugh, "Britain East of Suez—Facts and Figures." *International Affairs,* April, 1966.

Harrod, Sir Roy, *Reforming the World's Money.* London, Macmillan 1965.

Towards a New Economic Policy. Manchester University Press, 1967.

Hastings, Stephen, *The Murder of TSR2.* London, Macdonald, 1966.

International Labour Office, *Year Book of Labour Statistics.* Geneva, ILO, annually.

International Monetary Fund, *International Financial Statistics.* Washington, IMF, monthly.

International Monetary Problems. London, Federal Trust for Education and Research, 1966.

Johnson, Professor Harry, "The Commonwealth Preferences", *The Round Table,* October, 1966.

Economic Policies Towards Less Developed Countires. London, George Allen and Unwin, 1967.

The International Competitive Position of the United States and the Balance of Payments Prospect for 1968. Review of Economics and Statistics, 1964.

The World Economy at the Cross-roads. Oxford University Press, 1965.

Kaldor, Nicholas, *Causes of the Slow Rate of Economic Growth of the United Kingdom.* Cambridge University Press, 1966.

Kissinger, Henry A., *Troubled Partnership.* New York, McGraw Hill 1965.

Kitzinger, U. W., *The Challenge of the Common Market.* Oxford, Basil Blackwell, 1962.

Koestler, Arthur (ed.), *Suicide of a Nation.* London, Hutchinson, 1967.

Layton, Christopher, *Transatlantic Investments.* Boulogne-sur-Seine, The Atlantic Institute, 1966.

MacDougall, Sir Donald, "Britain and the Common Market". *Rotterdamsche Bank Review,* December, 1961.

Maddison, Angus, *Economic Growth in the West.* London, George Allen and Unwin, 1964.

Mayhew, Christopher, *Britain's Role Tomorrow.* London, Hutchinson, 1967.

Maxwell Stamp Associates, *The Free Trade Area Option*: *Opportunity for Britain*, The Atlantic Trade Study, Moor House, London, 1967.

The Military Balance. London, Institute of Strategic Studies, 1966.

Moore, Ben T., *NATO and the Future of Europe*. New York, Harper and Brothers, 1958.

National Institute Economic Review. NIESR, London, quarterly.

Nicholas, Herbert, *Britain and the United States*. London, Chatto and Windus, 1963.

Northedge, F. S., *British Foreign Policy*: *the Process of Adjustment 1945-1961*. London, George Allen and Unwin, 1962.

Pickles, Williams, *Not With Europe: the Political Case for Staying Out*. London, Fabian Tract 336, 1962.

Pryke, Richard, *Though Cowards Flinch*. London, MacGibbon and Kee, 1967.

Reddaway, W.B., in collaboration with J. O. N. Perkins, S. J. Potter and C. T. Taylor, *Effects of UK Direct Investment Overseas; an Interim Report*. Cambridge University Press, 1967.

Salant, Walter S. and Emile Despres, Lawrence B. Krause, Alice M. Rivlin, William A. Salant and Lorie Tarshis, *The United States Balance of Payments in 1968*. Washington, The Brookings Institution, 1963.

Sampson, Anthony, *Macmillan*. London, Allen Lane, The Penguin Press, 1967.

Steel, Ronald. *Pax Americana*, New York, Viking Press, 1967.

Strange, Susan, *The Sterling Problem and the Six*. London, PEP, 1967.

United Kingdom Balance of Payments. London, HMSO, annually.

Wells, Sidney, *Trade Policies for Britain*. London, Oxford University Press, 1966.

INDEX

Index

241